BALI, the most famous island in the world, is much praised for its spectacular scenery and unique and charming culture. Now it is fashionable also to lament the damage that it is thought to be suffering as tourists pour through its villages and temples.

Are they really so harmful? Could change really be prevented in an island which has long been adept at taking what it wants from the outside world and rejecting the rest?

Change is inherent in the Balinese way of life; or, as the Governor of Bali told the writer of this book, its culture contains 'many manifestations towards modernisation'. Now the process is faster. 'No man is an island,' the writer comments, 'and no island is an island either, in these days of radio, television, newspapers, magazines, books and travel.'

There are more questions than answers — but this book at least provides much basic information for understanding the past and the present. It describes the island's intricate social structure, discusses its religion, its arts and its crafts, tells a little of its history, and has chapters also on the economy, health, family planning, the major tourist centres and even wildlife.

There is much here for anyone interested in this island where so much is beguiling and almost everything is at least remarkable.

Bali has always been difficult to understand. Even mapmakers have been confused. The early European version, above left, is rough but the right way up. Upside down maps like the one below, however, persisted for nearly 200 years, almost into the 19th Century. For a modern one, see Pages 10-11.

The Balinese

by Hugh Mabbett

JANUARY BOOKS

Published by January Books Ltd,
35 Myrtle Crescent,
Wellington 2, New Zealand

© Copyright Hugh Mabbett 1985, 1989

Reprinted 1989

ISBN 0-473-00281-7

All rights reserved. No part of this book may be reproduced, stored in a retrieval system or transmitted in any form by any means, except when brief extracts are used for review purposes, without the written permission of the copyright owner.

Correspondence should be sent to
January Books Ltd
c/o Design Business
809 French Road #06-160
Singapore 0820

Printed by
Stamford Press Singapore

'BALI is neither a last nor a lost paradise, but the home of a peculiarly gifted people of mixed race, endowed with a great sense of humour and a great sense of style . . . and with a suppleness of mind which has enabled them to take what they want of the alien civilisations which have been reaching them for centuries and to leave the rest.' — from Dance and Drama in Bali, by Beryl de Zoete and Walter Spies, London, 1938.

PEDJENG. 20. 10. 00
1. METER.
W.O.J NIEUWENKAMP

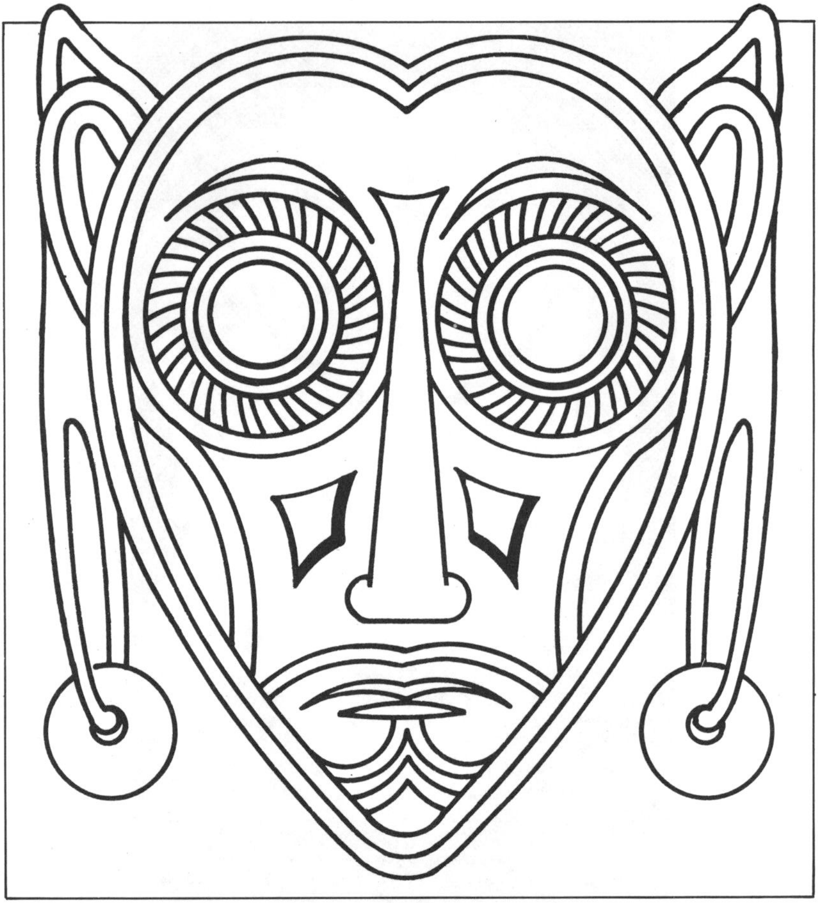

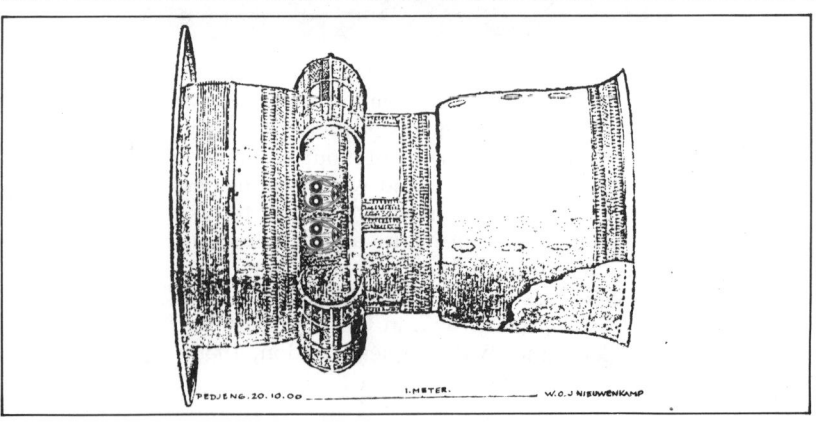

The Faces on the Cover

Bali has many faces. There are two on the cover of this book, one feminine and modern, one masculine and ancient. The feminine one belongs to a girl performing the legong, the most loved of all of Bali's many dances. She was drawn in 1984 by Beny Pournama, an artist from Jakarta who now lives in Pengosekan, a village near Ubud, the hub of Bali's cultural life. The masculine face, with its eyes like camera lenses looking deep into your mind, is from another age and could have come from another world. Yet its stretched earlobes — still found in Borneo, just across the Java Sea from Bali — denote its earthly origins. It is in fact from a huge, damaged kettle-gong of unknown age and history which lies today in the Panataran Sasih Temple near Pejeng, on the road to Tampaksiring.

The gong is known as the Moon of Pejeng, a name deriving from a legend which says it was once one of several moons that the Earth had in ancient times. One night it fell to earth and lodged in a tree, whence its continuing light disclosed some thieves at work. They hurriedly discussed ways of extinguishing the light, until one of them climbed into the tree and urinated on it until it cracked, darkened and fell to the ground. That is why it is damaged.

The largest of its kind ever found in Indonesia, perhaps the largest ever found anywhere, the gong is nearly two metres long and its sounding surface is more than 1.5 metres wide. The face shown here is one of four, all identical, which adorn the sides of the gong, each one about 20 cm high and all oxidised to a blue-green patina which reeks of age. Estimates of the gong's age range from 1,000 years to 2,000 years. Many Balinese believe it to possess magical power.

The Moon of Pejeng is often called a drum. It is not. Drums are percussion instruments producing sound by means of stretched membranes. Gongs are percussion instruments made of solid and naturally sonorous materials. This is a gong, but who were the gong-makers? Archeologists cannot even say whether it was made in Bali or imported and it is unlikely we shall ever know. It is an excellent mystery, and mysteries are much of what Bali is about. The drawing used here is based on a rendering by a Dutch artist, W.O.J. Nieuwenkamp, published in 1910.

For Charles and Lydia

Many people helped with this book. I would like to thank especially Njoman Oka, Gde Sukarya, Helene Vezina and the staffs of the Information Department, the Badung Government Tourist Office and Udayana University library in Denpasar; Cokorda Mas of the Mudraswara Foundation, Silvio Santosa of Bina Wisata, Han Snel and Oka Kartini in Ubud; Annie Berthe Simamora in Jakarta; Michael Sweet in Singapore; and also in Singapore Siva Choy and Ilsa Sharp, who put up with me during weeks of writing. To them, and to all those who gave so generously of their time and knowledge when I pestered them with endless and often foolish questions, terima kasih.

The extracts from Colin McPhee's A House In Bali which begin on Page 90 are included by permission of Victor Gollancz Ltd, London. The extracts from Willard A. Hanna's Bali Profile on Pages 184 and 186 are included by courtesy of Universities Field Staff International, Hanover, NH, USA. The extracts from Dick Bent's surfing diary which begin on Page 237 are included by courtesy of Tracks Magazine, Sydney, Australia.

The few prices mentioned in this book are in Indonesian rupiahs: 1,000 rupiahs = US$1 — more or less.
In Indonesian spelling 'c' = 'ch', 'a' approximates 'u' and a final 'k' on a word is often a glottal stop — you cut off the sound. So, as an example, 'cak' = 'cha!' — more or less.
Gods = God.

Contents

13	The beginning	120	Music
25	The original Balinese	129	Dancing
35	Family and village		The shadow play
	Working together		The trance dance
	The banjar	148	Painting
	The subak	163	Carving
	The pemaksan	169	History
45	The gentry		The Europeans
49	The language		A frenzy of death
51	The women		The wrath of the gods'
56	The calendar	194	No more Nyomans
	Occasions	200	Better living
	'Life-cycle' ceremonies	207	Better health
64	Cockfighting	213	Bali's wildlife
67	Eating, etcetera	223	Tourists in quarantine
	Something to chew on	231	Three Balinese places
77	Cremation		1 — Kuta
	The burning of widows		A word about the water
98	Religion	241	2 — Denpasar
106	Temples	245	3 — Ubud
	Besakih and other	250	. . and a Balinese journey
	ancient places	262	Books about Bali
	Other religions	263	Index

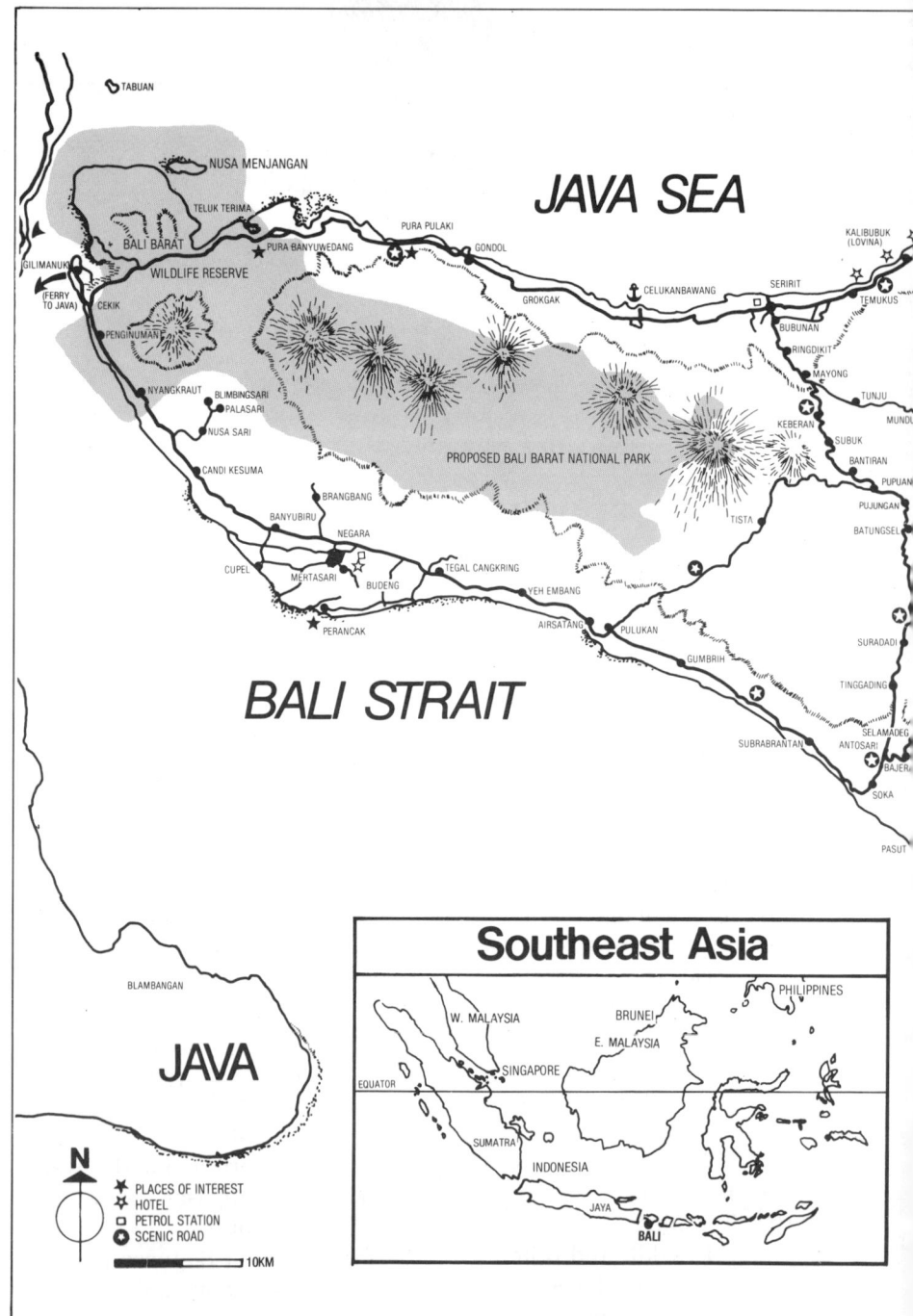

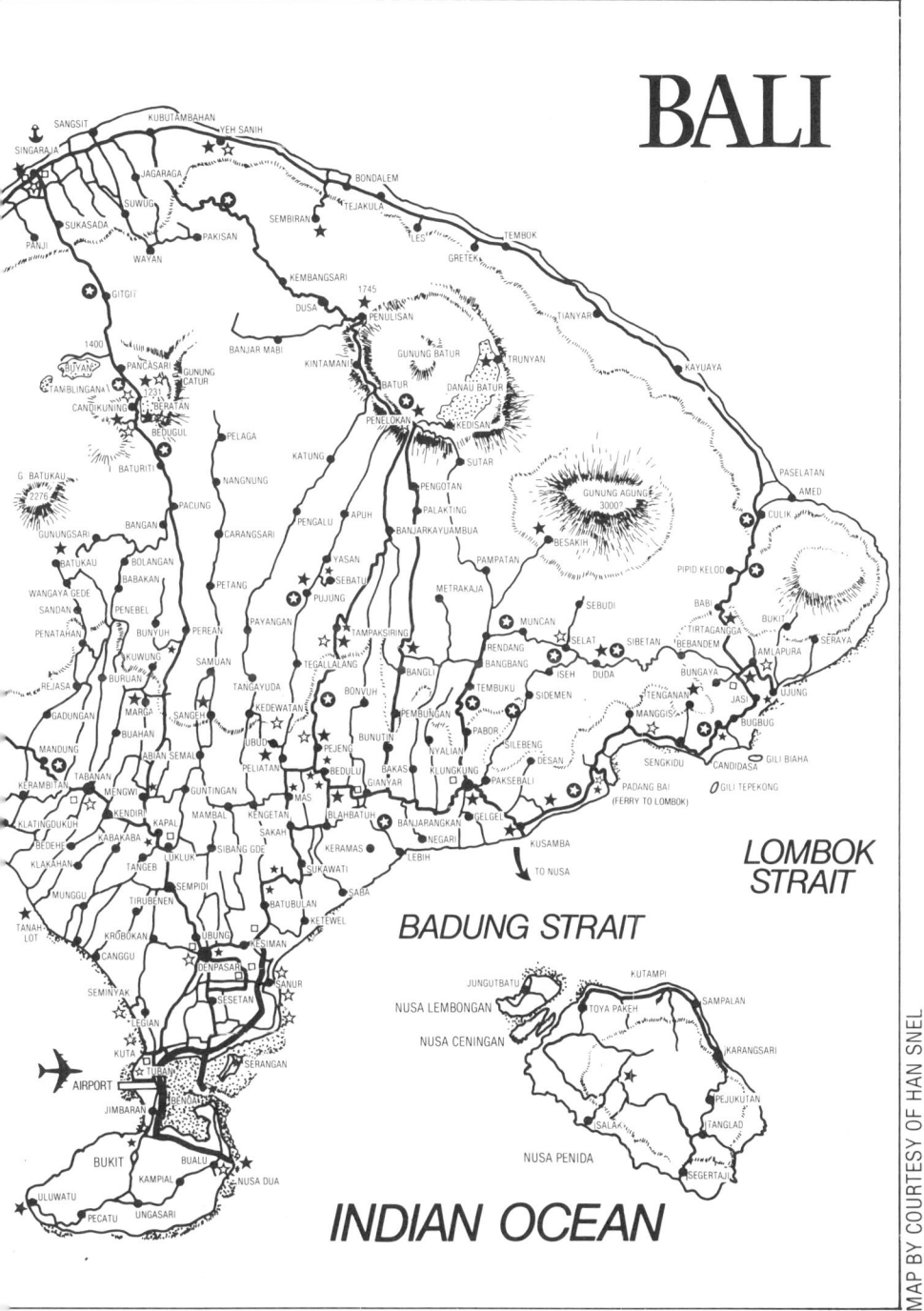

The Borobodnr t-shirt does not belong, but everything else in this picture, smiles and all, is Balinese.

The Beginning

he best way to arrive in Bali, the most famous island in the world, would be as a young and lusty adventurer about 100 years ago. Failing that, the 1930s was a good time for those well heeled enough to get along with Balinese gentry and Dutch colonial officials. But since neither of these courses is nowadays normally available, as good a way as any to arrive is by Garuda aircraft from Jakarta, the capital of Indonesia.

The flight takes ninety minutes. During that time I reflected that Garuda, as well as being the name of Indonesia's national airline, is important in Hindu mythology, and that I was flying to an island reputedly Hindu. Garuda is the eagle-like steed ridden by Vishnu which became the symbol of the mediaeval kingdom of Majapahit in Java, which at times included Bali in its embrace. Now Garuda is also Indonesia's state emblem   and thinking on that reminded me of the time I spent waiting for that state to give me permission to work on this book.

The Indonesian government distrusts foreign journalists but eventually I got my clearance because tourism is important to the Indonesian economy and Bali is central to the country's tourist industry. Perhaps my writing about it would help a little. Giving me a visa was an act of faith, but a cautious faith because it was a visa for only three months. As I ate my chicken lunch I wondered whether I could really come to grips with this hallowed island in such a short time. Only you, Dear Reader, as writers used to say, can be the judge of that. And perhaps my corrector too, because letters pointing out errors and omissions could be invaluable when work begins on an updated edition.

Bali is magic, all kinds of magic. Tolkien would have been astonished for here is an island with scenery to match his inventions, with people as remarkable in the flesh as his creations, with a way of life of such charm and intricacy that he would have thought again about his hobbits and heroes. Here we have a peasant community which centuries ago solved problems of harmony and co-operation which will vex the rest of the world for ever. Here we have creativity based on every person's certainty that he can achieve whatever artistic endeavour he sets his mind to. Here we have peasants who ruled their lords, lords who found solace in elaborate ceremonies and status seeking, gods who are invited to earth so everyone can have a party. . . .

What would Tolkien have made of a system of house measurement based on the physical size of the head of the household? Or of a community which so honoured blacksmiths that they were addressed with special terms of respect — so long as they held the tools of their trade in their hands? Or of an aristocracy with rules so intricate that at times a diner might take food with his left hand but not his right? Of a society where religion, custom and everyday life are inextricably and happily mixed? A society which believes totally in magic but has no call for fortune tellers, and which sees Heaven as just another Bali?

Tolkien would possibly have concluded that what the Balinese possess in full measure, and from which all else flows, is dignity. Note this man coming towards you along a footpath between two villages. He is marching strongly, his sarong tucked up around his thighs, his burden a shoulder pole with bunches of freshly picked coconuts at each end. His feet are bare and big in the dust, his chest is muscled, his hair combed, his moustache clipped like a film star's, his brow beaded with sweat. He is sturdy, confident, splendid. He smiles slightly as he passes. Here is a proud man, despite his humble calling, and the sense of dignity he represents is to be found at all levels in all parts of the island, among all Balinese.

Consider climbing a path through ricefields and orchards in the evening, rounding a corner and being confronted with eight bold breasts and four smiling faces over the concrete parapet of an irrigation channel used for bathing. There is no diving for shelter, no clutching for covering. Dignity wins and the encounter becomes a huge joke. You smile back, avert your gaze, or pretend to, and march on, leaving laughter behind — not mean and malicious laughter at your expense but open good humour.

A long-time resident I met in Sanur, a tourist centre, believes that the Balinese 'love a performance'. He advised me to watch a waiter, say, in action, turning the business of serving a meal into a theatrical production. Or to watch musicians — even those away from sight in the back row — as they toss their heads and gesticulate while playing. Or peasants as they thatch a house, or women as they march in procession carrying offerings.

There can be drama even in homely encounters. One night I was feeling my way down a completely dark village pathway when I saw two tiny red lights approaching. They were close together and, I guessed, well over two metres above the ground. They drew nearer and my puzzlement increased. Then they resolved themselves into the tips of two burning sticks of incense, atop a high offering, which it turn was atop a woman's head as she walked to a nearby temple. We wished each other a pleasant evening and continued on our way.

The confidence the Balinese have in themselves, which in turn must derive from the security of their family and community life, belies their often extreme poverty. The Balinese have such dignity, such physical sturdiness, such a disposition to smile easily, that it is easy to forget that most live spartan lives. There are many indications of this. Men tend ducks or cut and carry grass for tethered cattle. The ricefields demand endless labour. Women carry bricks from lorries or boulders from riverbeds. Children perform adult chores. Derisory sums of money become important.

Nonetheless, Balinese confidence in themselves means that a visitor who behaves reasonably will in general be treated reasonably. Despite the huge influx of strangers into their midst over the past two decades, the Balinese do not resent us. Their word for us, 'turis', remains totally neutral, unloaded and acceptable. If at times their prices are high, it is not so much that we must pay more as that the Balinese, their kin, must pay less. Our coming to their island helps the Balinese in their poverty. Our money is a gift from the gods, as it were, like a good harvest, and it would be absurd not to accept it with good grace.

Bali can be an endlessly complicated, even contradictory, island but some basic information can be readily dealt with. It is an island at the eastern end of Java in Indonesia, big enough to be the rather crowded home of 2.5 million people, far too small to figure significantly in any list of the world's islands by size. It is 5,426 sq km in area, slightly larger than the state of Delaware in the United States, less than half the size of Northern Ireland, just over twice the size of the Australian Capital Territory, ten times the size of Singapore.

Bali is one of the 24 provinces of Indonesia, which also includes two autonomous districts (Aceh in Sumatra and Jogjakarta in Java) and the 'special district' of Jakarta, the capital. The Balinese are only one of Indonesia's 300 ethnic groups and their language is only one of the country's 250.

Bali is smaller in size and population than the average Indonesian province but since it is important in Indonesia's economy as the country's primary tourist lure, it gets special attention from Jakarta. Economic growth rates exceed the Indonesian average. In 1983 tourism ranked seventh among Indonesia's foreign exchange earners, after oil, natural gas, timber, rubber, tin and coffee, and brought in nearly US$400 million. Without Bali the country's tourist industry would be much more modest.

There is a tendency to think the island has been drawing tourist hordes for decades. This is not so. Before World War II numbers were slight, the 1950s slid by without much action and for most of the 1960s Indonesia was not a country many people chose to visit. The Bali boom did not get under way until late in the 1960s. Since then it has been racing ahead madly as if desperate to make up lost time. French and Japanese consultants have estimated that foreign tourists to Bali will total 700,000 a year by 1990. When allowance is made for Indonesia's own domestic tourists, it becomes safe to assume that the island is on its way to entertaining a million visitors a year.

But back to basic information. A straight line from the eastern tip of Bali to the western is 145 km long, but the shortest distance by road between the two points, along the north coast, is 200 km. The shortest southern route is 210 km long. There is no central route because mountains get in the way. Gunung Agung (which means 'Great Mountain') was 3,142 metres high before a huge eruption in 1963 and is now 'about 3,000'. Gunung Abang is 2,152 metres; Gunung Catur 2,090 metres; Gunung Batukau 2,276 metres; and there are more of lesser height — much of the island is rugged. No fewer than ten of Bali's peaks are active volcanoes or were active until recently. As a result of volcanic activity, the island is fertile, as visitors appreciate when they see sticks stuck into the ground for whatever reason sprouting leaves.

Because Bali is at the eastern edge of an enormous time zone which embraces also all of Java and all of Sumatra, right to the western tip of Sumatra 2,500 km away, its hours of daylight take a little adjusting to. The sun rises in Bali ninety minutes before it does in western Sumatra, and it is broad daylight before 5am, narrow nightlight before 6pm. 'Some tourists think our people are lazy,' Professor Dr Ida Bagus Mantra, Governor of Bali, told me during an interview. 'That's because they don't often see people working in the fields. But most Balinese farmers have done most of their day's work before the tourists have even finished breakfast.'

They do most of their day's work early because Bali is hot and humid, with maximum temperatures at sea level around 30 degrees. These drop one degree with each 90 metres of altitude, and at night in mountain towns can fall to around 10 degrees. Rainfall in the south of the island where most Balinese live is around 1,800 mm a year, less than half that on the distinctly arid north coast and at the island's eastern and western tips. There is a distinct dry season between April and November, as this diagram showing the rainfall pattern at different stations over the year makes clear. I have taken the figures out as irrelevant; what matters is the shape:

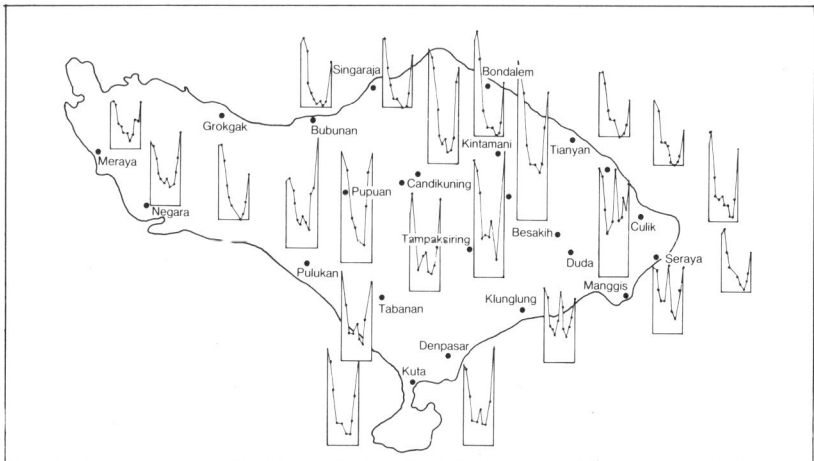

This rainfall pattern makes irrigation essential if Bali is to produce enough rice to feed all its people. The Balinese have developed the art of irrigation over at least 1,000 years, and in so doing have sculpted and tailored their landscape into the spectacular vistas that we visitors admire today. More important, the discipline that irrigation imposes has been fundamental to the success of the Balinese in evolving a marvellously co-operative way of life which yet leaves much room for individual freedom. The institutions they developed came in turn to shape aspects of their society and remain vitally important to Balinese culture today.

Another historical element which lives on is the division of the island, earlier into kingdoms, now into eight administrative districts, or regencies, based on the old kingdoms. The capital of the province of Bali is Denpasar, with about 260,000 people, which takes its name from two words meaning 'beside the market'; the second of the two words, 'pasar', has the same Persian origin as the English word 'bazaar'. Denpasar is also frequently known as Badung, its old name and the name of the regency which it serves as capital. A similar flexibility is found with Amlapura, also known as Karangasem; Singaraja, also known as Buleleng; and Negara, also known as Jembrana. In each case the town's name is interchangeable with that of its regency. The other four regencies are Tabanan, Gianyar, Bangli and Klungkung, each with a capital of the same name.

The most important of Bali's eight regencies from the tourist's point of view is Badung, which contains the airport, the resort towns of Sanur and Kuta, the coming resort of Nusa Dua and the port of Benoa, as well as the island's capital and largest town. Most visitors to Bali spend all their nights and most of their days in Badung. They cross into other regencies only during day trips to visit the cultural centres of Mas, Peliatan and Ubud, in Gianyar, or Kintamani, in Bangli, where they view the spectacular Gunung Batur volcanic crater. Only the more adventurous and more fortunate get to other parts of the island. This means that there are considerable areas which have escaped the tourist blight. This will remain so as long as the present policy of confining tourist development to a small part of the south of the island is maintained. The relevant chapter in this book is titled 'Tourists in Quarantine'. The system works well and is not likely to be changed.

If tourists break out of quarantine, it is likely to be by means of a remarkable contribution to the world's ideas about public transport. It is called the bemo. The first two letters of this word are short for 'becak', the three-wheeled, pedal-driven, man-powered successor to the rickshaw which ones sees in enormous numbers in Java, not so much in other parts of Indonesia. The last two letters of the word, 'mo', stand for 'motor'. So, a bemo is a motorised becak. The original bemo was probably a kind of three-wheeled motor scooter with room for three or four passengers. The streets of Denpasar are thronged with them, except they now have room for six, plus another in the driver's cabin. The word is applied nowadays also to the much larger vehicles which ply between the towns of Bali. Anything smaller than a bus is a bemo.

You catch one either by going to a bus station or by standing at the roadside waiting for one to arrive. During daylight hours you rarely have long to wait; at night you might wait till dawn. When a bemo stops for you, the conductor urges, indeed pushes you aboard among the other passengers, you agree on the fare, and away you go. The system is run by hundreds of independent operators who work together to maintain a kind of regularity along the highways but who otherwise compete for customers. They provide excellent service and impress many visitors as more efficient than the corporate or corporation services of their home towns. I mention all this because the word 'bemo' is much used in this book.

Every hour of every day among the Balinese I learned a little. I learned something when I asked a drinks hawker the time, and he glanced at the sun and gave a near-enough answer. At that moment three children marched past, singing 'Indo One, Indo Two, INDO STREE!' Perhaps it was an advertising jingle from television. They had a pig on a leash, and were walking it just like a dog. Later the same morning, a couple of days after arriving in Bali, I encountered something else, and mention it here to deal with an issue which could otherwise bedevil this book.

While walking along a sandy path — in the best of all possible worlds we would always travel along quiet, shady, sandy paths — I was passed by a cyclist, an Indian-looking man with long hair, beard and ear-rings. He reminded me of a man from Singapore then said to be in Bali. I called after him: 'Mohan!'

The cyclist skidded to a stop, looked back, said: 'Mohan? I was playing music with him last night.' One of those coincidences. We repaired to a coffee stall, as they say, and told each other of our doings. His name was Akah, not Indian but from the Moluccas, Maluku as Indonesia spells it, where people are taller and darker than the Balinese. Like many Moluccans he is an enterprising do-anythinger.

What he was doing in Bali was making music. What he really

wanted to do was return to Australia, where he had lived for some years, and pitch a tent on an opal field out in the desert. There he would collect stone which the miners had discarded as inferior, bring it back to Bali, and set superior craftsmen to bringing out its unsuspected wonders. He would make money. In the meantime he made music. And sometimes he made himself nervous.

I wrote earlier that 'Bali is magic, all kinds of magic'. Akah, unprompted, raised this theme. 'There's black magic here,' he said. 'Sometimes it's like a wall. Mohan feels it too. The other night he was playing and his fingers froze. He couldn't move them. The young Balinese were staring at him and he couldn't move his fingers.

'A musician projects to his listeners. Here the listeners can project back at you. They have lots of energy, these young people, but sometimes not good energy. They can make you do things. They do it to the girl tourists.' Akah's eyes shone and he waggled his beard. 'There's a lot of madness here in Bali.'

The Balinese religion and way of life may indeed have a dark side, as Akah said. The Balinese system of balanced good and bad, of gods and demons, says as much but not even scholars who have worked for years in Bali have attempted to record it in detail. I am not going to try, nor recount the further stories I heard which hinted at it. To do so would be as silly as devoting space to superstition, say, in a general book about England. I have included Akah's slightly absurd story merely to raise the subject of black magic so I can put it down again, and henceforth leave it out as beyond my competence. That anyone might be competent to write about black magic is a frightening thought.

Bali is famous because it is spectacularly beautiful and because it has a unique and attractive culture which this book will attempt to describe. It is also famous, this being the way the world works, because many people go there as tourists. 'It is Bali's fate,' an old friend, Allington Kennard, once wrote in a book review, 'to have been officially declared a paradise.' He also wrote, in the Singapore Straits Times, as follows: 'The old books about Bali are the best. This is as natural as Bali itself. We read and must be grateful that so much of the beauty, the legend and the romance of the "Isle of the Gods" remains in what has become the land of the tourist.'

He was right, and anyone who wishes to understand this fabled island must indeed read those books of the 1930s which made Bali famous — and whose writers lamented that they feared the damage

A German photographer, Gregor Krause, took the picture on the left about 1912 and published it in 1922. The drawing on the right is in a book published in the United States in 1930.

that fame would bring. Just how good they can be was illustrated in October, 1983, when an official magazine, Bali This Month, reprinted a whole section direct from Miguel Covarrubias' Island of Bali, published in 1936. Very little had changed since those days, the magazine said, in the way of life and social order of many people in the countryside and villages, and to some extent even in the towns.

Covarrubias was a Mexican who settled in the United States until he saw an album of 200 photographs of Bali by Gregor Krause which had been published in Germany in 1922. The photographs developed in him what he called an irresistible urge to see Bali for himself, and in 1930 he and his wife landed there to do so. They stayed a few months, returned home, then came back to Bali in 1933 to live there for several years.

The only aim of his book, he wrote in its introduction, was to present 'all that could be obtained from personal experience by an unscientific artist, of a living culture that is doomed to disappear under the merciless onslaught of modern commercialism and standardisation'. First editions of his work have become collectors' items but an Oxford in Asia reprint is available for those who do not want to wait for an original to come along.

Covarrubias' book remains outstanding but it is only a starting point in available reading. For decades Bali has brought out the best in good writers and the worst in bad. The island has inspired more volumes than perhaps any other comparable part of the world. The more that books have been written to fuel American and European fascination with Bali, the more have flowed forth to meet that fascination. But they have not always been improvements on the old. For example, Gregor Krause's album of superb black-and-white photographs, still as fascinating today for their technical excellence as for their artistry and content, continues to hold its own against today's glossiest productions.

Two other notable books of the 1930s (though one was not published until 1947, what with World War II and all) now readily available in reprints are Colin McPhee's A House in Bali and Hickman Powell's The Last Paradise. Many other travellers included sections on Bali in their accounts of Asian wanderings. To all these must be added two notable postwar books. One, only partly about Bali, is Revolt in Paradise, by an American, Muriel Pearson, writing under her given Balinese name of K'tut Tantri. The other is The Night of Purnama, by Anna Mathews, an account of experiences in a village on the slopes of Gunung Agung during a disastrous eruption in 1963.

Outstanding among other postwar writers is Clifford Geertz (at times in partnership with his wife Hildred), who when he can be understood amid all the sociology is often marvellous. For history there is none better than Willard A. Hanna, whose Bali Profile is by far the most comprehensive and compassionate history book available. For culture in general, I have relied much on the English translation of Urs Ramseyer's Art And Culture Of Bali. Other books are mentioned as I refer to information I gained from them.

There is no end to reading about Bali, so I was fortunate that ignorance of languages closed to me entire libraries of books especially in Dutch, but also in Indonesian, French, German, Japanese and other languages.

Lest all this gives the impression that this book is a mere regurgitation of other people's ideas, well, most books are. But I did do as much first-hand reporting as I could in the time allowed, I talked to as many people as possible, I travelled a good deal, and I returned to Bali twice to check my impressions. I gave myself sufficient exposure to cope, I think, with a problem central to all writing about Bali, the destructive effect of an excess of enthusiasm. No writing becomes so boring so quickly as that which results from transports of delight, though in Bali it is hard not to be carried away.

Consider the ricefields. These terraced panoramas fringed and decorated with coconut palms, bamboo, orchards and jungly groves

Do the ricefield terraces climb uphill?

at first sight have a stunning impact. Does one write of them then? Or after a week, or a month, or so much later that that first enthusiasm has vanished and cannot be recalled. There is no real answer. The sense of spectacle should no doubt be imparted but it would be a tedious travelling companion who continued to enthuse. I have tried not to do so, in this case of the ricefields for example, except in terms of admiration for the agricultural sculptors who created them. If I tried to cut farm plots out of a hillside as they do, the result would be a sliding, muddy disaster.

Why the bunds which hold back earth and water on steep slopes do not fall away is just one of many Balinese mysteries. Thinking about it led me to another marvellous aspect. Often I saw farmers

23

trimming soil from the earthen walls of their fields, sliding it down into the mud and spreading it around; perhaps, because that soil was once volcanic ash, it is excellent fertiliser. I also saw farmers moving soil to the tops and inside edges of the bunds, compensating for the higher levels which result when soil is added to the fields.

Over many years, this must cause fields to climb higher up the slope in a kind of reverse erosion. Such movement would be impossible to perceive — but imagine the effects over decades and centuries. Time-lapse photography would show the entire countryside to ripple, as if alive. The gods whom the Balinese believe live in a tiered heaven above Gunung Agung, and who have much finer sensitivities than we have, are surely able to detect such movement, and be reassured by it.

Perhaps these days they need such reassurance, as changes of other kinds sweep their island, if they are to remain convinced that Bali really is as eternal as their godly beliefs insist. How can it stand the pressures that modern times have brought? How has it stood them so well, so far? No man is an island, the poet wrote; and no island is an island either, in these days of radio, television, newspapers, magazines, books and mass travel. The world is endlessly complicated and there are more questions than answers. I climbed a volcano partly to ponder this matter, and from its slopes saw, in the distance, a village of gleaming rooftops. . . .

The Original Balinese

From Kintamani and Penelokan on the rim of the huge Batur crater, from the mountainside as we scrambled up and down the Batur volcano, there was visible a gleam of iron roofs across a lake, a huddle of houses trapped between water and the cliff behind. It was the village of Trunyan, our next destination, and our vehicle to get there turned out to be a canoe dug from a big treetrunk, patched with sections of old car tyres wherever water seeped through.

Trunyan figures in virtually every book ever written about Bali as one of the tiny number of villages which have retained the oldest religion on the island. Its people are usually called Bali Aga, from another pronunciation of the word 'aja', which means mountain; therefore, 'Mountain People'. The term is vaguely demeaning and Bali Asli, for Original Balinese, might be better.

We an Austrian man, a Swiss woman, a guide named Wayan Ngedap and I — paddled our own canoe across the lake, and enjoyed it though the craft was heavy and cumbersome. The day was bright now, after a misty morning, and breezy, and the temperature at that height, 750 m, pleasant. Crossing took about half an hour and we landed at the same time as a party of Javanese tourists who arrived by motorboat from Kedisan, at the head of the lake beneath Penelokan.

Many tourists come back from Trunyan with unhappy stories about unhappy people interested only in getting as much money as

25

they can from visitors. Bill Dalton's Indonesia Handbook says the village 'ain't much', that one is not really welcome, and that staying overnight is 'cold and scary'. But perhaps we were there at the wrong time. A couple of men were importunate and some children pestered us for ballpoint pens but otherwise we found the people much like other villagers in Bali, friendly when there was contact but otherwise not paying us much heed.

At first there seemed little to see. The village was different from others I had seen, with houses packed more closely together, without the gardens and trees to be found elsewhere. There is a big temple famous for housing what is said to be the biggest statue in Bali, three metres high, the village's patron guardian. Visitors are not allowed to see it and even villagers are admitted only on ceremonial occasions. From time to time 'virgin boys' clean the statue and paint it with a mixture of chalk, honey and water. The same boys used to take part in rituals in which they were dressed in great bundles of dried banana leaves and fierce masks, and set to running around the temple grounds whipping anyone they could reach. This tradition has been maintained but in a much watered-down form.

Another practice which has survived, and one much written about as evidence of uniqueness, involves disposal of the dead. No great Balinese cremations here, or even burials. The people of Trunyan expose their dead to the elements, and Bali's most unlikely tourist 'attraction' is surely the little jungle grove where this is done. We four canoeists got back in our boat and paddled around a rocky point, into a tiny cove, to see it.

There was a derelict temple gateway with cheap plastic bowls, the sort one washes plates in, on either side. Each bowl contained two human skulls and some longish bones. A sign in Indonesian was translated into English as, 'It is prohibited to destroy the cemetery'. Amid the trees behind the gateway, on the steep slope, were ten tiny plots, each roughly fenced with split bamboo only a couple of feet high, each containing a human body at some stage of disintegration.

One body had black, parchment-like skin on its face while its legs had been reduced to bone. Others appeared to have sunk into the earth or were partly covered in forest litter. There were no smells, nor flies, nor ants, nothing unpleasant, not even the bones scattered here and there. They were mixed with old enamel and plastic plates, scraps of cloth which had once covered the corpses, and a strewing of the old Chinese coins used throughout Bali as talismans which had been included in offerings. One of the little fences had a skull on it.

Wayan said the site had room for eleven bodies. When it is full, if another death occurs, the remains of the oldest body are unceremoniously pushed down the slope into a kind of rubbish dump of bones, old bamboo and forest debris. As a way of disposing of the dead it makes as much sense as any other — and I have yet to hear an explanation of why that little grove is not foul with the odour of decomposition.

When we were back in our boat, out from shore a little, we learned a little more about this mountain village's way of life, as opposed to its way of death. Trunyan really is virtually trapped between the lake and the precipitous cliffs behind. It has little room for farming, and not that much forest to draw fuel from. Burning or burying the dead would deprive the living of land or material they need to survive.

Looking back at the village we had just visited provided that little insight, and by chance a more important one. We had thought Trunyan to be accessible only by water and by a path along the lakeside but now we made out the faintest trace of a track zigzagging up the cliff behind. It leads, Wayan told us, to Trunyan's other half on the slightly more gentle slopes outside the crater. The lakeside village has about 600 people, the mountain one another 600.

We had been in Trunyan in school hours and the school had been a riot of noise and activity. Now the children were heading homewards, some of them up that precipitous trail. We could pick them out, tiny dots of colour, scrambling upwards, resting, scrambling upwards again. Children from outside the crater descend that almost unbelievable track each morning to go to school, climb back each afternoon. That distant glimpse taught me more about mountain life in Bali than anything I had seen before.

Meanwhile we travellers in our hollowed log faced a journey of our own. Our destination was Kedisan, right at the other end of the lake, another huddle of distant shining roofs. In between lay an expanse of choppy green water and a stiff breeze had come from nowhere to blow right in our faces. Even getting abreast of Trunyan again after visiting the cemetery was a dispiriting exercise. I remembered that only the previous morning I had been out sailing on the sea in one of Bali's beautiful and nimble fishing boats, flitting across the waves at a speed that made our present situation even more depressing.

Then a good and true Trunyan man intent on living up to all the harsh comments travellers have made about his village came into the picture. He circled our sluggish log with his motorboat and offered to take us to Kedisan for 10,000 rupiahs. His manner irked us and we plugged on paddling. He continued circling, waiting for us to give in, sure that wind and water would win in the end. Slowly he began lowering his fee, but this annoyed us even more as we struggled on, our clumsy craft lurching in the waves, our hands beginning to blister, our faces reddening in the westering sun.

'We love our little canoe,' the Austrian called out, and we drove on, all manner of new muscles in our shoulders and backs calling attention to themselves. Our inspiration to this effort, that man with his motorboat, persisted for more than an hour. His price came down to 2,000 rupiahs, we responded with a derisory 500, and he looked desolated. He was sure, so great the distance, so slow our progress, that we would give in. When he finally decided otherwise, having burned who knows how many rupiahs worth of fuel, we were more than halfway to Kedisan. Our victory inspired us to tackle the other half.

We got to Kedisan about two hours before dark. My companions had a motorcycle and wanted to be in Kuta, a seaside town, that night. I wanted to get to Ubud, about half as far away — partly to avoid another night and another bath in Penelokan, where the water is too cold to amuse. I faced the problem of climbing out of the crater: Four kilometres, very steep road, no certainty of bemos. It would be near dark when I walked out and there would be little prospect of transport to Ubud. My companions offered a solution, and a ride, and we screamed up that winding road, three on board, none of us small, in such style that the Japanese makers of that little 125 cc bike would have bowed and beamed with delight.

Before dark I was back in my hotel in Ubud, where the water as I washed off volcanic dust and the sweat of a long, hard paddle was refreshing rather than chilling. That evening I set about learning more about the Original Balinese, and that pursuit took me a few days later to the village of Tenganan.

Throughout the southeast Asian islands one finds occasional remnants of patterns of settlement in more or less concentric circles. Each circle represents a people retreating further into the centre of the island as new migrants settled around the edges. Successive waves produced successive retreats, so that the oldest inhabitants lived in the highest and most central areas, with more recent arrivals layered down the mountainsides beneath them. As I said, only remnants of this pattern remain, not enough to postulate a general rule. But if there were a rule, Trunyan, hidden away in the Balinese highlands, would be an example of it, and Tenganan would be an exception.

Tenganan is in the lowlands, it is only three kilometres from the sea, it is more or less midway along a much-travelled route betweeen the historic towns of Klungkung and Amlapura. Yet within its valley it has preserved for centuries elements of culture long lost in almost all other parts of the island. It has achieved this not through isolation, though its valley gives a measure of separation from the world outside, but through the villagers' absolute conviction that they are descended from gods.

This has produced an addiction to ritual remarkable even for Bali, coupled with entrenched conservatism and discipline. Ownership of much prime rice land, worked by share-cropping outsiders, has also helped, giving the villagers free time to engage in and perpetuate their ancient ways. The Tenganan villagers include some of the wealthiest landowners in Bali.

Not that tourists who arrive by bus, up a newly sealed sideroad from the round-island highway, see much evidence of either prosperity or addiction to tradition. What they do see are stone walls with narrow doorways, a wide, stone-paved street with stone ramps between its different levels, water buffaloes and wandering pigs, a long council hall, a cockfighting arena which is no longer used, and not many people.

'Since the village inhabitants' ritual life generally takes place early in the morning, in the evening or at night, foreigners guided through the hot valley basin in the early afternoon occasionally get the impression that they are moving through the lifeless streets of a ghost town,' Urs Ramseyer, a Swiss scholar who spent much time there, wrote in his monumental Art and Culture of Bali.

The ritual, legal and economic life of Tenganan is ruled by a council made up of all married people whose children are not yet married. As children marry, they supplant their parents on the council, which has the effect of making it an organisation of mainly young people. This has not made it any less conservative and it remains diligent in enforcing the old rules.

These rules are remorseless — and promise disaster. While most of the rest of Bali is adapting to change, Tenganan has tried to remain frozen, and as a result may not even survive. The rules prohibit polygamy, divorce and marriage to people from outside the valley. It is now clear that a community as small as this one cannot afford such strictness. Trunyan is distinctive partly for its method of dealing with the dead. Tenganan (which buries its dead) is bidding to become more famous because of a certain problem at the other end of the span of human life.

As I was shown through the village my guide, a local man, maintained a dolorous commentary on each house as we passed by: 'This house has no children. This house has only one. This one has only one old woman, living alone. This house is empty. . . .' And so on. The population of Tenganan, despite better medical care, is plunging downwards.

About the turn of this century the village had 700 people. Its population when I visited was 291, in only 106 families. My guide's precision about this, about the numbers of old people and of unmarried young ones, made it clear that population is a matter of pervading community interest. His further comments bore this out. 'Many women never become pregnant,' he said. 'Some have only one or two children, and three children is rare.' And, 'last year six people died but only three were born.' And later, 'Maybe it is because we are only one blood. Maybe we need to have new blood from outside — but that is against our tradition.' The idea that a tradition should ever be broken seemed to leave him in awe. It was surprising, he added, not really surprised, that girls from the village who broke the rules and married outside often had 'many' children.

Villagers who marry outside are exiled, even today. But that need not involve travelling to some Balinese Siberia. The village has three streets, West, Middle and East. East Street is where the outcasts live, those of them who do not move to Denpasar or other towns. The street looks much the same as the other two, though poorer, but the barrier is complete: Exiles never return, never re-enter their family homes, can never regain acceptance. East Street's residents produce many children.

A team of doctors from Basle in Switzerland has been examining Tenganan's population problem. When I was there the doctors had already recommended earlier marriages, girls at 17 and boys at 18, 19 or 20, than was general practice. But the more fundamental report was still awaited.

There would be a big ceremony when the doctors came back with their findings, I was told, though waiting for this to happen involved a deal of trepidation: What if the doctors said the villagers must change their rules, permit marriage with outsiders, bring in the 'new blood' which had so awed my guide? 'The council would have to talk about it for a long time,' he said. There would be much resistance to such a change, since approving it would imply that the gods from whom the Tengananese are descended had abandoned them. Little from the old ways would long survive such a blow to the community's pride. Already Tenganan has trouble maintaining one of its more exotic rituals, a kind of mating ceremony in which girls are spun through the air on a wooden ferris wheel. It is supposed to be an annual event but when I was there had not been held for three years, for a lack of young people to take part.

And what about those people in East Street? How insufferable they would be if the council ever had to agree that there was no real crime in marrying outsiders. And the people outside who are only too eager to look down on the Bali Aga? News of such a change would make the people of Tenganan a laughing stock. There would indeed be much to talk about.

In the meantime, while waiting for this crunch, life in Tenganan gets a certain lift from a persistent fascination throughout Bali, and beyond, with the village's most famous product. Tenganan is the only place in Indonesia, one of the very few in the world, making 'double ikat' cloth.

'Ikat' means 'to tie', and is applied to a process in which the threads which will make up a cloth are 'tied and dyed' before weaving. Binding the hanks of thread in careful patterns before dyeing means that the dye reaches only some sections. Several dyeings with bindings in different patterns can go into creating thread which can then be woven into colourful and unusual cloths, usually in sarong lengths. Normally only the warp, the lengthwise threads, or the weft, the crosswise threads, are dyed in this manner. In Bali most weavers prefer to dye the weft.

But the Tengananese centuries ago took the process further. They began dying both the warp and the weft, a mind-boggling operation since it meant envisaging where and how the two would intersect. It seems to me reasonable that such a creative urge should be rewarded with the utmost respect, even veneration, for the cloth which results. It became known as 'grinsing' or 'gringsing', meaning 'flaming' or 'iridescent' from its flicker of colours. (Another interpretation says the word means 'not sick', but this seems to have been forced from separate translations of the two syllables.) Throughout Bali this cloth is widely regarded as magical.

There is a steady market for even tiny scraps of grinsing cloth, at 1,000 rupiahs each, to be worn as amulets against evil. Large old cloths of good quality are described as priceless, or may wind up in well-endowed western museums. Pieces may be loaned or rented to help during illnesses. Even the water in which a grinsing cloth has been rinsed may have virtue: it is a remedy for curing a sick cow.

Just before going to Bali I read that only one woman in Tenganan was still making grinsing cloth, and that she was very old. I asked about her and was told that she had died. But three other women were back at work attending to the tieing and dying, and about ten were engaged in less specialised work of weaving.

The art lives on and perhaps will do so as long as there is a worthwhile market for grinsing cloth. The Balinese market may fade away, or continue to make do with old scraps, since the price of new grinsing cloth must be high, but tourism offers hope that the village will continue to produce. A good quality new cloth, 140 cm by 22 cm, will cost nearly 100,000 rupiahs — which is not an extraordinary amount for a remarkable product.

On the other hand, prices may go higher if production shows signs of ceasing, as well it might if the women of the village decide their time would be better spent in other ways. Embarking on the manufacture of a grinsing cloth is no light matter because much time and toil is involved. Just how much time it is difficult to say because work is never continuous. Claims that a good cloth takes five years to make mean simply that work may be spun out over that time. But the task of harvesting and spinning the cotton, collecting materials for the vegetable dyes, tieing and dying the warp and the weft, and weaving the final product — all this is surely an awesome one to contemplate.

The person in Tenganan who does so is always a woman, for the men seems always to have other things to do, such as showing tourists around, planning the next ritual ceremony, supervising work on their rented-out fields, running the village's half-dozen shops. Or making palm-leaf books. Pictures and text are cut into 2 cm-wide strips of lontar palm leaf with a small, sharp chisel, and then smeared with a mixture of lampblack and oil from a forest nut. When this mixture is wiped away, the cuts stand out black and sharp, showing often remarkable detail in a tiny area. The leaves are collected between split bamboo covers into books, usually Balinese calendars, which have an antique air and make excellent souvenirs.

I bought one from a jovial, grandly moustached shopkeeper who was whiling away the time playing jigs on a xylophone made with four iron keys, unlike the usual Balinese bronze ones, and playing a flute at the same time. He contrived to make two hands do three hands' work, and I was impressed. The xylophone, he said, came from a village in the hills behind and was made specially for tourists: 'So easy, we sell so many, [US]$50 each.'

Heavy rain began to fall and I stayed chatting with him until it stopped. He told me the village is 700 years old, that the Tenganan men are the only ones in Bali to wear earrings, that the village rules include a nightly 10pm curfew — loudly called out — for all unmarried young people. Anyone wanting to leave the village to go to work outside, or even to visit Denpasar, has to get the council's permission first; visiting Denpasar without permission could result in a 3,000 rupiahs fine.

I asked him about the village's dwindling population. Swiss doctors had taken blood samples from everyone and were looking for a solution, he said. I asked what would happen if the doctors recommended that the Tengananese find wives and husbands outside the village. 'Not possible,' he said firmly. 'Our law is very strong.' He smiled broadly and played another lively tune on his xylophone.

Most writers about Bali like to present a clear-cut distinction between the Bali Aga people and the rest of the Balinese. This seems a little forced. What we have is not so much a clear line as a blurring of the boundaries which has been going on for centuries. Nor does the lack of a really clear definition of what is Bali Aga and what is not help bring clarity. The conventional distinction has been between people who cremate their dead and those who do not, but in fact the great majority of Balinese are not cremated; they are buried to await the possibility of cremation, which is not quite the same thing.

Another complication is the stigma which has become attached to the phrase 'Bali Aga'. It must be presumed that many people in a position to avoid this slur do so. The spread of education and of the Indonesian language helps this process, because it is reducing the number of people who know only their dialects. Wayan, our guide up Gunung Batur, said that he could understand about three-quarters of the words spoken in Trunyan. Years ago he would have understood fewer; in time there will be no difference between his language and theirs.

In Batur I tried to explore this idea but the notion that some people might exist in a grey area between Bali Aga and the rest was firmly rejected. 'There are only three Bali Aga villages in Bali,' I was told severely. 'They are Trunyan, here in Batur; Tenganan, away to the east; and Sembiran.'

Covarrubias mentions Sembiran as one of 'many' mountain villages 'which have resisted the influence of Hinduism', along with Tenganan and Trunyan. Its temple in his day was a group of rough stone altars hidden in the jungle near a deep ravine, 'a dangerous, haunted place'. The dead were not buried but were wrapped in a cloth and left on a bamboo platform in the jungle for three days. If after three days the body had not been taken away by wild animals it was unceremoniously thrown into a ravine.

I went to Sembiran, by way of a heart-stopping walk up a steep 3 km road from a village near Tejakula, east of Singaraja. It is a compact village of iron and tile rooftops surrounded not by jungle, as in Covarrubias' day, but by orange groves and terraced maize fields. I could see little to set it apart from most other Balinese villages I had visited.

Later, as I sat at a coffee stall in the market, I was told variously that the village had once been Bali Aga but was not so now; that some people still practised the Bali Aga religion; and that it was not nice to call people Bali Aga anyway, or even to ask about them. This was done pleasantly enough, and was supported by instructions on where to see the village's excellent Balinese temples and shrines. Later I was told that the people of Sembiran no longer expose their dead but bury them — and that there are sometimes cremations.

It occured to me then that Sembiran, prosperous with orchards and farms and without any interest in tourists, was not under any pressure to proclaim its adherence to the old ways. On the contrary, it could benefit from becoming like the villages of the plains below. Trunyan, a community with little land and few resources, needs tourists for the semblance of an industry they create, and a demonstrated adherence to the old ways helps bring them in. Tenganan, as Ramseyer wrote, is so imbued with confidence in its divine origin that it will have extreme trouble changing even to save itself. But Sembiran, and presumably other villages like it, probably can see little reason to resist a slow transition to conformity with the rest of Bali.

Family and Village

hreads through the Balinese way of life can lead in surprising directions. Consider personal names. A system which I thought at first was exotic but not much else turned out to contain clues to the entire social system. As a result, what was to have been a kind of postscript has had to be raised to this point of prominence, introducing a chapter which will seek to explain the co-operative way of life which is Bali's outstanding achievement.

Most societies use personal names as a way of keeping track of family relationships. The great majority of Balinese almost deliberately use names as a means of forgetting them. A naming system which seems at first the very model of simplicity turns out to be intricate, difficult and destructive of conventional structure.

The visitor will quickly encounter the simple part. Most Balinese he meets, men or women, will be named Wayan, Made (with the 'e' pronounced), Nyoman or Ktut (or K'tut or Ketut). This is the system prevailing among the 'commoners', who make up about nine-tenths of the island's people, as opposed to the gentry, about whom more shortly. A commoner couple's first child is named Wayan, the second Made, the third Nyoman and the fourth Ktut. If there are more, the cycle may begin again, possibly omitting Wayan, a name sometimes reserved for the first-born; or all subsequent children may be named Ktut. Later in this book I have a chapter about family planning titled 'No More Nyomans' because if families stop at two, as they are urged to, they will have no Nyomans, or Ktuts either. There are regional and dialect variations, as when Made becomes Kade. Children are also given personal names but the four names which indicate the sequence of births are much used both inside the family and out, rather as in old China much use was made of 'Oldest Brother', 'Second Sister', 'Third Aunt' and so on.

Commoner names also include the initial name I (pronounced 'ee') for men and Ni for women, as a sex indicator and honorific. The I is to be distinguished from 'I.' which is an abbreviation in the western manner for Ida, a gentry name usually linked with Bagus, as in Ida Bagus Mantra, the Governor of Bali. Gentry names are much more complicated and do not necessarily include numbering elements. When they do, they follow the commoner pattern but with Gde or Gede (pronounced like an Australian 'good-day') or Putu for the first-born.

Now for the hard part, which begins with a hard word: Teknonymy. It means a system in which people are named not after their ancestors but after their descendants. Pan Seken means father of Seken. When Seken grows up and has a child, he becomes Pan someone else. In general a man or woman is known in this manner, after his or her first child, thereafter, though Pan may eventually give way to Kak, grandfather, or later still to Kumpi, great-grandfather. On the other hand, a man or woman who has never had a child retains his or her childhood name as a cruel and shameful proclamation of infertility.

This custom of identifying people by their children rather than by their forebears produces odd results. In the first place, to quote Clifford Geertz, 'Balinese parents view genealogy not as something which produces them but as something which they produce'. Time flows not so much from the past to the present as from the present to the future. The child is more important than the parent.

Second, the system causes forebears to be quickly forgotten as individuals, being lumped together more or less anonymously into an entire assemblage honoured in the ancestor-worshipping part of the Balinese religion. 'The Balinese rarely if ever know who began their local line,' says Geertz, 'do not really care, and regard it as mildly improper even to want to know.' This phenomenon whereby ancestors vanish into a mist of lore and legend he calls 'institutionalised genealogical amnesia'.

It begins right with the birth of a couple's first child, or at least as soon as the child has survived the first few dangerous weeks of life. Its parents become known as the mother or father of that child. It becomes impolite to use the parents' personal names which fade away through disuse. It is not uncommon for children never to know their fathers' or mothers' original names. Cousins may never know they are related. The 'extended family' concept which is so important in so many other parts of the world, where relationships are carefully remembered, does not apply to the commoners of Bali. This has important consequences in the conduct of village affairs.

Working together

Just before I arrived in Bali a celebration in Ubud, a town in Gianyar regency, had included a competition in which children were invited to climb a slippery tree trunk to win prizes hanging amid the top branches. The children failed, and failed again, until they agreed among themselves that competing was foolish. They formed a human pyramid, got one of their number to the top of the tree, and shared the prizes. That was a Balinese solution — and according to the man who told me about it, it was the solution the children were expected to arrive at.

It was the kind of solution Buckminster Fuller had in mind when

A village street, hub of the Balinese world.

he praised the island's co-operative society 'in which people love their work, love it together, and love to support and give happiness to each other'.

Co-operation in Balinese life, when it needs to be arranged, is handled through village institutions which must appear as blazing rockets of enlightenment to all those westerners who have played around with alternative life styles. None of them has yet devised a commune that really works. They all founder, or at least stray from their ideals, because of the problem of political control. Too few rules and there is anarchy; too many and there is resentment.

The Balinese answer has been to have rules for all situations but to diffuse responsibility for administering them among several and democratic organisations. The Balinese system never pushes a person into just one box as the western idea of co-operation so often does. The Balinese divide their community work among several boxes; if one does not suit, there are others to help diminish discontent and make life bearable.

The banjar

The best known of these boxes, though none is more important than any other, is the banjar. As you move around Bali you see numerous open buildings with signboards, Banjar This or Banjar That. The word cannot be translated though Dutch colonial officers perhaps came close with words meaning 'village republic'. The banjar is a busy organisation supervising many aspects of life in its village, or its ward if the village has grown too big for just one banjar to manage.

It works through a council of residents which attends to such matters as marriage, divorce, inheritance, and the building and maintenance of public buildings, markets, roads and bathing places; and when necessary to matters of law and order. The banjar is also involved in such 'life-cycle' occasions as 'birthday' celebrations for babies who survive their first three months, teeth-filings and burials (though not necessarily cremations).

The system has evolved and been made to work down the centuries because the villagers, the peasants, had little choice except to make it work. The village was their only support. They were tied to their land (not in a feudal sense but because they could not easily move elsewhere) and to their gods. To flee, to emigrate, to attempt a new life elsewhere, was to be foolhardy. (Eventually Balinese would be found in other parts of what is now Indonesia, as soldiers or servants or concubines, but it seems a large proportion of them were sold as slaves into those roles.) It was inevitable that a sense of village solidarity should develop.

I have mentioned that the Balinese commoners were not involved in an 'extended family' system. Within the village, it was difficult for any one family to become dominant and to rule. Much land was owned communally and could not fall under the control of any one family; and in any case families were not extensive enough to exercise political control. There was a political vacuum, or there would have been if the banjar were not there to fill it. There appears to be a direct link between the weakness in family structure which results from 'genealogical amnesia' and the importance of the banjar and other village institutions. The banjar came to be more important than family ties. No matter what squabbles might be going on in a village, when the banjar called everyone obeyed.

The banjar was effective because its decisions involved the equal participation of all families and because it operated through consensus rather than confrontation. Predictability would also have helped throughout most of Bali's history because there would not have been that many surprises to cope with; future shock had not been invented. Small size, usually not more than seventyfive families, also helped; if a banjar grew larger it would normally split in two. Each Balinese villager grew up to accept the banjar as an extension of himself and his family, far more important than the local gentry or the distant kings. His house was usually built on banjar land, he usually married within the banjar, his work groups and perhaps his music, drama and other clubs were formed within it.

In most banjars — in Bali there are exceptions to every rule — the council comprises most of the adults in its area, including the women because many banjar duties involve women's work. Generally, each male member brings along a female co-member, usually his wife. 'Adult' is variously defined as the state achieved on marriage, or on the birth of a first child, or on the death of a father leaving a vacancy for his son to fill.

With people living longer these days, this pattern has entered a state of flux. For example, in Balinese tradition a grandparent may be a person who should dutifully retire from an active role in village life. He is expected to trade influence for respect. Grandparents should act their age. But with many people remaining fit longer this hallowed progression away from influence and towards rather pointless status is being more and more often contested.

However it is constituted, the council appoints from its own members a chairman and assistants to the chairman to help run its affairs, though such appointment does not convey independent authority. These officers are responsible for keeping strict records of attendances at meetings and decisions reached. Meetings are usually held once every 35-day Balinese month, and decisions must be unanimous, based on a consensus which does much for village harmony but can hinder the acceptance of new ideas.

The banjar's officers also keep its financial records. Money comes in from levies (as on members' rice production), from fines and from commercial ventures, as when the banjar turns its building into a temporary disco for tourists. Fines can be imposed on members who fail to attend meetings or working assignments. The banjar is often also its own police force, or works in association with a government-run village security committee, and travellers may hear startling stories of how severely offenders are dealt with. In extreme cases it has the power to expel offenders from houses built on its land, and from the village.

The police role is so effective that the official Indonesian force rarely bothers to post men in the villages, and as a result Bali is one of the world's least formally policed territories in the world. Lt.-Col. Tawfiq Effendi, a senior officer at police headquarters in Denpasar, told me that the banjar was the main reason for Bali's extremely low crime rate — about 4,000 cases a year. By contrast Singapore, say, with a heavily policed population of similar size, has about 25,000 cases a year. The difference is marked even after guesstimating the numbers of unreported crimes. More, the great majority of Balinese crime is 'traditional', involving drinking, gambling and passion, and does not involve weapons or 'technology'. Armed robberies average about one a year, but, Col Tawfiq said, 'that one makes a lot of noise'. He added that most criminals in Bali came from Java and other islands.

Others I spoke to said the banjar is also the reason why there is little prostitution in Bali. Certainly Balinese women, as many male tourists have discovered to their chagrin, are untouchable, and those women from other islands who have filled this economic gap are not of the same quality. One explanation is that Bali is so small that the banjar would certainly learn if any of its women were engaged in prostitution and would enforce harsh penalties when they returned home. Another was that the reason lies not in fear but in a higher sense of morality based on religion.

The subak

As the banjar dominates civil life in its community, the subak — sometimes translated as 'agricultural society' — dominates the economic. The subak's main job is to run the irrigation system essential for growing rice, and essential therefore for survival. It is an association of the owners, tenants and sharecroppers of the ricefields within its area. It has been described as basically a temple group, tending temples involved in the worship of the gods of farming. But the subak is also directly involved in the farm programme, in the release and control of water to farmers who pay the subak according to the quantities supplied.

As with the banjar, members mostly meet every thirtyfive days, reach decisions by consensus, have the power to impose fines, and can enforce expulsions. The subak has been doing this for about 1,000 years, if references in old Balinese books are to believed. One seems to refer to the year 896 AD. Another dating back to 1072 AD refers specifically to a subak.

Today Bali has more than 1,000 of them, ranging in ricefield area from a tiny 3.5 hectares to one at Aseman of nearly 800 hectares. The average size is about 100 hectares. Since a subak's ricefields are often on a ridge between two deep gorges, or well removed from a river, the subak may have to tap water several kilometres away and bring it down through a system of channels, weirs, aqueducts and tunnels; some tunnels are three kilometres long. These systems can be considerable engineering achievements, and in techniques of managing water also the subaks have developed great skill.

The guiding principle is that, though land may be privately owned, the water is a gift from God and must be used for the greatest benefit for the greatest number. So well does this system work, on the basis of democracy, consensus and rules laid down in ancient books, that serious disputes between subak members, or between different subaks competing perhaps for a limited supply of water, are rare.

An institution as old and valuable as this deserves high-level recognition, and has it, in two forms. First, the government's campaigns to improve rice production are all channelled through the subaks, with all the compromises on both sides that this entails. On the one hand subak members must accept that perhaps new ideas are better than theirs; that engineers, for example, may be able to collect and divide water more efficiently than is possible with traditional methods; or that agriculturists may know of better methods or more productive rice varieties (even if the results do not taste so good). On the other hand, officials learn eventually that whatever may have worked in Sumatra or Java or Borneo is not necessarily right for Bali, and that subak members are not to be dictated to.

The subak's second form of official recognition is easier to find. It is the Museum Subak in Tabanan, more impressive as a building

Centuries of experience go into each planting season.

than it is informative, but a useful gesture. Exhibits include collections of farmers' tools, including a handmade wooden level, complete with tripod and plumbline, which could have been copied from a professional surveyor's one.

'Since ancient times,' says a card, 'Balinese farmers have used high technology to control the flow of irrigation water to their fields.' When I asked why wooden ploughs like those displayed where still being used instead of iron or steel ones, I was told that steel ploughs cut too deep, beyond the strength of harnessed cows to pull them. Muzzles which prevent cows cropping grass as they work and thus 'help their concentration' were also on show. The pretty Bali cow is generally taking over from the water buffalo; buffaloes though

42

bigger lack stamina. A large model of a tract of countryside attempts to show how a subak works but lacks sufficient explanation.

Examples of the success of the subak system are to be found not only in Bali but also in Sulawesi (Celebes) where Balinese settlements have emerged as a result of 'transmigration', the drive to move people from Java and Bali to less crowded parts of the country. Settlers from Bali have taken their subak and banjar systems with them as the best tools they have to help tackle the job of building new lives in strange surroundings.

The pemaksan

The banjar runs the civic life of the community, the subak the economic, but neither would be effective if it were not for a third organisation, the pemaksan, which relates to the moral sphere and administers temples and religious life. 'Congregation' could serve as a rough translation, with its members united in obedience to a single set of customary regulations and in worshipping in the same temple.

Bali has thousands of sets of three temples, with at least one set, or kahyangan tiga, in each village, sometimes more if the village is big enough. One of the three temples is the 'pura puseh', temple of origin, where the ancestral spirits of the present residents of the village or ward are worshipped. One is the 'pura balai agung', the great council temple, representing deities and demons who must be kept in a balanced relationship if the community is to avoid trouble and prosper. The third is the 'pura dalem', the temple of death, usually near a graveyard, for placating both the deities of death and the spirits of the dead who have not yet gone to heaven.

These three temples in a village may have identical congregations but this is not necessarily so. Part of the membership of any congregation may come from another village. Even within a village, the possible congregation of a set of three temples may be divided into three, each segment undertaking the main ritual burden of one temple and making only token offerings at the other two.

None of this means that the temple organisations control religious life. To say that would imply that the banjar and the subak are not involved in religious life; they are, very much. Perhaps all that can be said is that the temple organisations are the primary ones involved in religious life, so long as it is understood that virtually every other aspect of Balinese life is also in some way religious.

Though the temple organisations are more loosely organised than the banjar and the subak, they bear responsibilities just as demanding. The temples must be maintained, the rites must be observed, the dancing, drama and music must be of high standard if the gods are to be persuaded that the community is worth visiting and worth helping.

Just as the banjar and the subak are democratic, electing officials and giving them no power, so do temple congregations as a whole accept responsibility for the quality of their work, and for retribution if some act or omission should bring it on their heads. In this they are normally guided by written charters — incised on to the treated leaves of the lontar palm, treated with lampblack and bound into long, narrow books — which lay down rules of behaviour. It is said that no two charters are identical, and that differences between them can strengthen the unity of separate congregations.

These three organisations are three of the boxes I mentioned at the beginning of this section. They offer their members a diversity which would be absent if their lives were controlled by any one organisation, by anything like the single committee of a western commune or co-operative society. That the Balinese organisations operate on consensus rather than on the hard, majority-take-all democracy of the western world blunts still more sharp edges. More diversity results from the fact that any villager may be involved in further organisations, such as a group of artists or artisans, or an orchestra, or a project to build a new school, or to arrange a pilgrimage to a distant temple, or (nowadays illegally) to promote the career and profit potential of a champion fighting cock. The Balinese world may seem small but it contains many doorways into many boxes, providing niches of satisfaction for virtually everyone.

The Gentry

The people who make up the banjars, the subaks and most of the members of the temple congregations of the previous section of this book make up nine-tenths of the population of Bali. The other one-tenth is referred to variously as the gentry, the upper classes, the three upper castes. In Balinese they are the 'triwangsa', the people of the Brahmana, Ksatria and Weisya castes, the people in (or near) the palace of the king, as opposed to the Sudras, the commoners, the people outside the palace I have been writing about so far. Some of them like to believe that they are descended directly from high-born refugees from Java 600 years ago; some of them undoubtedly are because the refugees arrived in thousands, bringing with them both notions and names from a variant of the Hindu caste system.

The distant past apart, however, the gentry — this term is as good as any other — may fairly feel the world has treated them less than fairly. Before the Dutch took over Bali as part of their East Indies empire, the gentry were to be reckoned with, even if they did dissipate their energy by endless politicking among themselves over status. The Dutch incorporated them into their administration but they lost much in power and social position. Then came the Indonesian republic which offers them no real respect at all, and even took away much of their land during rural reforms in the early 1960s. The delights of noble birth have turned to sand which runs away between the fingers.

A fair proportion of gentry members is doing well, in government, or business, or the armed forces, on the strength of education and inherited money as well as talent. But the commoners are on their heels, doing as well in schools and universities, making more money often than the gentry do out of the tourist trade. This does nothing for gentry expectations that commoners should treat them with the respect due to people descended from the gods. (One result of this conviction is that the gentry, unlike the commoners, are interested in backward-looking genealogy and often know their family trees.)

Perhaps soon the gentry will have not much left except an idealised image of the past, their palaces and their titles — Ida Bagus for Brahmanas, the priestly and scholarly class; Anak Agung and Cokorda for Ksatrias, the princely and political caste; and Gusti for the Weisyas, the administrative and warrior caste, and for some Ksatria families as well. 'If my daughter were to marry a commoner,' an elegant Ksatria lady told me, 'I would never permit her to address me as Mother. She would have to use my title.'

And so, in an ideal world, would everyone else because one of the distinctions between gentry and commoners is that gentry are addressed by title always, commoners never. The commoners, through teknonymy, have a naming system which fits precisely with the absolute equality of the banjar and the subak. Gentry have no place in either, except when some unfortunate noble, totally impoverished, accepts his loss of status, accepts teknonymy and is accepted into the village as an equal. One of the problems of being descended from the gods is that descent can go too far.

The woman who would not let her commoner-marrying daughter call her Mother was perhaps being liberal. Not so long ago the daughter would have been disowned, exiled with her husband, possibly killed. Marriage was often a life-or-death matter, except for gentry men who often could do very much as they pleased. Ubud has a palace pavilion right opposite the village market, specially built so the local lord could sit and survey the passing crowd for comely young women. When one caught his fancy, he would send men to bring her in, normally into concubinage. The villagers twice knocked holes in the market wall so their pretty daughters could do the family shopping without being spotted and each time the lord sent men to block the holes. Gentry women enjoyed no such freedom to help themselves. Their prospects of happy lives rested with not making mistakes, with being linked with husbands of at least equal status, and — in days when widows were expected to immolate themselves on their husbands' funeral pyres — with having husbands who lived longer than they did.

Clifford Geertz has written fascinatingly on the gentry's preoccupation with status. Before the Dutch took over Bali completely early this century, he says, competition for status between gentry families involved not just marriage politics but also intrigue, assassination, coups d'etat and the like, often resulting in war. 'Just who properly belonged where, who had a right to how much and what sort of deference, was . . . just the sort of . . . question that could lead to bloodshed in the prestige politics of theatre-state Bali.'

Gentry families' relations with each other were endlessly burdened with concern that distinctions should be preserved. No two houses were ever precisely equal with one another. To eat with someone else from the same dish signified a precise equality that could exist only within a narrrow circle of kinsmen. In other cases, though eating together might be permitted, only a special relationship with the others permitted a diner to serve himself from a central dish with his right hand, eat with his right and reach for more food with his right. Diners not so specially related in rank were obliged to take their second helpings with their left hands. More distant relationships demanded that eating together be avoided. In some cases — this is all within the gentry — people of lower status might have to wait until the higher ones had finished eating and then get the leftovers. This could apply even between father and son.

If dining posed complicated problems, those involved in a marriage between gentry houses could be nightmarish. The safest of all marriages for a man to contract, for it neither demeaned him nor resulted in another family feeling demeaned, was with his father's brother's daughter — with his first cousin. It has been suggested that the harmony at times observed between a man's different wives could have resulted from their being cousins anyway. Among commoners marriage with cousins could happen by chance, from lack of knowledge. Among the gentry it was done deliberately. The dominating concern was that a woman, or girl, for this could happen during her early teens, must not 'marry down'. She could go only to an equal or a superior. A first cousin marriage avoided any suggestion that either family was lower in status than the other.

Inevitably this prohibition on women marrying down resulted in many women remaining unmarried because there were not enough men of uncontestably high status to go around. In Tabanan in the 1870s six of a prince's nine daughters never married. The problem persists to this day. If a woman did marry down she could be in desperate trouble with penalties including exile or death. The pervading point was that a daughter was property to be used to her parents' political and social advantage.

Being exiled for marriages which broke the rules and for other reasons was so common, especially during Dutch colonial times when rulers could not longer impose death penalties and when standards were changing, that an entire community of Balinese exiles developed at Perigi in central Sulawesi. One of my informants, no particular admirer of the gentry, laughed as he said that the exiles were sent off in disgrace 'but became prosperous'.

He laughed also as he told me how he had hired a contractor to arrange the carving of pillars in a pavilion of his new house in Denpasar. The contractor, a Ksatria, refused to have his men carve all surfaces because only a king could have such decoration in his house. My informant sacked the contractor, got another and went ahead. 'It's my house and I can do what I like,' he said. In the past he could have died for such insolence, or been sent to Perigi.

The existence of a gentry class in Bali has persuaded some writers that the island was therefore feudal but it was not. The word 'feudal' refers to a one-sided relationship between land-holding lords and peasants living and working on that land. The banjar and subak systems in Bali were so powerful that the gentry had little say in village and farming life. Gentry landowners either had to do their own farming or enter into share-cropping arrangements at times less favourable than commoner landowners could get.

Some service arrangements between lords and commoners existed but in general all that a local lord received for his superior status was a respectful form of address, a cast of extras (whom he had to feed) for his ceremonies, and an obligation to patronise artists and craftsmen. Often the gentry were strapped for money, relying on taxes they levied on markets and cockfights. Despite the brutality with which some of them enforced their laws, the gentry generally were less feared for their power than tolerated for the colour they helped bring into life. Yet they had to go along with the system because if they did not they lost status, and status, prestige, distinction was what gentry life was all about.

The Language

entry fascination with status and prestige gave the Balinese a special way of speaking to each other. To illustrate it, let us look at the other side of the world. In England jokes used to be made about the way horses sweat, men perspire and women glow. Or naval documents once referred — not joking, perfectly serious — to officers' ladies, petty officers' wives and sailors' women. Class-ridden societies inevitably produce such nonsense.

Balinese society was ridden by class, or caste, and its language reflects it, but with one important difference from usage in Europe, say, which makes it much more engaging. In Europe gentry folk used their language whatever the occasion, the peasants and workers theirs. There was no question of speakers adjusting their language according to their listeners, except perhaps by way of simplification.

In Bali practice was different and to a degree still is. People were addressed in their form of the language — as if in England a serf would talk posh to a lord, a lord use the lowest dialect imaginable when talking to a serf. In England it would be unthinkable. In Bali it happened.

More, the Balinese developed a system which required them not only to speak in the manner of their listener but also to use the appropriate style when speaking of someone else. Mention of the lord's head or house involved using lordly language even when talking to a commoner.

Eventually three distinct languages resulted: Low, middle and high. Low was used between intimates and equals and with inferiors. Middle was used with strangers and with superiors who were not members of higher castes. High was used with members of higher castes. But since no system of language can ever be that clearcut, intermediate versions also developed which made the system overcomplicated. In recent decades the decline of the caste system has brought further confusion.

The visitor to Bali today who hears only roadside exchanges, market banter and raucous exchanges in buses or coffeeshops may come to the conclusion that Balinese is loud, vigorous and coarse. Under the same circumstances, he could come to the same conclusion about any language anywhere in the world. If by chance he heard only the language of drawing rooms and polite society he would come to a quite different conclusion. It is hard to be precise on this subject.

What is certain, however, is that the system is changing rapidly. It is almost unknown now for strangers to ask each other the formerly mandatory question, 'Where do you sit (in relation to other people — that is, what is your caste)?' The low language is vanishing rapidly, not taught in schools and used, some children told me, 'only when we're angry'. The middle language, mider, is widely used instead, even on occasions when 'high' would have been compulsory. And if speakers are from time to time assailed by doubts about how to speak to strangers or superiors, they can switch easily to Indonesian. Very few people, very old or isolated in mountain villages, do not know Indonesian and it is common to hear children using it as they play.

Knowledge of Balinese will survive. A population of two and a half million is big enough to ensure this, it will remain a matter of some pride anyway, and it will remain essential for religious and traditional purposes. Education, indeed, may strengthen it because as young people are systematically taught more about their culture the language which goes with it mustbecome more important to them. I expect that the Balinese of the future will be bilingual in Indonesian and a form of Balinese rather like the middle language of today.

The Women

hatever the men of Bali do, the women work. Guides appear embarrassed by the frequency with which visitors comment on this, and the best of them think some of the comments unfair: they know that women work everywhere. But in Bali it is more obvious than in most other places, and not just because women are more likely than men are to catch the eye. They are often to be seen working while men sit and stand around.

One day I watched as a young woman prepared to move a pile of sand from the roadside to a building site. Normally this involves shovelling the sand into a dish which is then raised and carried on the head. This is easier if someone helps with the raising. There were men standing by, watching and joking with the woman, but none offered to help. She had to cope on her own. This she did, remarkably cheerfully, by putting the empty dish on her head, shovelling the sand upwards and catching it in the dish. Elsewhere it could have been a circus trick.

Women carrying headloads in the form of temple offerings is a much photographed Bali theme but they carry many other loads as well, from bricks and cement to water and rice. There is a story that men carry loads on the shoulders, never on their heads, but I saw enough exceptions to this to make it less than a rule. What is certain is that the headloads are often far heavier than the observer may appreciate. He sees the grace and poise but may overlook the sheer hard labour.

Watch the process of loading as a bucket of water, say, is raised for a child to carry home from a village standpipe. There is a moment of total concentration, then a slight to and fro movement of the head — precisely the movement so often seen in Indian and Balinese dances — as balance is found. There is also an instant of resignation in the child's eyes before she sets off. Then complete the observation by lifting a bucket of water to realise how heavy it is.

In an interview with Professor Dr Ida Bagus Mantra, the Governor of Bali, I asked about this common impression that women work harder than the men do. He was chary about the term 'hard-working' because it implies that the men are not so. It is not that men work less hard then women do, he said, but that their duties are different. In particular the men look after the fields and bear responsibility for many family and village decisions. The women look after the home and the market — and are free to make money as well.

Within the bounds of Bali's patriarchal society, women make the most of this 'freedom'. This is especially so at the frequent markets, places marked by abundant feminine energy and enterprise. The markets are worth visiting as much for the sight of women in action, the gleam of bargaining in their eyes, as for the goods on display. Long may it remain so. It is pleasant to buy food direct from a farmer, or from the person who bought it from the farmer, but it is pleasure not to be taken for granted. Modern shops owned by companies and staffed by wage-earners could do more to destroy Bali's way of life than a host of tourists.

Some commentators have found that relationships between Balinese men and women are in fact very balanced, without what one called 'sharp conceptual opposition'. Another thought it significant that he found male and female paired statues made of Chinese coins and sandalwood which are virtually identical; only their earrings were different. A system of names which uses the same terms for boys and girls points in the same direction. So does the process by which both father and mother take the name of their first child.

Women can own land and can supervise men working on that land. Men do cooking for ritual feasts. Men and women can play both male and female roles in dance and drama, though later in this book I have a woman dancer expressing herself clearly on the chauvinism of the men in her audiences. Music used to be a male preserve but in the schools and colleges girls now learn alongside

Women with offerings on their way to temple.

the boys. Men and women work together in many jobs — but women usually get paid much less for equal work.

Men tend to leave religious matters to the women. When men who had just danced in a village drama told me that in everyday life they were rice farmers, I asked also about the women who had danced with them. I was told they prepared temple offerings, which turned out to mean that they were housewives doing what all Balinese housewives do: Attend also to the religious side of family life. A man famous for his knowledge of the culture of his people took me to see offerings spread on a bed in his house. His wife was burning incense and praying. 'I don't know much about this,' the expert said. 'Women understand these things and know what to do.'

This could be an area where the culture is vulnerable. If a woman should decline to make temple offerings, say, on grounds that she is too busy with her job at the office, this would cause a family crisis. With more education and with more careers opening up for women, such crises may become more common. Perhaps more men will carry offerings? Perhaps temple rituals will be adjusted? In the meantime there seems to be no problem as all religious occasions draw big crowds.

Women also know more about marriage customs, though men keep a close watch on any issues of status which may be involved. A marriage between two families living close together and possibly related may be celebrated with nothing more than a simple ritual at the husband's household temple, during which the wife is presented to the husband's ancestors. This probably follows a period during which they have been sleeping together anyway, as the Balinese are flexible in such matters.

In a book published in 1936 a writer named Geoffrey Gorer produced a casual summary of the Balinese attitude to sex which reflects much that I heard in 1983. 'They are in no way romantic about sex,' Gorer said in his Bali And Angkor. 'They treat it as any other part of the ordinary business of life; it has no more intrinsic emotional importance to them than eating. This seems to me the only rational approach; we all have to eat to keep well, and we enjoy our food; we find a person who over-eats or is always thinking and talking about his food or indulges in odd diets absurd and disgusting and rather funny; greedy people lack a sense of proportion. For food substitute whatever word you use for sexual activity and I think you will have a very fair idea of the attitude of the Balinese.'

Where a marriage involves two distant or distinct families, however, issues of status and prestige arise. There are two ways to cope with these. One is expensive, calling for a good deal of ostentatious display. The other is commonsense — the young lovers run away together.

A book about Balinese customs published in Denpasar lays down the modern ground rules. Traditionally, it says, eloping should be done by night but now it can be done by day and still be considered valid. The couple cannot go directly to the man's house but must spend a few days in a third person's house. This third person has responsibilities in the affair which include being able to prove that the eloping is grounded in love. He must eventually report the matter to the village banjar. He must immediately separate the couple if there is evidence of force or cheating. It is the responsibility of the husband, if that is the right word, to get word to the girl's parents that she is safe and, well, happy.

In most cases the parents would know in advance, or at least suspect, what is going to happen and would tacitly approve. But if they are less than totally enthralled, they can give chase and try to drag the girl back, using force if necessary, so long as they do so before the couple reach sanctuary in the third person's house. Once the couple have reached that house, all the girl's parents can do is demand word from their daughter about whether she was a willing or unwilling kidnap victim. The institution is in fact called 'kidnap marriage' or 'runaway marriage'.

In addition to all this, I was told, the girl nowadays usually leaves a note to say she has gone willingly. If there is no such note, the affair may be considered an actual kidnapping and the police called in. If all is well, a simple (and inexpensive) ceremony follows — the Balinese equivalent of a rapid dash to the local registry of marriages.

This institution of 'runaway marriage' finds favour for an excellent reason in addition to its economy. It creates marvellous theatrical opportunities, with the girl's family raising a hue and cry, with the boy's family doing everything possible to thwart the pursuit. The girl may use the opportunity to show her spirit, fighting and shouting — just in case something should go wrong — as her lover attempts to spirit her away. It can be great fun, so long as enthusiasm does not ride so high that real fighting begins.

Normally the newly-weds will return to live in the husband's family home. If it is typical, this home is a collection of buildings behind one of the high, blank walls which line all village streets. Only narrow, inhospitable doorways, often at the top of a flight of steps and often with a barking dog in the entrance, break these walls — but within the walls the atmosphere is much more genial. Daily life continues around open-sided pavilions, and there always seems to be a great deal of it, mostly generated by women as they cook, clean, tend their children and prepare temple decorations and offerings.

Only in the evening does activity slow down, though women still find work for their hands to do as the family relaxes in the gloaming. The men talk about the day's events. Someone plays gently on a flute or — increasingly these days — a guitar. The children drop off to sleep in the arms of whoever happens to be holding them. This phase seems eternal though how well it will stand up to the spread of electric lights and television no one knows. Or can we take a pointer from a recent adjustment to the flights of steps which lead from the road to the family compound? Most now have a central ramp so motorcycles can be ridden in — and those ramps look as if they have been there for ages. May other results of modernisation fit in so nicely.

The Calendar

he Balinese, unique in so much that they do, have been ingenious also in measuring the passage of time. Most civilisations developed calendars based on the movements of the sun and the moon, on the seasons and on agricultural cycles. Though the Balinese system may have originated in some such manner, the connection is now remote and more important is fanciful play with weeks of different lengths.

Bali appears very early to have developed a three-day market week, every three days being perhaps how often kitchen supplies must be replenished in a hot climate. This week still operates, usually as a cycle among neighbouring villages so that hawkers can move from one to another and always arrive on market day.

Other purposes demanded periods of different lengths, and the result is a pattern (or to an outsider, a confusion) of weeks of different lengths. A week of one day is possible. And there exist also weeks of four, five, six, seven, eight, nine and ten days, each with a different, usually ritual purpose. The three, five and seven-day cycles are the most important.

An endless series of weeks would be inconvenient. A number of weeks need to be embraced handily within a longer period — call it a year, say. It would also be inconvenient to have many uncompleted weeks within a year. A year of 30 seven-day weeks works out well, because its 210 days allow also for 21 ten-day weeks,

35 six-day weeks, 42 five-day weeks, 70 three-day weeks. Four-day and eight-day weeks do not fit in but you cannot have everything. The Balinese settled on a 210-day year and built their religious life within it.

The insertion of an Indian solar calendar and then the western one lent a little more zest to the whole business. So did occasional adjustments for four-day and eight-day weeks. The result was a splendidly complicated creation which is still in use. Auspicious and inauspicious days could be calculated from the way weeks fell. A basic rule was that days when the first or last days of weeks of different lengths coincided were more sacred than others. When several such days coincided, those days were still more powerful, but whether for good or evil only a priest could say.

There was need also for another division of the year, so the lunar cycle was invoked as well, producing months. The fifteenth day of the lunar month, the night of the full moon, became known as Purnama. The end of the month, either the night without a moon or the night of the new moon according to different traditions, is Tilem. Both are sacred, and Purnama is a fine time to watch people attending temple. Even in workaday Denpasar, the numbers of people, young and older, visiting the great temple next to the Bali Museum is impressive evidence of the vigour of their religion.

The Balinese begin their New Year on the first day of their tenth month. This is because nine is both a sacred number and the biggest number (ten being a one and a zero). At least, that was one explanation offered me. One learns not to pursue too far the tendency to keep on asking questions. A New Year beginning on the first day of the tenth month implies a year of nine lunar months, which does not fit into the year of 210 days, so periodic adjustments are made. But the details were beyond me, and I can fully understand why even the Balinese must frequently seek help with their own calendar.

In the past much knowledge in this field was secret, or sacred, which amounts to the same thing. Anyone wanting to know the most propitious day for a cremation, for instance, would buy his information from a priest. There were calendars, and ingenious documents they were, but interpreting them called for rare and special skill and training. This has changed and those old calendars, or mass produced imitations of them, seem more valued now for the money they will fetch from tourists than for the information they contain.

This change is mainly the work of one man, Ktut Bangbang Gde Rawi, 73 years old when I met him at his home in Celuk early in 1984. Since 1950 he has been producing an annual calendar (for the western calendar year) which is one of the success stories of the island. His product was to be seen in virtually every home, shop and office I visited. Bangbang's name (sometimes spelt Bambang) is a household word not only among the Balinese but among other residents as well because all have need to keep track of their days.

Part of a Bangbang calendar, with 30-year-old portrait.

Not only his name is well known. His face is too, because his photograph appears on every page of his calendar — but it is the face of a young man. For more than 30 years he has left his portrait unchanged, not out of vanity but as a trademark. 'If I changed the photograph people would suspect that the calendar is not authentic,' he said.

Since his calendar is used in important and subtle matters, by important and subtle people, it must be beyond reproach. For this reason Bangbang has for many years maintained the trust of both government and religious organisations, and one, the Parisada Hindu Dharma, has become a joint producer. Its swastika emblem appears in the top line of every page's decorative border.

The calendar has currency not only in Bali but also in Balinese communities in other parts of Indonesia and even in other countries — because it is not just Balinese. Because there are Chinese and Christians and Muslims in Bali, he has included details of their calendars as well, and also of the Japanese calendar. 'It's an international calendar,' he said. 'I want it to be a calendar for the whole world.'

In theory priests should object to a calendar which makes people independent of their special knowledge, but Bangbang was careful from the start to involve them in his work. More, he is now a priest himself, after many years working for the government as a village headman. In spite of his age he is as busy as he ever was, and priests throughout the island, far from resenting his initiative, are happy to turn to his calendar to solve problems. There has been no trouble.

Bangbang says he enjoys the pernickety work of compiling his calendar, and only one aspect worries him. 'By July each year I must turn all the material for the following year's calendar to my son for typesetting and printing,' he said. 'I'm terrified of being late.'

Production is in Denpasar and the print run, according to his son, Made Bambang Swartha, is about 150,000 — he thinks. But he is not sure. The Parisada Hindu Dharma may print more. It is a good business despite this hint of vagueness, so good that while I was in Bali a pirated edition began appearing in the shops. It lacked the famous 30-year-old photograph, and some people I talked to said this lack plainly indicated an inferior product.

Occasions
Within the framework created by the Balinese calender, marvellous

occasions befall, such as Galungan. It is the first day of a ten-day spree which begins in the eleventh week of the 210-day year; sometimes it falls twice within a western calendar year. There is a legend that Galungan celebrates the death of a demon who was intent on taking Bali away from the path of true religion. A more general rendering is that it celebrates the creation of the universe.

The approach to this greatest of all Balinese festivals dominates life for days beforehand, just as Christmas, say, does in the west, but without the commercialisation. Six days before the festival there is a day for making offerings and for seeking mental and spiritual purity. The fifth day before the festival is called 'the second purification day'. The third day before the festival is the day for storing fruit in a warm container so it will ripen precisely in time for the occasion. The second day before the festival is given over to making cakes.

One day before, after all this women's work, the men come into their own, cleaning the temple grounds, building offering stands and killing pigs in preparation for the Galungan feast. In the home, work goes on preparing offerings and decorations, so that on Galungan Day itself the villages of Bali burst into fairyland.

The main element in this transformation is the penjor, said to symbolise the Serpent of Prosperity. Penjors are tall, splendidly decorated bamboo poles in front of each home, so arranged that each one dips towards the centre of the street. Each pole has fruit, rice and cakes hanging from it, so it becomes a symbol of fertility. This aspect is taken further in some with two coconuts hanging at the foot which, by at least one account, are even called testicles. 'We are tenant farmers of Earth. The penjor indicates our gratitude to God,' I was told. 'That is why it is decorated with the products of the soil, such as rice, coconuts and sugar cane.' Lines of penjors nodding throughout the villages are alone worth visiting Bali to see.

The occasion also sees numerous representations of 'Cili', a rice goddess, with a more or less abstract head and a huge head-dress. Typically it is made from palm leaf and tacked on to another leaf with little wooden skewers, but the form can also be found in cakes, or made from wood, baked clay or paper, or from old Chinese coins.

Galungan ceremonies begin at dawn, with the food prepared overnight being presented as offerings and with priests going through a chanting ritual of inviting the gods to descend from their heaven above Gunung Agung. Eventually drums beat to announce their arrival and the village streets come alive as families

A traditional 'Cili', or rice goddess, with her modern counterpart — a trademark for hand-loomed cloth.

head for the temple to worship. The priests invite the gods to accept the essence of the offerings, sprinkle the worshippers with holy water, and pour more holy water into their cupped hands for them to sip and spread over their faces, heads and breasts. All day long families come and go.

The day after Galungan is called Sweet Galungan and is given over to dressing in one's best, family reunions, visiting — and inevitably visits to the temples with offerings. The festival carries on quietly for its full ten days. Many people working in the towns take their annual leave at this time and spend the entire festival period in their home villages. The festival ends with Kuningan, a day for still more temple observances.

A completely different occasion is Nyepi, New Year's Day, a day of silence and inactivity. There are no cars on the roads, no people in the streets, no fires burning. Cooking was completed the previous day, which also saw offerings and ceremonies of exorcism throughout the island. While the priests dealt with evil spirits in their manner, the village children did so in theirs, roaming the streets with burning torches and home-made cymbals.

But the day of Nyepi itself is silent, and remains so for its full 24 hours. Traditionally it is a time for prayer, meditation and fasting. Tourists are sometimes told that Bali closes down for the day so that evil spirits will be deluded into thinking that all mankind has deserted the island, and will also leave.

Another island-wide occasion is a day devoted to honouring Saraswati, the Goddess of Learning. The Balinese, who always contrive to avoid the obvious, mark it with ceremonies and with a ban on all reading and writing. There are also numerous local occasions, so many of them that a calendar of events produced each year by the Badung Tourist Promotion Board lists nearly 500 temple festivals. The day for each of these is set by the Balinese calendar.

'Life cycle' ceremonies

The same calendar also determines to a large degree when various 'life cycle' ceremonies important in family life will be held, since each one needs an auspicious day. These ceremonies begin even before birth, as soon as it can be confirmed that a woman is pregnant, and are all designed to frustrate evil spirits. In addition the mother will observe various dietary prohibitions while the father may undertake not to cut his hair or not kill any animal until the child is safely born. He may read epic stories to his wife during this period, in the hope of influencing the child.

Purification and protection ceremonies are held soon after the birth, when the navel cord falls off, when the child is named, and after 42 days. For the first three 35-day months of his life the baby is not permitted to touch the ground (in some Ksatria families, this period lasts for 210 days). An explanation for this is that a new-born child has come direct from the world of the spirits and is holy, and his body must be kept free from dirt. Covarrubias says it is because the Balinese find repugnant anything in humans characteristic of animals — such as a child crawling. After three months, however, a ceremony as elaborate as the family can afford is held, and thereafter the child is a full-fledged family member. Another ceremony follows on the child's first birthday.

To a degree some of these occasions are independent of the calendar, though propitious days are always sought, but years later comes perhaps the most important event of the child's life. It is his

A Brahmana girl in Denpasar costumed for her teeth-filling ceremony.

or her teeth-filing ceremony, and the timing of this is considered very carefully indeed. It is the occasion when the child, or the adolescent by this time, abandons his residual animality and becomes entirely human. It is a ceremony which originates in the same abhorrence of animal behaviour that, according to Covarrubias, keeps a child off the ground for the first three months of his life.

The filing (sometimes these days reduced to a few token passes with a fine file) is directed at the upper incisors and upper canines, wearing them down to an even line. In Balinese eyes, it rescues a person from looking like an animal, and therefore running the risk of being treated as one when he seeks his place in heaven. If his teeth are doglike and uneven, he will not be admitted. Filing also reduces a person's liability to such animal passions as lust, anger, greed, stupidity, drunkenness and jealousy. It is essential, and it can also be a grand occasion.

There is only one grander, in fact, and that is cremation, about which more later, right after the following accounts of cockfighting and Balinese food and related matters. These are included at this point because they also involve Balinese antipathy to things animal.

Cockfighting

ne evening I sat watching television in a Denpasar coffeeshop. An outline map of Bali which appeared on the screen before a news bulletin reminded me of the kiwi of my native New Zealand, running from right to left. The Bukit peninsula in the south was one foot, Penida Island (joined in imagination to the mainland) was the other. The kiwi's long bill was missing but one cannot have everything. I felt I had made a discovery.

Later however I found that the Balinese were far, far ahead of me. In a long account of cockfighting in Bali, by Clifford Geertz, I came across this: ' . . . Even the very island itself is perceived from its shape as a small, proud cock, poised, neck extended, back taut, tail raised, in eternal challenge to large, feckless, shapeless Java.' I found this notion quite engaging. Soon I was to learn also that there is much more to cockfighting than simple excitement, that the frequent sight of men caressing their birds is only a small part of a complicated story.

Cockfighting is illegal in Bali, banned because of the gambling which accompanied it, but some fights are permitted for ritual purposes, as blood sacrifices to banish evil spirits from around temples. The day before Nyepi is an important such occasion. There is also a good deal of illegal fighting, carried on in defiance of the police and at risk of a night locked up and a 1,000 or 2,000 rupiah fine if caught. Visitors sometimes stumble on fights, whether with pleasure or not depending on their attitude to this activity, as when I encountered a session within four kilometres of the tourist town of Kuta. Sometimes visitors are present when the police strike, setting off a frantic scramble to escape.

Geertz and his wife, doing research work in a village away back in 1958, once joined in such a scramble — and found it worked wonders in establishing them in the villagers' estimation. They responded by adding cockfighting to their field of study, and it seems that Geertz watched no fewer than 57 fights to collect his data. The results, published in Daedalus, an American scholarly journal, in Winter, 1972, make fascinating reading.

Geertz remarks on the manner in which Balinese men identify psychologically with their cocks and explains that the double meaning in English works also in Balinese. It produces, he says, the same tired jokes and strained puns. He quotes other scholars who suggested that the Balinese viewed cocks as 'detachable, self-operating penises with a life of their own'. He notes that the word for cock, 'sabung', is used, as in English, to mean also a hero, warrior, champion, dandy or tough guy.

The fighting cocks which are to be seen in every village though fighting them is illegal receive extravagant care. They get special food carefully prepared, they are bathed just as ceremonially as babies, in tepid water with herbs and flowers. They are endlessly caressed, massaged and inspected. But, it seems, they are not loved. The problem is one we have already encountered: The Balinese revulsion from anything animal-like.

The Balinese man identifies with his cock not just as his ideal self or even as his penis, Geertz says, but also because it represents the feared and hated, but also fascinating, Powers of Darkness. The connection with these Powers is explicit. A cockfight is a sacrifice to the demons, to appease their appetites. In a cockfight, man and beast, good and evil, ego and id, creative masculinity and destructive animality, stand face to face. In a memorable sentence, Geertz says that the owner of a beaten bird takes its carcass home to eat 'with a mixture of social embarrassment, moral satisfaction, aesthetic disgust, and cannibal joy'.

The conduct of cockfighting encounters is governed by extraordinarily elaborate rules, written in palm leaf, or lontar, books, which provide for umpires, the timing of rounds (by a holed coconut shell sinking in water), the settlement of disputes, and gambling. This is as well because the turbulence as bets are laid before a well-matched bout can be akin to chaos. The fights I saw were all preceded by astonishing excitement. This chaos stands in intense contrast to the stillness that descends when the fight is about to begin, and to the animal fury of the actual bout, 'so pure, so absolute, and in its own way so beautiful, as to be almost abstract, a Platonic concept of hate'.

The point about a well-matched bout is important. Geertz says tremendous care is taken to ensure that the cocks in fights with heavy betting are as equal as possible — even if this means tying a stronger bird's steel spur at a less advantageous angle. There is tremendous pressure to make the match a genuinely even gambling proposition.

So far so good, but then Geertz offers a theory about why cockfighting is so important. It is made to be, he says, both 'a simulation of the social matrix' and also an opportunity to affirm, defend, celebrate, justify and bask in the prestige which is the central driving force of Balinese society. In short, he commented earlier in his account, much of Bali comes to the surface in the fighting ring because 'it is only apparently cocks that are fighting there. Actually it is men'.

In other words, a cockfight is 'a status bloodbath', a dramatisation of status concerns. A man virtually never bets against a bird owned by a member of his clan or village but will bet heavily against a bird owned by someone he is feuding against. And when the extraordinarily complex society he lives in produces conflicting claims on his loyalty, he will wander off for a cup of coffee.

Geertz says that almost all the Balinese he discussed the subject with said cockfighting was 'like playing with fire only not getting burned'. All manner of rivalries and hostilities could be activated but in 'play' form at times coming dangerously close to aggression but never actually crossing the line because 'it is only a cockfight'. Its function is not to assuage or heighten social passions but, 'in the medium of feathers, blood, crowds and money', to display them. It is not a matter of gaining status by winning or losing it by being beaten, since that does not happen. Rather it is a matter of learning what it feels like totally to triumph or totally to be brought low.

But only briefly. Each fight is a world in itself, from the matchmaking to the betting to the fight to the result, and the claiming of winning bets. And that is the end of it. No one congratulates the winner, consoles the loser or discusses the action. Attention turns to the next fight, and there is no looking back.

Eating, etcetera

ne evening I met two village boys taking two cows homewards. 'What are the cows' names?' I asked. 'Cow,' came the reply, using an Indonesian word. 'No, no,' I said. 'What are the cow's personal names?' This puzzled them. 'No personal names,' they said. 'Just cow.'

So, no Balinese equivalent of Buttercup, or Flossie, or Beatrice, and the other names which western dairymen bestow on their bovines. I thought it a little odd as these animals were certainly treated as pets.

I tried the same question on dokka (that is, dogcart) drivers. Did they have personal names for the ponies with which they spent their working lives? No. Just 'horse'.

With dogs and cats the picture became a little clouded but it seems the Balinese are reluctant to be overly personal towards their animals.

This may seem an odd way to begin a chapter about food, but bear with me. One of my best informants explained: 'We don't like to give animals human attributes, and giving them human names would be to do so. We must maintain a very strict line between animals and humans.' This is the reason why children have their teeth filed, as mentioned earlier. A person's teeth must be level, not pointed and fang-like. It is part of maintaining that strict line.

So, to food. Eating is an animal performance, necessary but not one to be dwelled on. Animals may think of nothing but food but ideal human behaviour involves acting as if one is not all that interested. The Balinese tend to eat quickly and quietly, and often alone. Even a 'feast' may involve just a nibble or two from one's portion, and the rest taken home to be eaten in private, or shared. At mealtime food is made available, people help themselves, and then retire to a corner of the house or garden. Dining is not normally a social occasion, and cuisine may have suffered as a result.

Bali, I think because of this, is not a gourmet's paradise. On the contrary, the visitor who tries to eat only local food is bound to have a pretty boring time, and before long to find himself eating Javanese or Sumatran or Chinese food rather than Balinese.

Or going back to the tourist hotels for imported goodies. He might even go to Kuta for what is advertised as a 'pig-in', a busload of tourists on an eating version of a pub crawl. They have one course here, get on their bus, have another course there, get back on their bus . . . and so on. Since they probably drink as well as eat their way around the tourist belt, and egg each other to excess, results can be horrible.

But back to Bali. I asked around Denpasar for a typical Balinese restaurant and eventually, after much effort, was referred to one in a street behind the Bali Hotel. It was a tiny place with a menu of only four items: Nasi campur, soto babad, gado gado and soto ayam. Nasi campur is 'mixed rice', a plate of white rice strewn with any meat and vegetable dishes available; most travellers get to know it well and it can be good, satisfying and cheap. Soto babad is a spicy tripe soup. Gado gado is a vegetable salad with peanut sauce, often an excellent dish, sometimes not. Soto ayam is a soup with chicken instead of the tripe that goes into soto babad.

I ordered a dish of soto ayam, and was fortunate to get it because minutes later a car-load of government officials arrived for lunch. 'All finished.' they were told. 'Ayyyyyuhh!' they said and rushed off. The time was 12.30pm. This was one of the few Balinese restaurants I found in Bali. None of its four dishes is especially Balinese; the same ones are served from end to end of Indonesia. In general restaurateurs come from other islands, other countries. Specifically Balinese dishes can be found normally only at roadside or market stalls.

But, but, but . . . there is a Balinese cuisine. I found it demonstrated to perfection in a palace garden in Kerambitan, near Tabanan. French tourists were ushered one evening into a fairyland courtyard where even the lawn was decorated, with patterns of flower petals. Each diner sat behind an elegant, once-only setting of woven palm fronds. After music and a little drinking, the meal was ushered in — a procession of servitors in traditional dress, two leading with a roasted pig held high, others with smaller dishes of fresh fish, chicken and duck and some splendid vegetable concoctions. It was first-class food in a marvellous setting.

The roasted pig, pig on a spit, of that occasion must come first in any list of Balinese dishes. Babi guling it is called in Indonesian, be guling in Balinese, with the word 'guling' meaning to turn, or turned. It is not suckling pig though tourists are often told it is. It is not

How to cook your pig, Balinese style.

hard to find if you do not try too hard — I tried until I lost interest and then found roast pig confronting me at every turn.

The pig, perhaps five months old and weighing about 30 kg, is stuffed with a chopped preparation of red chili, capsicum, garlic, red onions, turmeric, ginger, salt, tinke (a nut similar in taste to ginger), black pepper, whole peppercorns, aromatic leaves and coconut oil. The carcass is then stitched together, skewered, brushed with crushed turmeric and water to give it a golden colour, and roasted over a charcoal fire, turning slowly, for two or three hours. A refinement is to use an electric fan to keep smoke away.

Babi guling is a popular, common dish, not expensive, often served in proletarian surroundings as well as to tourists in palaces. A famous stall in Gianyar town sold a plateful, or banana-leaf-full, of rice, pork, crackling, stuffing, sausage and vegetables for 400 rupiahs.

Another Balinese specialty is a steamed duck dish which has achieved a measure of fame but which I found no more successful than duck dishes anywhere else, except in the Peking variant of good Chinese restaurants.

Sate, pronounced satay, meat on small skewers grilled over coconut-shell charcoal, is often fine, as much for the peanut sauce and the accompanying rice, onions and vegetables as anything, but only in three forms is it especially Balinese.

One, called 'wrapped sate', is made from fish meat pounded together with fresh coconut, garlic, prawn paste, chili, salt and lemon leaves. This sticky mixture is wrapped by hand around small skewers for grilling and can be excellent, though sight of the manufacturing process does not always enthrall.

The second sate I never tried because I decline to eat turtle. A vain gesture, perhaps, because it can have no effect on the slaughter of thousands of these animals described later in this book — see 'Wildlife' — but better than no gesture at all.

And the third sate? When staying at Tirtagangga, near Amlapura, I was told that dog sate was to be had in a village just down the road. I walked down the hill twice to find the seller, to observe and to ask such questions as, how much do you pay for a good dog, do you make sate from any old mongrels, how and where do you kill them, how do you prepare the meat, who are your customers, how much does a stick of dog sate cost, is it a thriving business — normal, reporter-like questions.

But the first day was Kuningan, a dog sate seller's holiday, and the second day was Sunday, a dog sate seller's holiday. On the third day I felt that other avenues presenting themselves would be more rewarding. I contented myself with being told that dogmeat is good for health and that eating it is entirely a matter of personal choice, free from caste or clan or religious significance.

Another meat which the Balinese eat without fear of religious complications is beef. Though the island is often called Hindu, it is not so in this and many other respects, about which more later. The attractive Bali cow, more deer-like than bovine, is reared in large numbers as a draught animal and for meat, not for milk, and beef and live cattle exports are important in the island's economy.

Some travellers come across feast day preparations, in a big home or a temple, and are impressed mainly by the scale of the operation.

This is men's business, and dozens may be involved in pounding turtle meat or pork, grating coconut meat and chopping spices, and stirring the pot in which the lot is cooked. One dish which emerges on these occasions is lawar, any food which has been cut into long, thin slivers and mixed with raw blood.

A more elegant preparation often served in homes, only rarely to be found in food stalls, is sayor urap, or creamed vegetables, a tasty combination of green vegetables, maize and beans, with spices and grated coconut. It is said to have reached its highest level in Klungkung regency.

Food in the richer private homes must be better than it is in the stalls and restaurants — it is so everywhere — and some dishes may be exotic indeed. Colin McPhee, writing in the 1930s, enthused over fish baked in banana leaves, ant-eater stewed in a bamboo tube, turtle in a crushed peanut sauce, skewered birds no larger than bumble bees, dragonfly larvae toasted with coconut. Fried dragonfly is still a delicacy. But such findings are rare.

One reason for the limited range of the cuisine could be Balinese reluctance to make the most of seafood. The sea around the island abounds with fish and other creatures but consumption is small; far more fish goes to local canneries than to local markets. The reasons could be cultural because the Balinese traditionally have regarded the sea, dangerous enough anyway, as a fearful place inhabited by demons — the reverse of the heavens. Necessity drove some of them to fishing for their livelihoods but it has never been a popular pursuit.

Whatever the islanders may lack in fish, however, they make up for in fruit. The king of all fruits is the durian. Some tourists may turn up their noses at it because it has a distinctive aroma. Indeed, eating durian has been described as eating the most delicious custard in the world in a public lavatory. It has been said to combine the taste of heaven and the smell of hell. In fact, much has been said about it. Alfred Russel Wallace, the English naturalist about whom more later, described the taste of durian as, well, indescribable, but he tried anyway:

'A rich butter-like custard highly flavoured with almonds gives the best general idea of it, but intermingled with it come wafts of flavour that call to mind cream-cheese, onion-sauce, brown sherry and other incongruities. Then there is a rich glutinous smoothness in the pulp which nothing else possesses but which adds to its delicacy. It is neither acid, nor sweet, nor juicy, yet one feels the want of none of these qualities, for it is perfect as it is. It produces no nausea or other bad effect, and the more you eat of it the less you feel inclined to stop. In fact to eat Durians is a new sensation, worth a voyage to the East to experience.'

In the presence of such prose one must be humble, but I shall add my own example of what a durian at the right time can mean. In Bedugul in central Bali the air is refreshingly cool, the view of the lake and mountain evocative, the lakeside temple exotic even for Bali. When to this I was able to add a perfect durian, to be savoured along with the view, that made my day.

Other fruits available in Bali, all locally grown, can be dealt with more briskly: Mangosteen (if durian has a contender for the title of finest fruit, this is it), rambutan, mango, papaya, banana (many varieties), coconut, pineapple, avocado, grapes, apples, sawo (also known as ciku, said to have originated in central America; a potato to look at but very tasty), jackfruit (the largest of all fruits, up to 90 cm long), salak (brown and scaly like lizard skin outside, crisp and scented inside), breadfruit, langsat, duku, jambu air ('water apple'), guava, passionfruit, palmyra or lontar nuts, nutmeg, pomelo, limes, oranges, starfruit, soursop and, therefore, sweetsop.

A friendly woman who has a food stall near the Campuan bridge in Ubud composes a fine dish by heaping various fruits on to a base of fragrant, freshly cooked black rice and topping the lot with palm sugar. In other places the es (ice) cendol is worth trying — jackfruit, palm sugar, coconut milk, perhaps other fruits, and a jellyish material, the cendol, made from mung beans or rice flour and coloured, usually green. Another possibility is culek, a dish of cooked pineapple, banana, coconut and palm sugar.

Cakes and sweets, usually based on rice flour or glutinous rice, abound and are worth trying. Many shops in Denpasar have interesting counters of such delicacies, and in Kuta women go from lodging house to lodging house carrying their wares in trays on their heads, usually in time for breakfast.

Their cakes go well with coffee, and here is a product which compensates for Bali's deficiencies in the matter of food. Bali coffee can be superb. Historically Bali's coffee (and pigs) did more to attract traders than did any other commodities. But the exported kind can never match that which comes freshly roasted from the market.

In Denpasar, sitting contentedly behind the antique grill of a shop his father founded more than 60 years ago, is a coffee dealer named Djuwito Chayadi. He has been in the business for more than 40 years, and the air about him is redolent with the smell of the coffee that has made him rich. Djuwito is contented because some connoisseurs regard Bali coffee as the best in the world, and his as the best in Bali. He sells it loose, still hot from roasting, and in plastic-wrapped packets and is thinking of putting it in tins as well. But there is no hurry. After 40 years, why rush? Perhaps one of his sons will do it.

Why is his coffee so good? Partly because he buys only the best coffee beans, each day letting his instincts work on the samples which farmers bring him from the higher mountain slopes. And then? Then there is a secret. All he will say is that his coffee is pure, without maize, rice, salt, sugar, margarine, coconut oil or any of the other commodities some other coffee makers add. This is not necessarily to make weight or to deceive. Many people in southeast Asia, particularly customers in old-fashioned coffee shops, like these concoctions.

I preferred the pure. I bought a kilo of Djuwito's coffee powder, ground and roasted that morning, warm in its brown paper bag, and took it home. Its redolence filled the kitchen. Balinese coffee in this style is instant in that you prepare it by pouring boiling water over it in a glass or cup. You add sugar but rarely milk, which is not available fresh in Bali anyway. Black is better. But the coffee is not instant, in that the powder does not all dissolve. You learn to stir briskly to help floating particles sink, and that drinking to the end means getting a mouthful of dregs. You also learn to consider this coffee superb.

With coffee so splendid, who needs tea? I did, until I learned that in Bali it is best not to bother. Tea usually comes readymade in vacuum flasks, a weakly flavoured hot water, often over-sweet, which gives you liquid intake without having to drink the possibly polluted water, but otherwise has little purpose. Lacking tea, you may from time to time drink rice wine, squatting by the roadside with the men (never women) of the village drinking clubs.

Something to chew on
As important as food and drink to many Balinese is what one ingenious writer has called 'Asia's quid pro quo', a quid of betel. Betel is widely used, especially by older people, and its signs are

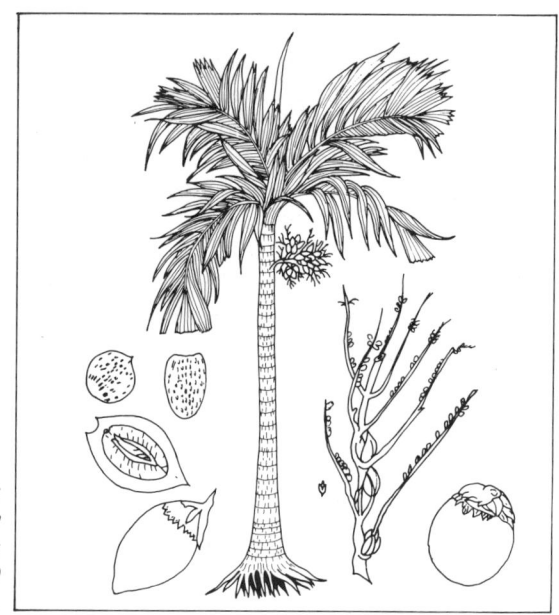

The areca nut palm, as depicted in all its parts by Rumphius, the famous pioneering naturalist 300 years ago.

everywhere to be seen in reddened mouths, blackened teeth and apparently bloodstained floors and pavings. It is entrenched in Balinese lore as a necessary offering to gods and visitors. Special tools and containers for preparing betel and offering it to guests have developed over the centuries, and some are splendidly ornate.

Strictly the word 'betel' means only the leaf the quid is wrapped in but it has come to be applied to the whole packet. Much more important in these mildly stimulating little bundles which people across half of Asia pop so often into their mouths is the areca nut, about the size of a small hen's egg, from a tall, thin palm tree which probably originated in Malaysia and is now found from Africa to Polynesia. In Malaysia it is called 'Pinang' and Penang is named after it.

Slivers from part of its hard nut make the first ingredient. The second is a tiny piece of purified lime. A small piece of pale, earthy material called gambir, prepared by boiling the leaves of a shrub related to the coffee and cinchona plants, is often added. (This gambir is not related to another, also known as gambier, formerly much used in tanning leather.) Other possible ingredients in the quid, depending on taste and local custom, include cinnamon, cardamom, camphor, nutmeg and turmeric.

The leaf in which all this is wrapped, and from which the quid gets its name, is from the Piper betle plant, a member of the pepper family. In India this leaf is called pan or paan, in Malaysia and most of Indonesia it is sireh, in Bali base (with the 'e' pronounced). In each case the word for the leaf is applied also to the quid.

An American writer, Fred Eiseman, to whom I am indebted for much of this information, says that in Bali the three essential ingredients of the quid — areca, lime and betel leaf — symbolise the Hindu trinity of Brahma, Vishnu and Siva (or, in Bali, Brahma, Wisnu and Siwa). This could have originated through nothing more than Balinese playfulness at work on colour similarities: Brahma is often thought of as red, and the areca nut is red; Siva is white and so is lime; and Vishnu is sometimes green, as is the betel leaf.

If it was once playful, however, it is now serious. Virtually every offering to the gods prepared in Bali, from the little ones on bus dashboards to the huge ones for the island's thousands of temples, include at least smidgens of areca, lime and betel.

Why the lime? The lime used in Bali is prepared from sea coral and would seem to have little in common with the other, vegetable ingredients. Eiseman says the areca nut contains an alkaloid which stimulates the nervous system of the body. Or rather, it would if it could penetrate the mucous membranes of the mouth. In the form in which it is found in the areca nut it cannot. But add lime and a chemical reaction occurs, its form changes, it can be absorbed and stimulation may result.

Users say the betel quid freshens the mouth, prevents them feeling hungry if they miss meals, helps digestion and strengthens the teeth. Some say they feel languorous if deprived of betel — which makes it a kind of indirect stimulant. Some writers have described it as mildly exhilarating. The areca nut is an accepted, and possibly effective, folk remedy for tapeworms. There are medical indications it causes cancer of the mouth.

...with a touch of spice

If you feel that you would like to take your exploration of things herbal further, Bali is a fine place to do it. The folklore relating to spices, herbs and traditional medicines is endless and supplies are right at hand.

A large stall in a big market right in the centre of Denpasar which appeared to offer only sticks and stones turned out to be an apothecary's delight. Here is a selection of the goods set out in more than 50 dishes: Star anis, sulphur, incense from Arabia in the form of black and white rocks, aluminium sulphate for clarifying water, gambier, mace, nutmeg, dried nutmeg flowers, cloves, tiny dried chillies, a yellow powder said to improve the complexion, various resins, and an entire chemistry set of seeds, twigs, leaves, barks, roots, shavings and funguses from the jungles and savannahs of half the world.

That was impressive, and impressive also was the certainty with which numerous customers knew precisely what they wanted. There is a world of expertise here just waiting to be tapped. Working out what chewing betel actually does would be just a start.

...And a postscript about Bali Belly

Many visitors find that this island of the gods, this earthly paradise, this home of celestial beauty turns their bowels to water. There is no way of knowing who will fall victim to diarrhoea. Some people exercise extravagant care and are smitten; others take absurd risks in an island which makes no pretence to high standards of hygiene and never feel even a twinge of doubt.

What should one do? Be careful. Eat only in clean restaurants. In cheaper places Bill Dalton's Indonesia Handbook suggests looking at the waiters because they eat the same food as they serve. If they look unhealthy, move on. Do not drink unboiled water. Most ice is prepared from treated water but if you feel delicate avoid it; drink beer or tea instead. Use commonsense.

And if the demon Bali Belly strikes? Proprietary medicines often do not deliver on their promises and may actually do harm while a good doctor could have you right in a day or two. Better than formal medicine, however, may be resort to one of Asia's best-known folk remedies. Medical researchers in India and Bangladesh have found that ricewater, the water in which rice has been cooked, can cure diarrhoea. So, ask your hotel to arrange a plateful of plain, soft-boiled rice for you. Some people know it as rice porridge or congee. The rice water works its magic by slowly releasing glucose into the gut and the solids give you nourishment. Do not add sugar, which could make your condition worse. But if your condition does worsen, get a good doctor quickly. They do exist in Bali and they have much experience of this potentially serious problem. Bon Appetit.

Cremation

oon after arriving in Bali I learned about a tourist who had drowned there and whose family had asked for her body to be cremated. The consul involved thought this would be no great problem because cremation is part of the Balinese way of life and death. He was taken aback, however, to learn that Bali has neither crematoria nor undertakers.

A dead body is the responsibility of its family and its community. They handle the rites of death, right to the occasional huge cremations which are probably as famous as Balinese painting and dancing — but they do not provide such services for outsiders. The consul ended up hiring two men with agricultural flamethrowers for a do-it-yourself operation in the consulate backyard which was marked more by efficiency than funereal solemnity. It was a difficult occasion because few westerners can much enjoy seeing a body reduced to ashes and a few charred bones.

A little more experience of Bali persuaded me to see this event in a light different from that of first encounter. The process began when a tourist official told me of a 'big' cremation about to take place. Anyone could go. In fact, anyone was invited, to add to the occasion. I wondered whether a British or American or Australian tourist official would invite any Asian or African tourist dropping into his office at attend a local funeral service, and decided he would not.

My more serious education in things Balinese was about to begin.

Nonetheless a certain reluctance attended my decision to attend this cremation because I wished to distance myself from the tourist hordes, from 'tourism'. But in the end a kind of sense of duty prevailed, and an engrossing and fascinating duty it turned out to be, a turbulent, grand, exciting and satisfying occasion. And educational as well, for a direct link it provided with that consulate incineration. I shall deal with cremation in some detail because of the light it casts on the Balinese situation today. Begin to comprehend Balinese cremations and one begins to comprehend a great deal about Bali.

The dead man was Anak Agung Ngurah Jono, an important personage of Puri Saren Kelod, in Carangsari, 30 kilometres from Denpasar, Bali's capital. He had died a month earlier, after a long illness, at the age of 45, leaving a wife, five daughters and three sons. At the time of his death his family network numbered more than two hundred people who between them had raised eight million rupiahs for his cremation.

I arrived early by bus from Denpasar and found people beginning to gather. A 30-man gamelan orchestra, one of two present, one on each side of the gateway to the dead man's home, was playing, its music brittle and loud in the warming morning air. On the roadway nearby stood an intricate, ornate, dragon-like creation of timber and tinsel, its hollowed black and gold trunk (originally the trunk of a small tree) just large enough eventually to contain a cloth-wrapped corpse.

Beside it was a towering structure with nine pagoda-like roof tiers which indicated that the dead man was of high rank. Both dragon and tower were mounted on wide platforms of thick, green bamboo poles lashed together.

One of the dead man's sons gave me a strip of white cloth to wear around my waist. (Later I learned always to carry a sarong and sash wherever I went, so as to be ready always to make a gesture towards being properly dressed before entering temples or other sacred places.) Then the son gave me a glass of rice wine and answered my questions. All around were men wearing sarongs, shirts, white head-cloths. The women were more elegant, in single-colour blouses, many of then black, contrasting sashes and their best batik, songket or tie-and-dye sarongs.

The son took me through the gateway into the family compound, past a priest reading from an old Balinese text with another man rendering it into modern language. No one seemed to pay either of them much heed. We went to view the coffin, or rather the pile of splendid cloths which covered it as it stood in an open-air pavilion. Many women were gathered here, some all in black, all of them serious. Another group of women, perhaps more distant relatives, in another pavilion nearby were less stern, more chatty with one another.

We passed into another courtyard — this clearly was a very prosperous family — to sit in yet another pavilion with relatives and friends of the family, among them an amiable clove farmer I had met on the bemo coming from Denpasar. We talked about Ngurah Rai, a Balinese hero whose name I knew because the airport where I had landed a week earlier is named after him; he was from Carangsari.

More rice wine was distributed. I was introduced to an elderly man, his teeth and lips richly stained with betel, who had made the dragon-like creation, or naga, standing on the road outside, waiting for the coffin. The work, a labour of love for he admired the dead man, had taken him a week, he said. The naga form was dictated by considerations of rank and region. Other shapes used include bull, cow, winged lion, deer and a mythological creature with an elephant's head and the tail of a fish. In earlier times, up to, say, World War II, the forms to be used were strictly prescribed but today many of the old rules mean little.

I took my leave and returned to the roadway. Many more people had arrived. The gamelan orchestra played lustily, its sole flute nevertheless a clear and reedy wail through the drums, gongs, cymbals and xylophones. The players, uniformed in red head-cloths, cream tunics and batik sarongs, were deep in concentration, intent upon their interlocking rhythms. The morning was changing from warm to hot, the air from balmy to humid. Coconut fronds and the decorations on the naga and the cremation tower hung motionless.

Hawkers had arrived, setting up shop in the shade of any convenient tree or building overhang, or spreading their own awnings. One was using a small loudspeaker, graphic medical drawings of male parts and a small live snake crawling around his hands and arms to sell energising potions. Others displayed trinkets, posters of heroes and film stars, cheap clothing, books, cold drinks in plastic buckets packed with ice.

They had come from miles around and were intent on selling to the villagers who crowded around, eager for a little entertainment while waiting for the main event to get under way. But they were not the only vendors hawking their wares. A different class of trader was also arriving in strength, set upon selling much more expensive items to the foreign tourists who were also sure to turn up.

About 11 am — the cremation procession was to begin at noon — they did so by coach and limousine from the luxury beach hotels of Sanur and Nusa Dua, all casual wear and funny hats, cameras and video gear and often distressing manners, sweating and serious and diligent about enjoying themselves. The hawkers flocked around them offering hand-carved chess sets, sarongs, replicas of antique paintings, jewellery. Some tourists seemed to resent this, others accepted it as due recognition of their money but made a dour business of bargaining all the same.

Meanwhile the Balinese in general contrived to ignore this avalanche of outsiders, displaying a facility I came to observe often in the weeks ahead. When they wished they could render the strangers in their midst totally invisible, absent, of no account. It may be this ability as much as any other which has permitted Balinese life to survive so well despite the pressures arriving from outside. On this occasion in Carangsari, despite the tourists' numbers and strangeness, the Balinese paid them no heed, concentrating instead on making the most of what was, after all, a family and community occasion.

By this time elements of the coming ceremony, previously a matter mainly of a few organisers looking harrassed but not actually doing very much, are picking up speed. Adjustments are made to the coffin's coverings, to offerings on various altars, to the naga and the tower, with its many decorations and its huge, backward-facing image of Bhoma, Son of the Earth, a wild-eyed, fanged creature with enormous wings. There is a flurry as a long white cloth is laid along the ground from the pavilion where the coffin lies, through the gateway to the tower outside. A man climbs a watchtower to begin beating a rhythm on two hanging, hollowed, wooden logs, forehanded to the left, backhanded to the right. The gamelan becomes louder, the faces of the people more excited, the hawkers — running out of time — more importunate.

Suddenly, action. Women in black file forth, raising the white cloth high. Men follow with the coffin, carrying it to the tower where it is manhandled into position high above the ground. A xylophone player is already seated alongside, adding to the din. A priest strug-

A pause for adjustments during the Carangsari cremation procession.

gles with a long white cloth to lash the coffin into position, for reason which will soon become obvious. Tourists jostle for position to take pictures and swear in sundry European languages when one climbs so high on a wall as to block the view of the others.

Noise swells. Everyone is shouting and the gamelan is ever more vigorous. One of the orchestras lines up behind the tower, playing instruments swinging from bamboo carrying poles. There is a rising human clamour as men position themselves alongside and within the two bamboo carrrying platforms. Perhaps fifty of them raise the naga on high and rush off up the road. Another party, even larger, lifts the platform with the coffin and tower, with everyone shouting.

The tower rocks to one side, then to the other. The priest high up besides the coffin holds on with one hand, flourishes a leafy wand — much studied by anthropologists for its detail and symbolism — with the other. The din of music and voices is fantastic. The xylophonist plays on, though his position is even more precarious than the priest's because he has no spare hand to hold on with. Within moments the tower is high on men's shoulders, rocking, dipping and soaring its way along the road in pursuit of the naga.

The pace is high. One must run to keep ahead. The noise is relentless. I scribble, 'What a way to go!' and dash on, trying to keep up with the women leading the way. They hold aloft the long white cloth as a kind of tow rope except they are not so much pulling as in danger of being overrun. Oddly, they do not seem to move all that rapidly but they cover the ground at a great rate. By holding the cloth above their heads the women are symbolically helping to carry the platform with the coffin.

Tourists, villagers sprint alongside. Some tourists give up, red-faced and drenched with sweat, and turn back. Others pound on, dashing here and there along the ricefield bunds for a different kind of picture. From time to time the tower is halted, spun, lurched from side to side to confuse any spirits so evil as to want to follow the dead man. The excitement is delirious, intoxicating.

But what is this? Trouble? The shouting around the tower, the cries from the straining carriers are suddenly panicky, alarmed. The tower rocks frighteningly. The women with the white cloth look back in something like terror. An old woman falls to her knees and prays. A tumult of movement seethes around the base of the tower and the shouting verges on screaming. Slowly the tower steadies and order, if that is the right word, is restored.

The mad dash continues, tower following naga to the burning ground, an open grassy area amid the ricefields, ringed by coconut palms, about a kilometre from where the procession began. The tower surges to a lurching stop alongside the already resting naga. The exhausted carriers, sweat-soaked, seek rest in the shade. The gamelan musicians find their own patch of shade, play on.

The trunk of the naga is opened up, with decorative frills which happen to get in the way being summarily discarded. Not that the man with the betel-stained mouth who made it minds — he is as busy with the demolition as anyone. The coffin so elaborately brought to this point is handed down from the tower, carried three times around the naga with the women leading, torn apart so its cloth-wrapped contents can be stowed inside the trunk.

A phalanx of men in white head-cloths ring this new centre of activity, arranging ritual items upon the body and adding more — some carried all this way on women's heads — which are handed up one by one. The presiding priest chants and the gamelan plays on but the tension is fading away. One feels release from the surging, roaring excitement of the procession which had enfolded even some of the tourists.

The tower, now useless, is tipped on its side with a crash and stripped of its more valuable trimmings. Back at the naga a bucket of holy water is handed up through the row of white head-cloths and poured over the body. The bucket is handed back down — a variation on traditional practice which would have seen earthenware containers used, and then smashed. Tourists standing on tiptoe right behind the presiding officials hold their cameras high, lenses pointing downwards, to record every last splash. Elsewhere around the cremation ground other tourists continue their dealings with hawkers or pick strips of tinsel from the fallen tower as souvenirs.

Men manhandle a tower through the streets of Denpasar.

A whiff of smoke appears. I try to check an account which says that matches, being deemed unclean, are never used to light a funeral pyre and that a magnifying glass to concentrate the sun's rays is employed instead. Answers are confusing, which is another element of working in Bali that I shall become accustomed to. One man says matches were used, another insists on a cigarette lighter, a third finds the idea of using a magnifying glass so remarkable that he turns to discuss the point with his friends — which leads to other matters and the subject is quickly lost. I am unable to locate the man who started the fire, which in any case is becoming a subject of observation its own right.

People who have been milling around the naga move back, those who have been idling on the outer perimeter of the cremation ground move closer, and a circle forms. The gamelan falls silent for the first time in three hours as players join the watchers — but only briefly because children are quick to seize the chance to use the abandoned instruments. What they lack in skill they make up with gusto.

The flames lick up around such decorations as the naga has retained, and I am confronted with another puzzle. There is no pile of firewood and I realise that the bamboo of the carrying platform and the woodwork of the naga do not comprise nearly enough fuel to render a body to ashes. The mystery is soon explained, however, in a manner to illuminate that story about a tourist being incinerated by men wielding two agricultural flamethrowers. The burning power at this Balinese cremation turns out to come from two more of these same instruments, linked by plastic hose with a drum of kerosene hanging in a coconut palm, to supply gravity feed. Perhaps that poor tourist had not been so badly treated after all. The flames roar. The crowd stands and watches, then sits and watches. The naga is quickly a charred ruin and the body, still recognisable with head, arms and legs, falls through into a corrugated iron trough.

The toppled tower is also ignited and the two fires produce frequent loud reports from exploding bamboo. The two men wielding the flamethrowers thrust them closer and closer to the body, reducing it rapidly to ashes and charred bone fragments. The crowd, which has been dwindling for some time, breaks up rapidly now and people head for home, having had what can be described as a holiday outing.

Miguel Covarrubias, writing about Bali in the 1930s, was much impressed by the lavish cremations of his times. 'Strange as it seems,' he wrote, 'it is in their cremation ceremonies that the Balinese have their greatest fun.'

Beryl de Zoete, who was in Bali for years about the same time as Covarrubias, found that cremations were scenes of vast hilarity, and continued: 'There may be an element of bravado in the hysterical mirth of a Balinese cremation, a kind of euphemistic challenge to death. Perhaps the noise is merely to frighten away boetas [evil spirits], and the manoeuvres with the cremation tower an attempt to mislead them, since they can only see straight ahead; or it may be the ebullition [?] of rather macabre high spirits. Certainly it has the effect of banishing gloom from a funeral.'

Clifford Geertz, a more recent source of essential information about Bali, has described cremations as 'a bit like a playful riot,' though he follows this up with intricate explanations of how the events are laden with completely unplayful significance. For example, a royal cremation, as well as being dramatic, splendid and expensive, was also 'thoroughly dedicated to the aggressive assertion of status . . . a headlong attack in a war of prestige'.

Geertz lists cremations, at least in the past, as central to the island's 'absolutely astonishing degree of invidious distinction' — along with subtle differences in titles, elaborate etiquette, highly developed language differences, precise dining, seating, precedence and marriage rules, and enormously detailed regulations governing building design and decoration.

When the ashes and charred bone fragments of the cremation I had been watching were cool enough, they were gathered into the shell of an unripe coconut with sweet-smelling flowers and other items. Then the ceremony moved to the seashore — a long drive — for a brief and simple ritual during which the ashes were scattered on the water. There were also more ceremonies later. The timing and nature of these later events varies with caste and region, and with personal, family and community preferences, as do other aspects of cremations and, indeed, of numerous other elements of behaviour; Bali

The culmination — flames begin the work of cremation.

is a difficult island to be precise about.

As a result of all this activity on behalf of the deceased, his soul is liberated from the body and is free to fly to the heaven which stand in tiers, one above the other, high above Gunung Agung, the live volcano which dominates much of Bali. There it will live as in Bali, although under more ideal conditions, until it is time for it to be reborn within its circle of blood relatives — perhaps, in theory at least, as his own grandchild.

Belief in rebirth, reincarnation, is basic to the Balinese religion, about which more later. But at this stage it is necessary to explain that I shall not be calling that religion Hinduism. In fact, there is a case to be made that if the first Europeans to encounter Bali had not had earlier experience in India the Hindu label would not have been applied. These Europeans perceived the superficial similarities with Hinduism, and by the time awareness of important deeper differences had penetrated the label was too firmly stuck to be removed.

Here is a comment from Covarrubias: '[Various elaborate cults] are the backbone of the Balinese religion, which is generally referred to as Hinduism, but which is in reality too close to the earth, too animistic, to be taken as the same esoteric religion as that of the Hindus of India.'

In his excellent Bali Profile, Hanna has this to say: 'In Bali there is no creed, no dogma, no conviction about salvation or damnation by reason of adherence to any metaphysical doctrine. But there is an immense deposit of mystical and spiritual manifestations which the villagers constantly re-experience in daily life, always aware of the living presence in nature of the ancestral and divine spirits.'

On the doctrine of reincarnation, Geertz says it is known in Bali only in a 'vague, general and rather idiosyncratic way,' while 'the entire dharma-karma-samsara doctrine [of Hinduism], as an effective social belief, is absent.'

Hanna says that the Balinese religion could be described as an archaic form of much modified Hinduism, 'but certainly it is not a Hinduism which any Indian Hindu, ancient or modern, would recognise as approximately his own system of beliefs, values, and dogmas.' He suggests calling it Balinism, and so I shall.

In Indian Hinduism rebirth is linked with virtue. The more virtuous one's life, the more agreeable one's next life. Rebirth within one's family is not, so far as I can discover, a goal; in fact, such a desire could be seen as a kind of selfishness and lead to a penalty for a lapse from virtue. In Bali, those scholars who have involved themselves with Indian texts in the course of religious studies say that promotion to a higher caste is possible; but others more concerned with folk beliefs say that in practice promotion is a little considered element. The prospect of demotion, on the other hand, to rebirth as a dog or a snake or a poisonous mushroom, may be more widely accepted and may be a force in Bali's remarkably high standard of morality.

On the possibility of promotion, a mountain sage I met had it both ways: 'Reincarnation is usually back in the family but a person can be reborn into a higher caste if he has been good and virtuous, and lower if not good. But that is not the point. The only real promotion is to Nirvana. If you're reincarnated, you're not pure.'

On the other hand, rebirth in the world of the living is to be considered proof that a dead person's descendants have fulfilled their obligations properly. In this sense a full-scale cremation is as much, or more, for the living than for the dead. In Carangsari that day, there was no doubt Anak Agung Ngurah Jono's family could fairly feel they had done well.

There was a time, inevitably, when cremation was not known, and the history of its spread through Balinese society is in large degree a history of that society as well. The Bali Aga people have resisted the trend and as a result today form communities among the most remarkable on the island.

In its earliest forms in Bali cremation appears to have been confined to the nobility and the priesthood but after the 16th Century rule of a king named Batu Renggong the custom began spreading throughout the populace. How pervasive that spread was, however, is a question impossible to answer, and even today estimates of the proportion of people cremated are more like guesses, ranging from about ten percent to thirty or more.

Most upper caste people are cremated, and as these upper castes make up about a tenth of the population the lower estimate above is easy to arrive at. What is not known is how many members of the fourth caste, the commoners, are cremated. This would be a difficult figure to arrive at even if cremation followed closely upon death but it does not necessarily do so. Each village has a burial ground and here corpses are interred until a cremation can be arranged — perhaps decades later, and perhaps tagged on to the cremation of a more important figure. Covarrubias records a cremation in 1934 for a man who died in 1906, and also the eerie sight of men opening graves to find remains for cremation, 'shouting with delight at the discovery of a blackened jawbone or a femur'. This aspect has not much changed today. The ritual opening of a grave, by no means an uncommon sight, is as much part of a cremation as the actual burning.

The principle is that there will be a cremation eventually, because a person who is not cremated remains a separate and possibly dangerous soul who must be ceaselessly appeased with graveyard offerings. But it seems that in practice the intention to cremate is often deferred for so long as to vanish entirely. The considerable cost of a cremation big enough to reflect well on the family is a factor in this, but equally important could be a kind of inertia, and a lapse in memory, and even a tendency to assume years later that the overlooked event has in fact taken place.

The day after the Carangsari cremation I had the interview with Professor Dr Ida Bagus Mantra, the Governor of Bali, which I mentioned briefly when writing about Bali's women. The Governor is a big man with an impressive record as a scholar and administrator, and was for some years Indonesia's Minister of Culture. Now he is back in Bali, his birthplace, with at first glance contradictory assignments — to help preserve a unique culture, to promote development and also to help bring in still more tourists. I met him in his office, which is itself a showpiece of Balinese culture, in an enclave of elegant new government buildings a mile from the heart of Denpasar. The architectural style is based on traditional temple and palace design. We spoke mainly about change.

When I suggested that Bali had been subjected to more change in the previous decade than in much longer periods previously, he commented that these were changes 'in the environmental sense only and not in the spiritual and cultural senses'. He expanded on this point when I asked if Covarrubias — along with many other more recent writers — had been right or wrong in predicting disaster if the tourist flow continued.

'He was wrong,' the Governor said. 'His book is still worth reading as a source of information but his stress is more on the ritualistic than on the dynamic and deeper aspects of spiritual life. There is some imbalance in his method. He ignored the more dynamic and spiritual aspects. He did not pay enough attention to Balinese culture as adjusting and developing.' Then, in a remarkable phrase,

'Balinese culture contains many manifestations towards modernisation.'

I cited the use of kerosene burners at the cremation I had seen the day before as an example of change and asked if change to this degree was acceptable. 'Kerosene burners do not alter the spiritual and cultural aspects,' the Governor replied. 'It's practical to use kerosene, it's a matter of a new environment, an adjustment in the spiritual environment. Who knows, but in the future we may have a crematorium powered by electricity — it's not a religious matter, just a practical one.'

The interview moved on, its other points to be produced at appropriate stages in this book. The point here is cremations as a fundamental part of Balinese life. In time I came to agree with the Governor. It does not really much matter if, for example, the bodies of important people are no longer reduced to ashes on pyres entirely of fragrant and costly sandalwood. Nor does it matter that formalin or in some cases even morgue freezers are used to preserve bodies until cremation arrangements have been completed. What is important is that such changes permit the institution to survive, that people brought up to regard cremation as important can anticipate eventually being cremated themselves. Without technical adjustments, without the Governor's 'changes in the environmental sense', this would not be possible.

And the tourists? They do not really matter. They do not figure in the equation except as extras to give a cremation a little more verve and excitement. The problems they pose are different, as reference once more to that story about the tourist's flamethrower cremation makes clear. By this time I had come to regard as acceptable the part about the method used. More difficult was the part of the narrative which followed, which I have not so far mentioned.

On the morning after the cremation the consul and a small number of friends took the ashes to the beach at Legian, the girl's favourite resort, to complete the ritual. As the party waded into the water, beach idlers gathered to watch. Among them was a European tourist, male, completely naked except for his hat. When he learned what was happening he removed his hat, held it over his breast, and stood at attention. 'It was like something out of a Fellini movie,' the consul recalled.

Weeks later in a small town in the west of Bali I was the only outsider watching another cremation, and another demonstration of adjustment. The height of the tower, for instance, was regulated not so much by custom — I was told quite seriously — as by the height of the electricity wires across the road. Similarly, the style of the event was determined not so much by custom and status as by financial ability.

The occasion was just as exciting as my first cremation had been. The procedure was similar, except that a small boy, the dead woman's grandson, dressed entirely in white, was seated astride the coffin throughout, clinging on desperately during the ritual rotations. There was much noise and excitement, and the scene as the procession thrust its way down a narrow lane between bushy banks and then splashed through a shallow stream was memorable. The actual cremation was on a high, exposed and breezy ground, and the fuel was kerosene.

But much that is traditional and symbolic remains. The structure, termed bade or wadah, in which the coffin is carried to the burning ground is laden with symbolism. It represents the cosmos as Balinese tradition envisages it. Its base, a stylised representation of a flattened-out turtle bearing winged serpents — or nagas — is intended to bring to mind the underworld of demons. The platform above this, where the coffin is placed, represents the world of man. The tower with its tiered roofs stands for the world of the gods, the number of tiers indicating the status of the dead person and the heavenly level to which the departing soul aspires: one for a commoner, three or five for lesser gentry, seven or nine for ordinary lords, eleven for a king. The tower is known as meru, a word from India, where it refers to a cosmic mountain at the centre of the world. Why only odd numbers of tiers are used is another Balinese mystery, but a pervasive one, since the pattern applies not only to cremation towers but also to Bali's thousands of temples.

Because the number of tiers is dictated by the caste or rank of the dead person, it is not an element to be trifled with. But today the rules are a little more relaxed than they were in the 1930s, when Colin McPhee, an American student of Balinese music, watched the cremation of another Anak Agung. Later he wrote in his *A House in Bali*:

'Before the palace gates the wadah, the tower which would bear the body of the old Anak Agung to the cremation ground, stood glistening like a Christmas tree. It rose high above our heads, a complicated structure of bamboo, and from the many little roofs that ascended pagoda-like above the platform high up where the body would rest there fluttered fringes of tinsel and gold, fringes of tissue paper dyed every colour of the spectrum. . . . But even as I stood admiring this wonderful affair, the Anak Agung [the son of the dead man] came up with the Brahman priest, a troubled look on his face. Something had gone wrong.

'He had, it seemed, in his characteristic and exuberant love for the grand gesture, built a wadah with eleven roofs. This, however, was above his rank. . . . The sarcophagus too had been built above his station. This the priest reluctantly agreed to overlook, since it was too late to change it, but he insisted with quiet firmness that two roofs be removed from the wadah. It was a bitter pill. Reluctantly, the Anak Agung gave the order, and three men climbed the tower, to disfigure it before the eyes of the world.

'Do not take a picture of it, said the Anak Agung sombrely as we stood watching side by side. . . .'

The cremation went ahead, on a grander scale, more turbulent, but not all that different from the one I saw in Carangsari. A month later McPhee watched the final stage of the same event, something not to be seen today, which involved also the remains of other people whose cremations had taken place along with the Anak Agung's. Here is his description:

'. . . later I went down to the sea to wait for the wadahs to arrive from Saba with the ashes of the dead. . . . Far off in the distance there was the sound of bright processional music, the melodious ringing of the g'nders [xylophones in the gamelan] and little gongs above the rapid beat of drums and cymbals. The music grew louder. Across the fields and down the road to the shore the procession of wadahs approached.

'They were tall delicate spires of white, now decorated only with gold foil and a thousand little mirrors, and as they travelled along the road the gold and mirrors flashed in the sun as though the wadahs were lit with candles. In their fragility, their loftiness, their paper-white radiance, the slender towers celebrated this final and lovely rite when the ashes, the last earthly relics, would be dissolved completely in the sea. Now the soul was free at last, free to float away, join its forefathers, merge, said some, in the ancestral home.

'Along the sand the wadahs were set in a row. While men and women waded singing out into the water as far as they dared, to cast away the ashes, boys climbed the quivering towers to tear away the streamers, the gold, the precious little mirrors. Now the wadahs were set afire. One by one they fell with a crash. In the dusk the fires burned themselves out, and to the sound of music the procession returned to Saba.'

Why this emphasis — Bali's and mine — on this theme? Is it not macabre? Well, no. Death is inevitable, life after death is assured, and a well-conducted cremation which will ensure the best of that afterlife for the dead person is cause for great satisfaction. Is it not destructive, that so much money should be spent on these events? Perhaps but they also add colour to life, they enable families to demonstrate unity and worth, and in any case extravagance is not necessarily essential — if it were families would bankrupt themselves to buy firewood instead of using kerosene.

There are two reasons why cremations are important, apart from the satisfaction they bring. The first is that they embody in one way or another the essentials of Balinism, that term which is so much to be preferred to any which refers to Hinduism. Second, changes in the physical aspects of cremation — such as the use of kerosene — relate directly to other changes taking place on this fabled island, and offer hope that change in general will help it survive. Lack of change is much more to be feared than change itself, because when Bali ceases to change it will die.

McPhee wrote about the 1930s. In more recent times the Balinese have still from time to time contrived to present a grand show in the old tradition. As recently as 1979 a cremation in Ubud featured a tower twenty metres high and drew a reported 100,000 visitors. Nor is it inconceivable that such occasions will not continue, though perhaps with a switch from old money to new, from the decaying aristocracy of the old palaces to the modern rich of trade and tourism. A commoner's cremation I watched in Denpasar was just as grand as the one in Carangsari. Whether or not the Balinese will adjust the rules which regulate such matters as the number of tiers on a tower it is impossible to say — but if they want to they will.

The main forces working against cremation are, of course, economic and social: the cost of an impressive event, and changes in the thinking of younger and more educated people. But there are also forces working for continuation of the tradition, such as the improving economy, the arrival of such cost-cutting devices as kerosene for fuel, and the shortage of land for burials in a crowded island. The time may already have arrived when cremation, perhaps shorn of its status implications, makes more sense than burial; permanent burial, that is, rather than burial pending a cremation which may never eventuate. The time may soon arrive when the Governor's apparently whimsical comment about an electric crematorium may turn into something firmer.

I found everything connected with cremations — seeing them, discussing them, reading about them — fascinating, but not all visitors to Bali are as impressed as I was. Here is a passage from a 1930s novel I shall refer to again, Vicki Baum's A Tale of Bali, in which a Dutch official, Boomsmer, laments his posting in Singaraja, in those days Bali's main port. The format is fictional, but there is no doubt that Boomsmer had his counterparts in real life:

'The natives were dirty and spat out their betel juice even on the office stoep. They were eaten up with rabies* and ringworm and fever and were too stupid to have themselves cured. They had innumerable superstitions and tabus, and the higher castes were even worse in that respect than the lower ones. The petty rajas, who after all were no better than bare-footed peasants, squatted about among the litter of their puris [palaces] and thought themselves the most mighty sovereigns on earth because they could have the heads and hands of their subjects hacked off when they had the mind.

'But when one of them died, then he was wrapped in white linen and kept in the house till the stink rose to heaven. Boomsmer shuddered at the recollection of this charnal stench and took a quick nip of gin. . . .'

The burning of widows

The cremation I saw, exciting though I found it, was a bland affair by contrast with the one McPhee had watched nearly 50 years before; and that by turn was much less memorable than one a Danish adventurer named L.V. Helms recorded nearly a century before that. He was in Bali for little more than a year, but during that time the raja of the state of Gianyar died and was cremated with full ceremony and ritual in December, 1847. Helms' account, one of the best there is from those days, is notable for the detail it includes of procedure and equipment, of the vast scale of the occasion with, for instance, five hundred men carrying the eleven-tiered tower,

There is no rabies in Bali.

and of the enormous crowd which gathered.

But what sticks in the mind most is his description of how three women, concubines of the dead raja whose body was being burned, were burned alive with him. 'It was a lovely day,' he wrote, and the Balinese dressed in their best flocking in across the lawn-like terraces of the endless rice fields 'looked little enough like savages, but rather like a kindly festive crowd bent upon some pleasant excursion'. Such was the impression of plenty, peace and happiness that it was hard to believe that three women, 'guiltless of any crime, were, for their affection's sake, and in the name of religion, to suffer the most horrible of deaths, while thousands of their countrymen looked on'.

They would do so by leaping into a fierce, bright fire from a bamboo platform seven metres above. They were carried to the scene on three platforms following the huge one which contained the king's body, and, according to Helms, showed no fear. 'Dressed in white, their long black hair partly concealing them, with a mirror in one hand and a comb in the other, they appeared intent only upon adorning themselves as though for some gay festival. The courage which sustained them in a position so awful was indeed extraordinary, but it was born of the hope of happiness in a future world. From being bondswomen here, they believed they were to become the favourite wives and queens of their late master in another world.'

They showed no fear even when the flames had consumed the gorgeous wooden image of a lion in which the raja's coffin had been placed, and continued to behave 'as though making ready for life rather than for death'. A plank was pushed out over the flames and oil was poured on the fire, causing flames to leap to a great height. The moment had arrived.

'With firm and measured steps the victims trod the fatal plank; three times they brought their hands together [in a gesture of reverence] over their heads, on each of which a small dove was placed, and then, with body erect, they leaped into the flaming sea below, while the doves flew up, symbolising the escaping spirits.

'Two of the women showed, even at the very last, no sign of fear; they looked at each other, to see whether they were prepared, and then, without stopping, took the plunge. The third appeared to hesitate, and to take the leap with less resolution; she faltered for a moment, and then followed, all three disappearing without uttering a sound.'

An old Dutch rendering of a widow throwing herself into the flames.

It was a sight never to be forgotten, Helms wrote, bringing to one's heart 'a strange feeling of thankfulness that one belonged to a civilisation which, with all its faults, was merciful and tended more and more to emancipate women from deception and cruelty'.

Commenting on Helms' description, Geertz says his use of the word 'bondswomen' is surely wrong, because if they were they would have been stabbed before being thrown on the pyre. Only proper wives of the lord had sufficient status to leap alive into the flames, sometimes stabbing themselves at the same time.

A Dutch account of the same occasion, included in Covarrubias' book, said that the fire in which the three women were to die had been burning since morning and threw off a glowing heat. Before the women leaped down, it added, oil and rice spirit were poured on to the fire to produce flames nearly three metres high which must have suffocated the victims at once.

At the moment of sacrifice the women, arrayed exactly as for a feast, 'glanced one towards another to convince themselves that all was prepared; but this was not a glance of fear, but of impatience, and it seemed to express a wish that they might leap at the same moment. . . . They immediately leaped down. There was no cry in leaping, no cry from the fire; they must have suffocated at once.

'One of the Europeans present succeeded in pushing through the crowd to the fire and in seeing the body some seconds after the leap — it was dead and its movements were caused merely by the combustion of the materials cast upon the flames. On other occasions, however, Europeans have heard cries uttered in leaping and in the first moments afterwards. . . .

'During the whole time from the burning of the prince till the leap of the victims, the air resounded with the clangour of numerous bands of music; small cannon were discharged and the soldiers had drawn up outside the fire and contributed to the noise by firing off their muskets. There was not one of the 50,000 Balinese present who did not show a merry face; no one was filled with repugnance and disgust except a few Europeans whose only desire was to see the end of such barbarities.'

It must be added, however, that commentators agree that such sacrifices were voluntary and that women who decided to die in this manner were treated with enormous respect. In the days that remained to them they were cossetted and constantly reminded of the beauty of the life they would live among the gods. One writer said that when the time came to die they were so thoroughly hypnotised that 'they jumped into the fire as if it were a bath'.

Covarrubias' book also includes a translation of a Dutch 17th Century account of twentytwo women slaves being killed and their bodies burned so they could continue to serve their mistress, a queen, whose body was burned at the same time. 'They were divested of all their garments, except their sashes, and four of the men, seizing the victim, two by the arms, which they held extended, and two by the feet, the victim standing, the fifth [man] prepared himself for the execution, the whole being done without covering the eyes. . . .

'Some of the most courageous demanded the poignard [dagger] themselves, which they received in the right hand, passing it to the left, after respectfully kissing the weapon. They wounded their right arms, sucked the blood which flowed from the wound, and stained their lips with it, making a bloody mark on the forehead with the point of the finger. Then, returning the dagger to their executioners, they received the first stab between the false ribs and a second under the shoulder blade, the weapon being thrust up to the hilt towards the heart.

'As soon as the horrors of death were visible in the countenance, without a complaint escaping them, they were permitted to fall to the ground ... and were stripped of their last remnant of dress, so they were left in a state of perfect nakedness.' The bodies were washed, covered with wood and burned, the greater number of their pyres being already in flames before the body of the queen arrived in its huge tower. When two sons of the same king had been cremated a short time before, a total of 76 women had been stabbed and burned in the same manner.

On occasion men as well as women were sacrificed in this way. Captain Thomas Young, an English mariner who visited Bali in 1775, recorded that one of his men, Ishmael Jerrybatoo, 'a man of veracity', told him of such cases. A man who determined to die in his master's funeral pyre was venerated and caressed wherever he went. On the fatal day, he would dance on a stage erected beside the fire, working himself into a fit before skipping to the end of a loose plank which tilted and dropped him into the flames.

Such a practice could have led to the frequent practice of commoners being cremated with lords. Covarrubias records the cremation of 250 commoners being tagged on to, as it were, the cremation of a minor lord. Geertz in 1957 saw a cremation in which no fewer than 460 other bodies were burned at the same time as that of a high priest.

As the Dutch progressively gained control of Bali in the last decades of the last century and the first years of this one, they put an end to the burning of widows and concubines, as the British did in India. Some 'secret' immolations are reported to have occured after that but it is probable the custom had completely died out by the 1920s. If it continued later, it was more in the form of wives committing suicide so they could be cremated with their husbands.

Religion

ou stand, a long time ago, on a green ridge between two deep gorges with crashing cataracts. A smouldering volcano fills the sky to your right. Thunder rolls continuously and lightning flashes among black clouds ahead of you. Patches of sunlight illuminate more mountains to your left. You turn around and see the shining line of the dangerous sea. Vegetation flourishes all around you, concealing who knows what wild animals. At night, often, the stars gleam as if close enough to touch from the top of that frightening volcano. Inexplicable ills befall, inexplicable benefits arise. You understand none of it. So you grab eagerly at any ideas which might help you come to grips with Bali's awful mysteries, and you do so again and again.

So what do you have, as a Balinese, many centuries later? Scholars will say you have combined in your religion elements of nature worship from those early days, ancestor worship but with your forebears transformed into faceless and anonymous deities, Mahayana Buddhism, Indian Sivaism, some demonic practices from Tantrism, and a touch here and there of other Hindu elements as adapted by the Majapahit Javanese of Indonesia's middle ages.

The result is unique. Hindu and Buddhist elements in your religion no longer contain the austere message that this is a world only of the senses. You have replaced this kill-joy notion with an image of the universe as a delightful compound of fantasy and realism. Fantasy permits belief in a separate world of gods, realism lets you imagine the gods as people, divine and earthy at the same time. They are invisible and very much whatever you want them to be. You can believe them undepictable or you can carve images of them as you think they should appear, and keep them in house and village shrines. If the point were pressed you would concede these various gods to be aspects of one God but it is more homely to think of Him, or Her, or It, as many.

What you want the gods to be is benevolent. Here you seize upon the idea of the sacrifice or offering, a banquet to which the gods are invited. The offering becomes the central item in a system of ritual obligations which seek both to win favour for yourself and your community and to help the gods in their ceaseless battle against evil.

In this your community is just as important as you are. Its interests are yours. You belong where you were born (or, in the case of a woman, where your husband was born). Your belief commits you to a kind of ancestor worship. If you have no Balinese ancestors you are not, cannot become, a Balinese. You may live with, and even as, the Balinese, but you will never be one.

Just as you cannot have just one side of a coin, or the warp of a cloth without the weft, you cannot have good without evil. To remove one would be to destroy the other. If you have gods you must have demons engaging the gods in constant battle. The correct execution of rituals will not so much help the gods to victory, since a final result is impossible, as help the two sides maintain a balance. Therefore, according to Urs Ramseyer in his Art and Culture of Bali, pious Balinese go through a life full of rites whose purpose is to cleanse what is unclean, reconcile what seems irreconcilable, compensate, worship and appease, avert danger, obtain nourishment and secure a happy life and a good rebirth beyond this one.

Among these rites the offering is paramount because of the obligation it imposes on the god or demon receiving it. Fire (in the form of burning incense), rice, flowers and water (which is sprinkled on the flowers) are basic to all offerings but more are added as the occasion indicates. These additional items can include pork, chicken, fish, onions, ginger, alcohol, betel chew ingredients, rice, fruit, cakes and so on.

Eventually the idea of sacrifice culminates in towering and colourful structures which women carry on their heads to their temples. (Special plates are used, with a spike rising from the centre. A banana stem may be speared on to the spike in an upright position, and the components of the offering fastened to the stem with slender palm or bamboo skewers.) Once the gods have accepted the essence of these offerings, the material remains can be taken home. This means that offerings can be offered only once and that there is no place for plastic replicas. It also means that the Balinese can make their offerings and eat them too. For these reasons alone the religion of Bali seems safe from the tawdrier aspects of some other religious practices.

Thus you — you are now a visitor to Bali — begin to understand a little of what is going on around you, as when a little girl in school uniform, with a yellow sash added, comes with a tray into the garden of your lodging house. She places a small square basket with the basic components of an offering — flowers, rice, betel chew ingredients, oil and holy water — on a ledge. She may light a small stick of incense, or pour a few drops of holy water over the offering, or flick water from a flower held between her third and index fingers, and make an elegant fingers-bent-back gesture to waft the essence towards its divine recipient. Or she may place a small square of banana leaf with a few grains of cooked rice on it on the stoop. She smiles at you, goes on to repeat the performance elsewhere. A dog comes and eats the rice but its essence has already been accepted. Much of the litter in some streets originated as offerings.

You also begin to understand a little about what is going on when your bemo or taxi stops at a roadside shrine for driver or attendant to rush out, lay an offering, clasp his hands briefly in prayer, and dash back. He has created an obligation on a god to get your vehicle safely through the next stage.

For the real thing, for the real outpouring, however, you must go to a temple festival. Bali is said to have more than 20,000 village temples and each one has at least one three-day festival every Balinese year of 210 days. It is not hard to find a festival, but I still managed to get to my first by accident, by going with the crowd.

I was going from Ubud to Denpasar and could not understand why the bemos were so crowded; or, in those early days, why so many women were in temple dress and carrying small bowls of offerings. I asked two where they were going and they replied, 'To the beach'. Eventually I found a place in a bemo and learned that the crowds were on their way to the beach at Lebih, near Gianyar. I went along — partly because the bemo was soon so packed that I could not have got out with disturbing many people between me and the door.

Eventually we all fell out, into a stream of people walking down a long avenue of coconut palms running towards the sea, both sides lined with hawkers. Women who had been nursing offering bowls carefully in the bemos placed them on their heads. All offerings were modest in size; the towering structures appear only when the temple is within walking distance.

On the beach was a rough, palm-leaf replica of a temple layout, with enclosure, stand for two crowned priests, drum tower, shelter for offerings, a shelter in which masked dancers were entertaining an enthralled crowd, and another shelter in which a puppeteer and his musicians awaited their turn to perform. People peered over the palm-leaf fence into the masked dancers' 'dressing room'. The two priests, one with a black crown, one with red, rang their bells and intoned.

They were not the only priests. All around this temporary temple a mass of people, well dressed, more women than men, were bringing offerings to priests who had taken up positions along the beach, amid the fishing boats. It was a breezy, brilliant occasion with sea, sand, sky, priests in white, women in their colourful best, men in batik shirts and head-cloths, boats brightly painted, trees and mountains behind.

Offerings arrived brightly wrapped, sitting atop heads, often with a brightly embroidered or beaded pad between. When the offering was placed before a priest, a solemn chanting, praying and sprinkling of holy water ensued. Women prayed, hands to foreheads while their fingertips held small flowers. Priests and their priestess wives (mostly also in white, most comely) sprinkled water on the offerings with graceful flicks from flowers held between their third and fourth fingers. They also distributed wet, uncooked rice in handfuls for people to press to their own and their children's brows, temples and throats. Some of the grains remained stuck on for a long time, often appearing to form a pattern. Holy water poured into palms from long-handled coconut, brass and silver dippers was sipped and spread over face, head and breast.

Then people picked up their offerings, strolled back along that crowded avenue, pausing perhaps for snacks, to where the waiting bemos were being packed solid for the trip home. An obligation had been fulfilled and a good time had been had. Here is Ramseyer again: 'The Balinese religion [is] fundamentally a system of rules of behaviour which the believer must follow if he wishes to establish the right relationship between the opposing powers inside and outside his body.' And here is Geertz: 'Religious rules are fairly clear, and if one is properly cautious one need not worry — and instead one can have a good deal of pleasure at the gods' festivals.'

It is as if behaviour is more important than belief. Right action more than right thinking is what produces right results. It is not a matter of fervour or sentiment; it is a matter of the correct execution of duties for the enjoyment of an invisible audience of gods and demons. In Bali, says Hanna in his Bali Profile, there is no creed, no dogma, no scripture, no conviction about salvation or damnation by reason of adherence to any metaphysical doctrine. Unless he is a high priest, a Balinese does not need to study sacred writings, perform prescribed prayers or reflect profoundly on virtue and vice. It is enough to make daily offerings and always to participate actively in village and temple affairs.

Though this religion is commonly referred to as Hinduism, and though it may be called a much modified form of an archaic style of Hinduism, it is not a Hinduism which any Hindu would recognise as approaching his system of beliefs. The Balinese religion has been described by Geertz as public, social and civic, with an emphasis on ceremonies and ritual rather than on theology, communion or religious ecstacy. As I mentioned when writing about cremations, I follow Hanna's suggestion that the Balinese religion can best be called 'Balinism'.

That not even priests — let alone laymen — know the meaning of the chants which are so important during rituals is further evidence of the special quality of this religion. 'All too frequently the words of the pemangku [priest] make no sense, either to himself or his fellow villagers, presuming that they try to comprehend,' an outstanding Dutch scholar, C. Hooykaas, noted in his A Balinese Temple Festival. Comparisons between old texts and modern renderings have found numerous variations and corruptions but these seem not to matter. A priest once told an American scholar, Jane Belo, when she asked the meaning of certain words: 'I do not know and I would not dare to understand.'

Nonetheless, says Hooykaas, drawing on 40 years' experience of old Balinese literary material, Sanskrit stanzas from India handed down through the centuries have survived, if not accurately, at least in recognisable form. A reason for this seems to be that priests, lacking understanding of their chants, have concentrated on what they consider to be correct pronunciation. They came to believe that

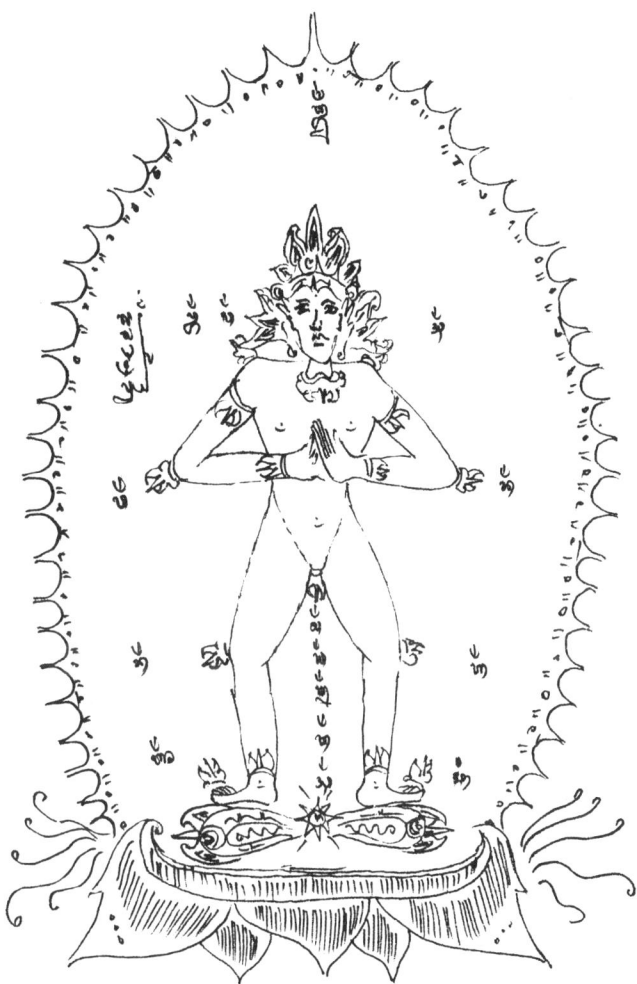

The gods are invisible but if you wish you can depict them. Here is Tintiya, the Almighty, also known as Sanghyang Tunggal, in one of his frequent representations. This version is from a drawing on cloth, done by a Denpasar priest to hang in the doorway of a new house.

if words were not pronounced correctly they would not 'work'. There is even a tagline to chants in which the priest asks forgiveness for any defects in pronunciation.

Priests thus are not so much religious leaders or teachers as technical specialists. There is no pulpit, no preacher, no teaching.

No one has been elevated above other people as a guru whose views must be honoured. No one stands between a worshipper and his god, telling him what to say. The priest's job as a technical specialist is to help produce desired results. What these results might be is indicated in a typical sequence in a temple ceremony: A prayer to attract the gods' attention and to invite them to descend, perhaps with smoke from incense to show them the way; a prayer describing the descent; a prayer inviting the gods' companions to descend; a prayer of homage; a prayer inviting the godly party to partake of the offerings; a prayer to thank them for attending and to wish them a safe journey home. All praying is accompanied by ringing of the priest's handbell, for emphasis and punctuation.

If there is an intermediary between the Balinese worshipper and his god, it is not a priest but a medium. Some temple occasions are designed to induce trances. Throbbing, persistent music, chanting and heavy incense are used. If all goes well members of the congregation will become detached from this world, at it were, rocking back and forth, speaking loudly and perhaps moving to more vigorous activity until they have to be restrained. A particular priestly function is knowing how to deal with trances and help people out of them. Trance mediums are often in fact priests but this is more a matter of disposition shaping a career than an essential requirement. After a trance session the medium feels exorcised of his problems and other worshippers present share the same release to some degree. Attendance at trance dances — see the chapter on Dancing — can bring similar relief.

The gentry have their own priests, from the Brahmana caste, who see their role as similar to that of the Brahmans in India. They are known not as pemangku, commoner priests attached to temples, but as pedanda or padanda, they tend to be more scholarly, and they are involved not so much with temples as with families, both gentry and commoner, though they are called on to officiate at temple ceremonies. More important, they prepare the holy water which is essential for virtually any religious occasion, a commodity so important that the Balinese religion at times is called Agama Tirta, the Religion of Holy Water. The pedandas' 'clients' consult them when the technical help of temple priests is not sufficient. At their highest levels these priests may be seen as guardians of sacred knowledge and mythic history — knowledge often passed down from father to son.

Is Balinism under threat? The most important process under

way involves a hitherto unknown degree of precision as a result of formal religious education in schools. There are now five principles of the Balinese religion which seem not to have been so well defined in the past. They are belief in the Almighty; belief in the Atman, or soul; belief in reincarnation; belief in cause and effect; and belief in Moksha, release from the cycle of existences.

The first point to be made about these five is that they seem to permit no distinction between Hinduism and Balinism. It seems that Balinese scholars assigned the task of defining their religion for textbook purposes have looked to India for source material. The result is now being officially propagated through the government's Religious Affairs Department and through missionary organisations.

Yet nothing ever happens on its own. There are indications also that just as this official system is gaining currency, so there is also a trend back to Balinism as it was before Indonesian independence brought official concerns for precision and definition. Some observers claim to have seen in these two movements a conflict between those who would restore caste to its former status and those who would resist this. Caste has no stance in the formal Indonesian position on such matters, which permits no distinction between people on grounds of birth. There is no way of knowing how this process will develop, but simply by promoting interest in religion it could be creative.

Nor, despite the spread of general education and with it perhaps a good deal of scepticism, do the temple festivals, the primary manifestation of Balinism, appear to be suffering. They have maintained their position and could in fact have gained from Bali's greater prosperity. Just as official support for music and dancing is helping to counteract westernisation, so does a growing awareness that Bali needs to protect its culture for economic reasons if for no others. Besides, the Balinese enjoy their religious occasions and will continue to do so.

A final point favouring the survival of the Balinese religion in a distinctive form — perhaps much changed, but still unique — lies with Bali's position within Indonesia. The flood of tourists may causes stresses but it also helps the Balinese realise that their way of life is different from that of other Indonesians. They are a distinct community, and the more they learn about Indonesia as a whole they more they realise this. Increasingly they know that if they cease to be special they will vanish in the tide. They are not going to let this happen.

Temples

n the early stages of work on this book I wrote to James Michener, the American author, to ask about the origin of the world 'Bali-ha'i' in his book Tales of the South Pacific, used later in the film and musical versions. 'Bali-ha'i was an island of the sea,' he had written, 'a jewel of the vast ocean. It was small. Like a jewel, it could be perceived at one loving glance. It was neat. It had majestic cliffs facing the open sea. It had a jagged hill to give it character. It was green like something ever youthful, and it seemed to curve itself like a woman into the rough shadows formed by the volcanoes of the greater island of Vanicoro.'

Vanicoro was in Melanesia in the southwest Pacific, thousands of kilometres away from Bali, but decades later some tourists still confess that they have long taken the song 'Bali-ha'i' to refer to the even more spectacular Indonesian isle. There is no doubt that part of Bali's fame today arises from this mistake.

Michener replied that his Bali-ha'i was a fictitious name for an imaginary island and had no connection with the real Bali. There is a kind of cultural connection, however, between Bali and the south Pacific that Michener found so engaging, and you can find it in the most difficult places of all in Bali to understand. These are the temples. The word is inadequate unless you resort to fanciful notions indeed.

Imagine that you wished to pray to your god or gods, and instead of going into a building went into an open field. Imagine that part of that field came to suit you very well, so you put a fence around it. You would have the essence of something very like a Balinese temple. Try a different line. Imagine that instead of going into a building you found a tree which you decided could well be inhabited by your god or gods. Or a rock. You found that this tree or rock suited you very well, so you put a fence around it. You would in fact have something very like an early Polynesian temple — or an early Balinese one.

There is a deal of evidence that the ancestors of people now living in Polynesia at some stage migrated east from Asia. Anthropologists will go on arguing the toss about precise connections for ever but it seems certain that the idea of the Balinese temple goes back to that age. A later development was the concept that the gods living in their tiered heaven above Gunung Agung could be invited down to earthly temples, and from that came the perception that a roof would get in the way. Once that had been settled the Balinese were on their way towards temples as they exist so numerously today.

How numerously? The figure of 20,000 is often used, along with 300,000 household temples (in an island with a statistical 480,000 households) and countless minor altars, but probably no one really knows. Certainly there is no organisation, no temple bureaucracy to keep track of such rather pointless detail.

I have mentioned when writing about the pemaksan the three temples in each village: the temple of origin, the temple of assembly, the temple of death. Then there are family and clan temples, agricultural temples, district and state temples and six 'divine homes' of island-wide significance. There is no complete agreement on what these six are and sometimes the list contains more than six names, but temples at Besakih, Uluwatu and Tanah Lot (about which more later) are always among them.

All temples have in common the fact that they are open to the sky, that their walls and gates are more impressive than anything found within, and that there is an identity of overall style. It has been claimed that no two temples in Bali are identical. This is a statement impossible to verify but it seems important that it be true, as an indicator of the absence of central direction and the power of local initiative.

The need for gateways to be impressive is said to derive from the pleasing notion that you approach a temple as through a jungle, as if it is a sanctuary in the wilderness. Vegetation carved sometimes profusely on the main gateway and the wall around it is to strengthen this idea. Then you enter through the 'split gateway', the outstanding Balinese architectural feature. Throughout Indonesia even the most stylised rendering of this gateway is instantly recognised as indicating Bali, and it is often the first feature to attract the tourist's eye.

The split gateway does not always indicate a temple, however. Palaces and even modern hotels also use it, palaces with some justification. A temple is a 'pura', a palace is a 'puri', and both words derive from a Sanskrit word meaning 'fortified town' which is much used to end placenames such as Jodhpur, Udaipur, Jaipur, Nagpur and dozens of others in India, and Singapore. Today's distinction between palaces and temples seems not always to have obtained. But should hotels and other commercial buildings use the split gateway? They do so so numerously, and often impressively, that perhaps we should accept this as just another Balinese adaptation.

The gateway looks like a tower or monument which has been split precisely down the middle and the two halves then pushed apart to create an entrance between them. Theories about the origin of this remarkable structure abound. It represents the two halves of a cosmic mountain split and placed in Bali as Gunung Agung and Gunung Batur. It represents the two halves, male and female, which make a whole. It represents, if you count the vacant space as well, the Hindu Trinity of Brahma, Vishnu and Siva.

Buckminster Fuller, the geodesic dome man, wrote that Balinese people had told him the vertical gap in the gateway represented the gap between once-united Bali and Java. This proved, he said, that Balinese 'legend-supported' memory goes back 30,000 years. Though in English the structure is usually called a 'split gateway', the Balinese words 'candi bentar' actually mean something like 'high monument'.

Within the split gateway of every temple is a courtyard leading directly to a doorway enclosed in another monumental structure, just as lavishly decorated as the gateway but with a roof. The first courtyard is a kind of antechamber where preparations are made for entrance to the more important courtyard within the doorway. The inner courtyard is for altars, shrines for the gods during their visits, and for offerings.

Inside this area the most impressive structures, second only to split gateways as symbols of Bali, are high, slender, pagoda-like structures of wood and thick, black thatching, named merus. They were mentioned in the chapter on cremations, when the number of their tiers indicate the rank of the dead person. The name is important, coming directly from classical Hindu mythology: Meru is the cosmic mountain at the centre of the world.

In a way the split gateway and the covered doorway also represent Meru, but the pagoda-like version carries the imagery forward more spectacularly. The number of tiers, or roofs, never more than eleven, reflects the status of the god to whom the meru is dedicated. Eleven is for Siva, nine is for Brahma or Vishnu, and so on down, always in odd numbers. They may also reflect the status of the owners of the temple, or the status of people permitted to

A festival in progress in a small village temple near Legian.

worship there, and it may in fact be impossible to sort out which is which. The centre of a meru is an open shaft down which gods are sometimes said to descend to a temple.

Scholars have created an industry out of trying to interpret the significance of various structures within Balinese temples, so perhaps it is not surprising that at various times the meru has been associated with the Egyptian pyramids, the Babylonian ziggurat, the Tower of Babel and, less speculatively, with Borobodur, the huge Buddhist monument in central Java.

Another distinctive structure is the padmasana, literally 'lotus seat', the throne of the supreme god, Siva, or Surya, the sun god. It is found in temples throughout Bali and also in the gardens of countless private homes. Usually the padmasana is a small stone column topped with an empty stone throne set so that it faces away from Gunung Agung, or sometimes away from the east. The base of the pillar is usually a representation of a turtle, the mythological base on which the world rests. On top of this base are often two carved serpents, indicating animality. Then comes a representation perhaps of mountains, to indicate the physical world of man, with the godly seat placed well above this. Even in small and simple padmasanas the throne is about two metres above the ground, to keep it above the heads of worshippers, and in big and elaborate versions it can be much higher, with steps to enable people to place offerings. The structure signifies the entire cosmos, from demonic depths to the heavens. Its similarity to the structure in which a body is carried to cremation is obvious.

These, then, are among the features that enable a Balinese temple to serve also as a stage on which the worshippers become actors, the priests become directors and the gods and demons become an invisible but critical audience. This metaphor is from Ramseyer, who also explains that temple ceremonies are only part of the process of worship. Preparations, including repairs, can take weeks and can so pervade village life that the actual performance is just an extension of all that work. Ramseyer says it is not uncommon to get the impression that the Balinese are either preparing for a ceremony, taking part in one or clearing up after one.

The temple serves as a stage, and one of the attributes honoured on this stage is purity. The old Balinese (who were not alone in this) believed that a menstruating woman was unclean. A woman who concealed menstruation and made offerings in a temple could be fined. A woman who for some reason unconnected with pregnancy or age did not menstruate was forbidden ever to enter a temple. This is all written in the lontar books, and this is why so many temples have notices in English advertising this prohibition. A typical sign says, 'For the sake of the holiness and our safety, we kindly regret women being menstruation not to enter the temple'.

These notices cause much indignation among tourists and are presumably much ignored.

Besakih and other ancient places

Of all the temples, by far the most famous, the most potent, is Besakih 1,000 metres up on the slopes of Gunung Agung, 22 kilometres from Klungkung. Ancient and austere, it is the only temple which serves the whole of Bali. Offerings are made here on behalf of the entire population. It is the essence of all temples, the mother temple, the holiest of them all.

That it is not just one temple but an entire complex of them, with nearly 200 separate structures, makes no difference, since Besakih as a whole has been hallowed for centuries. There is evidence that almost 1,000 years ago a Buddhist sanctuary stood on the same ground and some students claim that it dates back to still earlier times. This antiquity sets Besakih apart from the numerous temples of the plains below, and so does its simple and evocative appearance and setting, often with mountain mists turning the merus and gateways into stark silhouettes.

The complex contains 40 temples, including one for each of the former Balinese kingdoms, many clan and family temples, more honouring deified ancestors. The main one is called Pura Panataran Agung, a series of terraced courtyards containing more than 50 shrines and merus. The visitor will see six courtyards but may be told there are seven, in accordance with a Hindu doctrine of the seven levels of the world; opinions differ about where the seventh terrace is to be found.

A colourful book titled Bali — Once In A Lifetime Ceremony, published by the Parisada Hindu Dharma in Denpasar in 1981, contains a step-by-step account of the contents of the terraces. The approach to the first terrace is by steps flanked by stone statues of Mahabharata and Ramayana heroes carved as recently as 1935; the major shrines and their contents are listed; and two shrines on the topmost terrace is said to symbolise 'the doctrine of dualism that characterises all creation'. The terraces and the gods honoured there, the book says, have been likened to a history of the creation of the world.

In 1963 the celebration of the most important Balinese religious occasion, Eka Dasa Rudra, was ordered for Besakih, it seems for political as much as for religious reasons. In the event, Gunung

Besakih simplified — in fact it has more than 200 structures.

Agung chose that same year for a spectacular eruption which is discussed later in this book (in The Wrath of the Gods section of the History chapter). Scholars argued that 1963 was the wrong year for the festival and that the correct year was 1979. And that was when the 'once in a century' purification festival was actually held, to bring harmony and good fortune and to strengthen the spiritual life of all who took part. The book mentioned above gives a mass of technical detail and colourful illustration, but neglects to explain that 'once in a lifetime' and 'once in a century', phrases used to explain how often the ceremony is held, mean more or less the same thing: A century of Balinese 210-day years comes to less than 60 years.

Some visitors find visiting temples in Bali quickly ceases to be enthralling, as does visiting churches in a European city. In general they do repay a little effort if you happen to be near, however, and at least two, in addition to Besakih, are worth a special journey.

One is at Uluwatu, splendidly set on a clifftop high above the sea on the western edge of the Bukit peninsula south of the airport. A recently improved road leads to it and to a stretch of surfing water nearby. The second of these two extraordinary temples is Tanah Lot, 31 kilometres west of Denpasar, not so much high above the sea as almost in it, since you can cross to its tiny island only at low tide. It is one of the most photographed temples in Bali because it stands silhouetted against the setting sun. Both Uluwatu and Tanah Lot are believed to have been founded by a wandering Hindu saint, Sang Hyang Niratha, who had an eye to this-worldly sites as well as a mind for other-worldly matters. He is said to have chosen to die, to achieve oneness with the divine, at Uluwatu.

The traditional heartland of the Balinese religion lies not on the seashore or on the mountainside, however, but in a tract of country in Gianyar regency. This tract, little more than ten kilometres long, contains a series of sacred or once-sacred places of antiquity.

A convenient place to start seeing them during an outing from Ubud, say, is Yeh Pulu (Yeh means water or spring). You come on it almost by surprise, though you are looking for it, after walking through a village and along paths through the ricefields. A stone cliff two metres high and 25 metres long has been carved into a homely frieze of everyday life, either in a primitive style or never finished. For centuries it lay buried, perhaps after a volcanic eruption, and thus preserved; since it was excavated in 1925 it has been exposed to the air and may eventually crumble away. The frieze was possibly once part of a hermitage.

An easy walk away is another ancient creation also recently excavated, named Gua Gajah. This is a difficult name to translate fairly. Literally the words mean 'elephant cave' but the 'elephant' here is Ganesh, the elephant-headed Hindu god who is never known by any name which means elephant. His head is incidental to his nature, merely the result of a childhood accident when his original head was lost and he was given another in its place.

The cave is in a valley where, a guidebook surmises, 'followers of Hinduism and Buddhism once lived peacefully side by side'. They cut a tunnel into the rock and then a crossway at the end of it, so the result is shaped like a capital T. Today a small image of Ganesh stands at one end of the crossway illuminated only by a tiny oil lamp.

In his four hands he holds an axe, a small drinking vessel with his trunk dipping into it, a ring of beads and a broken tusk. The axe and tusk represent Ganesh as a god of war while the beads and small vessel represent him as a god of wisdom. These attributes tell a devotee that all obstacles and dangers can be overcome, that we learn from experience, and that we can become wise.

At the other end of the T crossway is a 'triple linga', sexual symbols whose coming together creates life. There is said to be a parallel between this effigy and a three-throne padmasana at Besakih. There are niches inside large enough for a monk to sit crosslegged in, meditating.

The entrance to the cave is elaborately carved with a massive deity, all bulging eyes and arched eyebrows and huge teeth, with his enormous hands appearing to hold the cave entrance open. He represents Bhoma, son of Vishnu and Pertiwi, goddess of the soil, Mother Earth. As he is carved at Gua Gajah, his eyes look to the observer's left, and on the left stands a small building sheltering three old statues. One of them, believed to be nearly 1,000 years old, is of a plump woman surrounded by children, named Hariti.

In Buddhist mythology, Hariti was a demon who loved to eat children until she was converted to Buddhism, when she became their protectress. Her fangs indicate her origin as a demon. In Hindu mythology, Hariti is a goddess of fertility who together with her husband, the god of wealth, signifies prosperity. In Bali, Hariti became known as Men (Mother) Brayut. A woman with many children is likely to be known as Men Brayut.

With political changes in mediaeval times, Gua Gajah ceased to be a hermitage. An earthquake destroyed part of it and filled an elaborate bathing place. A temple was built on the site. Only this century did archeologists rediscover the cave and it is now much more frequented than ever before, but by tourists. 'The feet that come now . . . come with a different step,' says one of Bali's homegrown publicists, Silvio Santosa, who also has a smooth translation for Gua Gajah: 'The Elephant Cave without an elephant.' There is a speculation that it is named after a hermitage in central India.

From Gua Gajah the road from Denpasar, 25 km behind, climbs gently. It passes a museum with huge stone coffins and other relics of pre-cremation days. It passes the temple, famous for the skill of its priests in finding auspicious dates, where is kept the huge Pejeng gong which bears the powerful, mask-like face on the cover

The 'split gateway', Bali's outstanding architectural feature. — From a drawing by W.O.J. Nieuwenkamp published in 1910.

of this book. It passes Gunung Kawi, where you descend many, many steps into another old hermitage with meditation cells carved from the rock. Amid the cells you must walk barefoot and are exhorted not to talk loudly. You do not want to. The valley around the hermitage is lush and loud with the sound of running water.

And so to Tampaksiring, another focal point of the Balinese religion, another tourist haunt. It has a 1,000-year-old temple, Tirta Empul, which stands around the most famous freshwater spring in Bali, with water bubbling up through sand as if boiling. Hundreds of people use the bathing place a few metres downstream, men and women in separate compartments. There is a banyan tree spectacular even by Bali's standards, with its knobbly roots encasing a cube of old bricks.

Bali's southern slopes are today well-watered, yet the religion and the culture make much of water. The religion is sometimes called Agama Tirta, the religion of holy water. Many springs are sacred. The word 'yeh' for water occurs frequently in place names.

It is as if the slopes were once much drier, water once much less taken for granted, today's lushness therefore the result of irrigation, of human endeavour. This possibility makes Bali still more remarkable.

A legend about the origin of the spring at Tampaksiring says that once upon a time a demon set himself up as god and refused to let people perform their customary rites. As a result the air over Bali became so dirty that the true gods could not see through it. Eventually Indra and other deities were ordered down to clean up the mess.

The demon fled — with his flight later becoming various additional tales — and eventually reached Tampaksiring, where he poisoned a river so that his pursuers, drinking from it, died. This made Indra so angry that he shot an arrow into the ground to create a fount of perfectly fresh, clean water, which he used to bring his companions back to life. The spring is Tirta Empul. Then Indra went on to deal fittingly with the demon.

The Dutch built a resthouse on a hill overlooking the spring, much to Balinese indignation. President Sukarno of Indonesia turned it into a palace where, the story goes, he could look down on women bathing at the spring — and then send for any beauty he fancied. One had a daughter as a result, and today this daughter runs a small handcraft shop in the slummy tourist area below the springs. She has two children of her own, her mother was still living when I was there, and Sukarno's sons accept her as related, visiting her whenever they are in Bali. The palace is now an official guesthouse for state visitors.

Other religions

Not all Balinese are Balinists. There is a small community of people, fully accepted as members of the Balinese community, who style themselves Buddhists and live near Amlapura, in a village aptly named Budakling. An informant told me this name derived in part from 'Kalinga', the Buddhist realm in India once ruled by the Emperor Asoka. Another said the second part of the name derived from an Indonesian word, 'keliling', indicating 'around': Budakling — where the Buddhists live.

I walked there from Tirtagangga ('Water of the Ganges') and found the house of the priest. He is a gentle old man, Gde Wayan Dilantik Dharma, with white hair, white whiskers, a mouth ruined by betel. He told me eight of Bali's 14 Buddhist priests lived in Budakling and that the total Buddhist population of the island was around 1,000. But they are not strictly Buddhist. Their faith includes elements of Balinism: 'Siwa and Buddha mixed together.' The teaching has been 'unified' with Balinism. For example, though Buddhism strictly denies caste, all the Buddhist priests are Brahmanas. There are no commoner priests at all.

The Indian god Siva, in Bali Siwa, is represented as holding a lotus flower. The language of prayers is Sanskrit, not Pali as in Buddhism elsewhere. 'Buddha Dharma is the same as Hindu Dharma,' the old man said. 'It includes both Siwa and Buddha.' On government forms the villagers enter their religion as 'Hindu-Buddha'. I asked if anyone coming to the village, not knowing it was Buddhist, and watching the ceremonies would notice any difference from those in Balinist temples. The answer was, No, the differences are so slight as to be hard to detect.

There is a story that Budakling not long ago was a last refuge for Bali's Buddhists. Their community over the centuries had moved eastward from near present-day Denpasar to Padangbai, and then still further east and up the mountainside to its present retreat. This movement suggests a degree of persecution, but if it were so it certainly is not so now.

The reason six of Bali's 14 Buddhist priests are not in Budakling is that they are out tending to the spiritual needs of members of their flock, emigrants from Budakling, in Gianyar, Sukawati, Batuan and Celuk, all places handy to Denpasar. And many ceremonies are judged to be improved if a Buddhist priest sits next to the Balinist one. If there were a tide flowing against the community, that tide has turned.

More conventional Buddhism in a Balinese setting is to be found on a hillside west of Singaraja, at the Brahma Vihara Arama. Here Balinist artisans from Ubud, working from photographs, have decorated a colourful building with stone panels depicting Buddhist themes. There are also Buddha statues, a temple bell from Thailand and a bo tree, of the family of the tree the first Buddha was sitting under when he became enlightened.

The vihara was opened about 1970 by a local Brahmana man who studied Buddhism in Java before returning as Bhikku Giri Rakkito Thera. His teaching is along Therevada lines though his teacher was a Mahayanist, and the vihara is popular also with many of Bali's Chinese families. When I visited, on the pillion seat of a taxi motorcycle from the highway below, I was told that about once a year people from Budakling would arrive by bus and ask 'very simple questions'. Other visitors included Balinist priests, better educated, who would engage the bhikku in more learned discussion, and some of the villagers living nearby had actually become Buddhists. In 1982 the Dalai Lama paid a visit.

A shopkeeper in Negara, a town in west Bali, took pity on me when I asked what the district had to offer the visitor. 'Just a few kilometres from here,' he said, 'we have the biggest Catholic church in eastern Indonesia.' And not just a church — an entire community up in the hills. And a few kilometres further west, a community of Protestants, with another big church.

The history of these communities says much about Bali before World War II. Enlightened Dutch officials for decades were engaged in a running war both with Christian missionary organisations and with politicians back in Holland to keep missionaries out of Bali. They could see no good coming from the disruption of the tightly woven Balinese way of life that could result and could point to active Balinese opposition to the idea. But from time to time they lost their battles, missionaries were admitted, and the number of converts grew. Colin McPhee, writing in the 1930s, mentions both the expulsion of a Canadian churchman and a report in a Canadian newspaper about 'Balinese laying down their idols'.

Converts to other religions were exiled from their villages and generally had no choice except to go to the then rapidly growing town of Denpasar to find jobs. Soon the number of these outcasts became a problem, and the two settlements near Negara resulted from a Dutch attempt to find a solution. Catholics were given land at a place now called Palasari and Protestants went to Blimbingsari.

As they went to their new homes their faith was surely tested because though the distance was not great the change involved was momentous. From predictable village life these exiles headed for unknown jungle places where everything they had ever heard told them they would be in perpetual danger. Any one of them could have changed his or her mind, and agreed to undergo the purification rituals which would have reunited them with their families. Instead they went voluntarily to years of hardship as they tried to make their land productive.

Today their settlements are beautiful — as beautiful as Balinese villages. The Catholics number about 1,500, in 180 families. Their church, which had recently celebrated its 25th year when I visited, has room for 700 worshippers and is ornately Balinese in its decoration. Schools and a clinic stand nearby, and beyond are clove and coconut groves and rice and maize fields.

At Blimbingsari (named after the starfruit), a community of about 1,700 Protestants in about 300 families pays tribute to the 30 men who arrived as pioneers in 1939 to begin making homes in the jungle. Their settlement has succeeded so well that it has even generated emigrants of its own, to another Balinese community in Sulawesi (the Celebes) founded by Balinese exiled for breaking caste rules.

The Blimbingsari community recently built a big, open-style church as splendid in its modern way as the Catholic one is in the traditional. Its three-tiered roof represents the Trinity, water flows behind the altar, there is a Balinese drum tower to summon worshippers, and the gateway is like that of a Balinese temple — but with a broad, welcoming entrance instead of a narrow one.

Both churches have Balinese pastors and the schools associated with both teach Balinese music and dancing, but with Biblical rather than Ramayana themes. This raises interesting questions about the links between religion and culture. In Blimbingsari I was told, 'We're all Balinese. If the culture can be separated from the religion it can be very strong, no matter what happens to the religion.'

Finally, Bali has considerable Muslim and Christian communities throughout the island, some traditional Chinese temples have maintained their congregations, and there is a Gandhian ashram, superbly set beside a perfect beach, which becomes Bali very well. Because the ashram is Gandhian it does not talk much about itself or engage in teaching or missionary activity; instead it hopes for 'recognition by action'. It is run by fascinating people and garners fascinating residents. The regime is fairly strict, starting at 4 am each day, including four hours of assigned work each day, and prohibiting smoking and drinking. Where is it? Anyone interested in such a place will surely know how to go about finding it; and anyone not interested does not need to know.

Music

he way of life described so far in this book is a vehicle for astonishing creativity. In dancing, in painting, in carving, the Balinese display far more talent than one would reasonably expect of any community. Chapters will deal with each of these in turn but first comes music, from which flows so much else.

The word one encounters time and time again when reading or talking with people about Balinese gamelan music is 'brilliant'. The Encyclopaedia Britannica, for example: 'In contrast to the introspection of Javanese music, the Balinese gamelan exudes a music of brilliant sounds with syncopations (displaced accents) and sudden changes, as well as gradual increase and decrease in volume and speed and feats of fast, precise playing.' No matter that the word 'brilliant' has a special meaning in music — 'a high proportion of high harmonics above the fundamental'. Give the word its normal meaning and it is still clear that here we have something special.

Note that phrase 'fast and precise'. Here is an opinion by an American musicologist, Mantle Hood, writing in a 1967 collection of academic reports on Indonesia, edited by Ruth McVey: 'For most Western ears Balinese gamelan is immediately attractive, for the simple reason that it corresponds more closely to the Western idea of dynamic contrasts, of sudden shifts from fast to slow and loud to soft. . . . Thirty to fifty players perform . . . to a standard of perfection expected in the west only from a string quartet.

'Balinese musicians seem to operate on the principle that if two players play interlocking parts as fast as possible — that is to say, each player plays every other note but at his full capacity for speed — the result will be a performance twice as fast as either of them can play. These shared or interlocking parts require the most precise rhythmic timing.'

Colin McPhee, another American, the outstanding foreign scholar of the Balinese gamelan, said that while the Javanese version was soft, shockless and refined, the Balinese was dramatic, hard, vital, almost feverish — 'as contemporary as jazz'. It so fascinated him that he lived in Bali on and off from 1931 to 1939, and after World War II continued his studies while working as a composer and lecturer in music at the University of California in Los Angeles. In 1947 he published his account of life on the island, A House In Bali.

In the early 1960s two Balinese, Cokorda Mas of Ubud and Wayan Gandera of Peliatan, spent two years at the university with McPhee, teaching students the Balinese gamelan. They also helped McPhee with a book, Music in Bali, which is likely long to remain the definitive work on its subject. McPhee died in 1964, after seeing the final page proofs of his book but before it was published.

Cokorda Mas, 'Cok Mas', still lives in Ubud, where he has turned his family home into the headquarters of the Mudraswara Foundation, dedicated to Balinese music and dancing. He remembers his California stint, and McPhee, with affection. His foundation both teaches and presents regular performances of music and dancing, and Cok Mas is also much involved in plans for a 'Museum of Gamelan'. It will not be just a place for lifeless displays, however; it will be a research, teaching and performing centre as well, and he is confident it is not far distant. Support is coming in from other parts of Indonesia and overseas and the district government has told him land will be no problem: 'If you have the coffee and the milk, we have the cup!' The museum may be near Bedulu, Gianyar, in Bali's cultural heartland.

In the meantime progress in preserving and developing the gamelan is impressive. 'There are more gamelans in Bali now than ever before,' Cok Mas says. 'When I was a boy Ubud had only one. Now it has four. And it's happening everywhere.' Others echo this view, and if views are not enough gamelan music is heard throughout the island. More, the players often are startlingly young, and a visit to the KOKAR conservatory of music and dancing in Denpasar offers a sight which may still astonish (and perhaps alarm) some older players. At KOKAR and other training centres, girls take their places alongside the boys in the gamelan groups, and another barrier has fallen.

But then, the gamelan has been knocking down barriers for decades now, ever since the Dutch conquest of Bali was completed in the first few years of this century. As the old courts gave up their rituals of formality and display, their gamelans were sold to village groups or given as payment for what were once feudal services. It was this that brought the big change from the Javanese tradition, from soft to hard, from aristocratic to popular, from classical to jazz. Since then experimentation and development have never ceased.

When McPhee arrived in Bali — lured there partly by chance hearings of German records made in the 1920s — he found 'a literally unbelievable' musical situation. The phrase is by Mantle Hood, quoted earlier, from his introduction to McPhee's book. 'With a population of approximately one million, . . . there were literally thousands of active music clubs and dramatic societies. . . . A village was poor indeed that did not possess at least one gamelan to play for temple festivals.'

Young composers were creating bold new music, breaking down the rigid classical forms, showing great freedom and ingenuity. At any festival new compositions could be heard. McPhee noted that they seemed to come into being overnight, filled with melodies of originality and grace. Old melodies, sacred and secular, were woven into new music and given fresh life through shortening and new orchestration. And also through night-after-night practice by those clubs that wished to master the increasingly difficult compositions and play them with the technical perfection that audiences expected.

All this, it must be noted, was an entirely Balinese phenomena. There were too few tourists in Bali, virtually no demands for commercial performances, for them to have had any effect at all. Were such changes to happen today, tourism would be blamed but in those days, and I believe still today, change is inherent in the Balinese way of doing things. Shortly we shall look at the welter of events which enveloped the dance scene in the 1930s, and musical transformation was part of the same phenomenon. People who complain about the changes which tourism is bringing to Bali would do well to ensure first that there are not other phenomena involved.

The gamelan, the recurring word in all this, is not an orchestra. An orchestra is a group of musicians. A gamelan is a group of musical instruments. Great diversity is possible within the group — Cok Mas plans to collect 24 for his museum, all different — but the instruments can be divided into six sections. There are melody instruments with metal keys for the basic melody, more instruments with metal keys to ornament the basic melody, and gongs to punctuate the basic melody. There are gongs — 'idiophones' some call them — to accompany and enliven certain combinations of dance steps, there are 'sweetening' instruments to play around the melody, and there are drums to lead the orchestra and communicate with the dancer. The woodwork which supports the metal parts is often splendidly carved and coloured, usually in red and gold.

The instruments with metal keys 'work' not just because of the keys but because each one is suspended over a bamboo resonating tube. Keys and tubes must both be filed and trimmed during tuning until a precise relationship is found. When in use, the player strikes the key with a mallet held in his right hand, then a split second later damps the key with the fingers of his left hand. Foreign students told me that this split-second sequence during high speed play is one of the most difficult aspects of the gamelan to learn. But they do, and occasionally a foreigner progresses far enough to join a local group.

The most important player, the lead drummer, links the instruments together. In Ramseyer's words, not only does he 'tie the dance to accents in the music but also receives signals from dancers about imminent breaks, changes of tempo or dynamic acceleration and passes them on to the orchestra by beating certain patterns'. He achieves an actual drum language by using his palm, his fingers near the palm or his finger tips on different parts of the drumskin.

The drummer usually has a follower who works with him in creating what McPhee called 'an elaborate continuity of hand and finger strokes that controls the tempo of both dancers and musicians'. Once the three basic elements of melody, punctuation and drumming had been co-ordinated with movement and gesture, he wrote, the whole elaborate polyphony could be added without confusing the dancer. 'In the last analysis it is the drumming which is her guide, controlling her speed and preparing her with accented cues for an approaching pause.'

One of the greatest of drummers, by all accounts, is Anak Agung Gde Mandera of Peliatan, whose name crops up again and again in all recent discussions of Balinese music. Here is a comment from Njoman Oka, the doyen of Bali's many tourist guides and an authority on his island's culture, on the Peliatan gamelan which Mandera,

Gamelan musicians at a barong dance ..

though he is 80 years old, still guides: 'His music is out of this world. It goes into your heart. It fills you up. You never get tired.'

The first time Balinese music travelled overseas was in 1931, when a party of musicians and dancers from Peliatan, near Ubud, went to Europe. It was a time of wide-eyed wonder for all concerned. For men and women from a small and isolated Balinese village, a journey around the world by ship and train was akin to fantasy. And for their audiences, a revelation. The party won rapturous applause in Paris and then went to Amsterdam where, a survivor told me, Queen Wilhelmina of Holland (which then ruled Indonesia) gave each member a piece of chocolate. Mandera was a member of that party.

In the 1950s, after the break caused by world depression and world war, Mandera and other Balinese musicians and dancers were travelling again, to the United States, Mexico and Europe, later to Australia. They usually travelled on government sponsorship, as cultural ambassadors for Indonesia. More tours were undoubtedly considered, and surely are often mooted today, but hard economic reasons stand to prevent Balinese music and dancing being much seen abroad. Since the real thing demands a full gamelan, a touring party of at least 40 or 50 people is involved, and the costs are high, too high normally for commercial ventures.

. . *and at a village celebration, with child.*

The contrast with Indian dancing's place in the entertainment and cultural world is marked. Most major cities offer expert Indian performances more or less regularly, but Indian dancers need only small musical groups. More, most cities have Indian communities eager to sponsor artists and to help keep costs down. The Balinese must make do without this support. The best way to see their performances is to go to Bali.

Mandera's tours punctuated his working life as a surveyor and later as village head; but a village head of such status that once President Sukarno came to call, giving Peliatan its most exciting day in years. Mostly, however, Mandera lived for his music. In 1938, the Peliatan gamelan, A.A. Gde Mandera leader, won a contest between five regencies with music which was 'like the rays of the sun gently caressing the skin'. The words are McPhee's, who also described sitting with Mandera to listen to a remodelled gamelan producing 'the most beautiful sound ever heard on the island'.

This effect had been achieved by a slight change in one of the five tones of modern Balinese music. The second tone had been raised and made sharp — and that was enough to produce a scale which McPhee said he had heard earlier in ancient flute melodies in Japan.

Today Mandera lives quietly, managing his musicians and a

small restaurant, receiving visitors on a porch where caged birds are so exuberant that their noise can interrupt a conversation. The whole of his sitting room wall is covered with plaques and certificates, including a big panel 'commemorating the triumphant America Tour, 1952, of the Dancers of Bali and Gamelan [as if Gamelan was another island], A.A. Gde Mandera, Artistic Director'.

None of this is to suggest that Mandera is alone in his expertise. Far from it. As has been stated, Balinese music is the opposite of courtly and classical. It is popular, folksy and pop, outdoor rather than indoor, and the field abounds with musicians and music lovers who know exactly what they like and why they like it. This is only to be expected in an island where music is so important and of such venerable ancestry, where music rises like incense to the heavens as a vehicle which the gods may use for their descent to Earth.

There is a theory that Balinese music originated in the sound of priestly bells, as dancing may have originated in priestly gestures. But that is only one theory. Another is that it owes much to the pounding rhythms of rice being husked. Women standing around the trough, raising their heavy wooden pestles and crashing them down, must observe a certain rhythm if the pestles are not to collide with each other. To this rhythm they are said long ago to have added a routine of rapping the side of the trough, and to have enhanced the effect by raising the trough off the ground, laying it on crossbeams, to improve resonance. Interwoven rhythms beaten on the hanging slit-drums in each banjar could also have contributed. Add to these the need to entertain the gods, and a naturally talented people could not be restrained, especially once the aristocratic houses had lost their cultural domination.

The kebyar is a good example of the development of modern folk music. Early this century some village musicians in north Bali began transforming the traditional gamelan. They dropped some instruments, changed some others and produced a distinctive and exuberant form of music. They called it kebyar and it swept the island, with professional chauffeurs important in the process — they were often also fine musicians who would spend time with local music clubs when away from home. The kebyar gained fame first as purely instrumental music which permitted a gamelan group to display its skill, and then as accompaniment for dancing. Old musicians — Bali is not alone in having conservatives in all cultural fields — complained bitterly about the new music's loudness and lack of discipline, but the rage continued.

McPhee comments that such music's freedom of form, lavish and varied orchestral effects, bold syncopations and intricate passage work was 'a new flowering', a release from the forms of the past. When a famous dancer, Mario, showed how this new music could be matched with a scintillating new dance, about which more in the next chapter, there was no looking back.

By the mid-1930s gamelans throughout the island were being dismantled and their gongs and keys were being recast in new alloys suitable for the new music. McPhee says that only sacred ensembles were spared so they could continue to provide music for rituals. The rest were remade to provide the tempestuous rhapsodies that the Balinese demanded, and that some visitors found totally entrancing. 'The clear, metallic sounds of the music were like the stirring of a thousand bells, delicate, confused, with a sensuous charm, a mystery that was quite overpowering,' McPhee wrote.

A traveller today can be just as entranced. Again and again in Bali, after sunset, one hears gamelan groups practising and performing, hour after hour. By day one hears and sees children at play on the same instruments, which have the practical advantage of being virtually indestructable. So long as they are treated with reasonable respect, no real harm can come to them, and this helps hugely in ensuring that children learn their father's skills. It is as if a western symphony orchestra left its instruments out for all comers to work on. Who knows what talent might develop from such an admittedly expensive experiment with fragile instruments? Western children perhaps would be reluctant to try but no such shyness restrains Balinese children, who are brought up to believe that they can succeed at anything, so long as they try hard enough.

The instruments they play on are not necessarily old. Indonesia's hard times cramped a lot of enterprise for decades but now that economic conditions are better the demand for new gamelans is rising sharply. Banjars are the main buyers, an old sentiment that no community is complete without its own gamelan having come strongly back to life. Far from their overall numbers declining, gamelans are increasing.

One of the makers trying to meet this demand for new instruments is Pan Wicarna — 'Father of Wicarna' — in Banjar Munduk, in Wayan, a small town along a side road in the mountains about 20 kilometres from Singaraja. He has been making gamelans since childhood, and now he is over 70. His raw material comes from old gongs imported from Sulawesi or other islands where they are no longer greatly admired, or from an alloy he prepares himself: Three parts copper and one of tin, possibly some zinc, lead and iron, and perhaps smidgens of gold, silver and arsenic as well, but he does not talk about them. Give him two months' notice and he will make a 'gong besar', or complete gamelan set, for six million rupiahs.

Or rather, the workers in the foundry next to his house where he has lived all his life will do so. There were five of them when I called, in the simplest imaginable worshop. Two of them were blacksmithing in the forge, shaping keys heated in a glowing bed of burning charcoal. The third worker was a woman sitting in a pit who worked a push-pull bellows whenever a key was returned to the charcoal for reheating. And there were two men working tirelessly with files, shaping and tuning the keys, adding their special noises to the clangour of the foundry. And there was another sound as well, gamelan music from a tape recorder, just to remind the workers of what their toil was all about.

Pan Wicarna's gamelan's are workmanlike, adjustable to nearly all demands of Balinese music, religious or secular. But once in a long time comes the construction of something different. Tenganan, the Bali Aga village in east Bali, posed a special problem for Swiss musicologists interested in its extremely ancient gamelan, known as selonding, made up of 40 tuned iron keys suspended by leather straps over eight trough-shaped resonators. It is believed to be copied from a divine original, parts of which survive. It is so sacred that even a fleeting and accidental touch by an outsider weakens its power, leading to an elaborate reconsecration. Plainly there was no question of the Swiss students learning from these instruments.

The answer was a completely new set. Never having been consecrated, it would be free from taboos. A local blacksmith was given the job, and that is how the Basle Museum of Anthropology has a complete replica of a gamelan that many Balinese, no matter what mixed feelings they may have about the Bali Aga, surely feel is the most magical on their magical island.

Dancing

was in Peliatan checking on a story that Charlie Chaplin had once ended a dance performance he had been watching by taking a turn on stage himself, reducing the villagers to hysterics. Covarrubias mentions that Chaplin performed a hilarious parody of a Balinese dance but gives no details. I met people who knew of the occasion, almost 50 years previously, and then at last, in converse with a benign old man, struck gold.

When I mentioned Chaplin, his face crinkled, his eyes almost vanished into the folds of flesh around them, his toothless mouth opened wide, and he fell into helpless, silent laughter. Unable to speak for mirth, he gestured, the widespread, two-handed movement of a drummer. And who better to make that gesture, for he was none other than Anak Agung Gde Mandera, the famous musician I wrote about in the previous chapter? It turned out he had been the lead musician on that delirious occasion, and the memory of Chaplin mimicking Balinese dancing all those years ago was still enough to render him speechless.

But Chaplin in Bali in the 1930s was not just a clown at large. Before he attempted his parody he had watched numerous dance performances in Java and Bali in the course of at least three visits to those islands, and understood much about them. 'The Javanese dance the Idea, the Balinese dance the Action,' he commented, and that is a sound starting point for any attempt to understand this fascinating aspect of Balinese life. In Bali the dance exists for its own sake, for its vigour and vitality alone.

All manner of settings are involved. One might leave one's lodgings at dusk, walk a mile along a poorly-lit village street, dusty or muddy according to the weather, find one's way to a temporary building of bamboo and thatch, pay a derisory sum, sit on a cheap iron chair — and see a show of such brilliance, colour and beauty that when all is over you wander home in a daze. Such a performance anywhere else in the world would be bannered and ballyhooed and would cost no small sum to see. Such a performance would grace the cultural life of any great city. Its leading performers would be famous, their names blazoned outside their theatres. In Bali such shows are part of everyday life and the performers remain anonymous beyond their own communities. Such shows are the Balinese community at work, or at play, or at prayer, depending how one looks at it.

Settings for dance performances include, in addition to temporary bamboo and thatch buildings, temple courtyards, the forecourts of old and rundown palaces, the gardens of the tourist hotels, banjar buildings, and in Denpasar a cosy little outdoor amphitheatre in the Art Centre. That was where I saw my first performance of what has become Bali's best known entertainment for tourists, the kecak. It is a splendid event in itself and useful also as an illustration of how Bali caters for tourists without destroying, or even demeaning, itself.

Everything about the kecak dance bespeaks antiquity. There is a priest performing a brief ritual before the show; there is a tall and many-armed oil lamp with its flames providing the only illumination; there is a total lack of music, the chanting performers providing the only sound. And what sound! 'Cak, Cak, Cak,' goes the chorus, rising and falling as 50 men or more gesticulate in unison, the lamplight throwing weird shadows. It seems utterly primeval.

But in fact the kecak dates back only to 1932. In that year Walter Spies, a German living near Ubud, about whom more later, became consultant to a German company making a film to be titled, in English, 'The Island of Demons'. For the film Spies took a chorus from a sacred trance dance, added as many men as his stage would hold, and worked in a passage from the Ramayana, the Indian epic which crops up in numerous forms in southeast Asian cultures.

The dance was an instant success and is still performed regularly and enthusiastically for tourists. It was designed purely for show and has no religious or ritual significance at all. Yet the kecak is entirely within the Balinese spirit, if not tradition, and it would be a brave or foolish critic who tried to deride it on grounds that it is not several centuries old.

While I was in Bali, as if to confirm the dance's cultural integrity, villagers in Bualu, near the new Nusa Dua hotels, won an award for staging the best kecak in Bali. These villagers had never been noted as dancers before but in their preparations for the contest they had spared no effort, getting a good teacher and rehearsing night after night. Their award-winning performance was superb, full of vigour and drama, and audiences of tourists from the nearby hotels were a certain prospect.

The villagers will make some money and — more important — enjoy themselves. Eventually perhaps their performance will lose its verve and another group will take over as Bali's best, but in the meantime Bualu and Bali are both better for their efforts. Would this be any different if the kecak, a superb and evocative entertainment, were 500 years old, and not just 50?

Any doubts I may have had on this point vanished one evening in a village near Ubud where I saw a kecak staged as part of a five-day temple festival. About 80 people took part and villagers packed in so closely to see them as to stand amid the outermost performers. It was an exuberant occasion with dancers having trouble restraining their mirth. Later, as if to endorse the Balinese-ness of the kecak, I encountered part of it in a tiny village in north Bali, far from the tourist belt. The men of the village were enlivening a drinking session with spirited chanting straight from the kecak, with help from a tape recorder, and they surely had no doubts about its place in their way of life.

If the kecak is Bali's most popular dance with the general run of tourists, the most popular with aficionados, foreign and Balinese alike, is the legong. It was a legong that sent me home in a daze that night from that temporary building of bamboo and thatch. It is the legong that Covarrubias terms the archetype of the delicate and the feminine, the finest of Balinese dances, and about which his book goes on for page after page. It is old but, since really old records make no mention of it, not necessarily ancient. The girl on the cover of this book is a legong dancer.

In its pristine form the legong is danced by two pre-adolescent girls, 'as alike as two breasts', with a third as their attendant. The dance, vigorous and rapid, has only slight dramatic content and its

Ratih Iryani — as a student of economics and, facing page, a talented dancer — says it would be an embarrassment for any girl from Peliatan not to dance.

overriding interest lies in the unison of the two girls' movements, precise even to the flickering movements of their eyes. This precision is not readily attained. Long before these children can impress an audience they must master the basic legong pose, since translated to other dances: The feet at right angles to each other, the knees bent and turned out, the spine curved, the shoulders pushed back, the arms bent slightly and lifted so the elbows are slightly higher than the shoulders, hands at right angles to the forearms. It is a pose which one sees endlessly in Bali, in paintings and in stone and wood carvings as well as on the stage.

In earlier days a legong dancer could well attract a ruler's attention and become a wife or concubine as soon as she reached sexual maturity — which in any case would put an end to her legong career. Jane Belo, who studied aspects of Balinese dancing in the 1930s, wrote that she believed the choice of children as dancers rested on 'the very impersonal quality of their performance'. They could be trained in a fixed traditional pattern and danced with a purity which conformed with the Balinese ideal of what a dance should be.

I talked with a young woman who as a child had mastered the dance and had since progressed as close to fame as Bali permits any of its performers. She is Cokorda Istri Ratih Iryani, a principal dancer in the Peliatan group, one of Bali's best, born in 1963 — and named

Iryani because 1963 was the year when Indonesia took West Irian from the Dutch. She is a beautiful and intelligent woman whom I shall shortly quote at length for the illumination her comments cast on dancing in Bali today.

When I met her she was dancing her way through university, earning enough to finance her studies in economics. The previous evening I had seen her dancing, with two of her sisters also in the cast. Ratih's family has been producing dancers and musicians for generations and was much involved when Balinese dancing first burst into the consciousness of the outside world. Anak Agung Gde Mandera is her grand-uncle. Her mother, Anak Agung Anom Styari, was only 11 years old when she went to the United States and Europe as a dancer with a troupe after World War II. The tour lasted ten months and Anom remembers such details as taking ten encores in New York, meeting Bob Hope, Dorothy Lamour and Bing Crosby, and seeing a film they had made called Road to Bali, which she thought not really about Bali. Other overseas tours followed.

Here now is Ratih's account of her dancing career, straight from my notes. She spoke in English: 'I began learning dancing when I was seven, in the same year that I began going to school, going to my grand-uncle [Mandera] after school. I don't recall it being very difficult. I had been seeing dancing virtually every day all my life, and as I was young my body was very supple. I found learning easy but remember not having enough time to play with my friends. I would be in school from 7am to 10am, go home for a meal and be at the dance class from about 11am till evening, with a rest of about two hours in the course of the afternoon. The learning was not difficult but I remember that the climb down to the river for our bath and up again was painful because my legs were tired.

'When I was nine I began dancing with music and costume. Up to this time there had been little music, just a drum and voice for timing. My mother also gave me lessons. When I was nine I also gave my first public performance, in the legong in the temple. I had many experiences preparing for my first public dance. First I had to pray for the spirit of the dance to come. After that I was very happy — but during the dance my helmet fell off, and once I slipped on a flower. Later I learned more about how to put on the costume. I finished dancing the legong when I became a lady and learned the bumblebee dance, another classical dance, which I still dance. [The bumblebee dance, the oleg tambulilingan, tells of two bees falling in love in a beautiful and romantic garden, and symbolises a Balinese courtship.]

'Dancing occupied my interest to such an extent that I did not take much part in school sports, only playing some badminton. Now dancing is my life. I never stop. If I stopped I would be very sad. Once when I was sick and could not dance I was very sad. At 14 I began teaching as well as dancing. I wanted to teach my young sister but she wanted to play and to learn kung-fu. But later she was embarrassed to be a non-dancer in a family of dancers and agreed to learn. I took other students as well to make up a class of ten. Sometimes my sister would cry because she did not want to learn, but then she would realise again that it is an embarrassment for any girl from Peliatan not to dance. Everyone here must dance.

'In 1981 I was in a party of 42 people who went to America to dance. My older sister was also in the group. I was happy to go but also worried about a school exam. If I failed it I would have to repeat a year. But I worked hard when we came back five days before the exam, and I passed. We were five weeks in the United States and in Mexico. In New York we worked very hard with two shows a day, each lasting two hours.

'Now I'm very busy. I'm in the second year of my economics course in Udayana University in Denpasar, taking the maximum number of subjects permitted. And I dance here in Peliatan two or three times a week, and I also dance at the hotels sometimes on most other nights of the week. I must go to university because I want a career separate from dancing.

'When I get older and weaker people will not want to see me. Later when I look older and people do not like to see my face I may dance the dances where you wear masks. Here everyone is an expert and everyone can criticise, and a poor dancer is openly criticised and told to leave. Dancers can be criticised also just for not being beautiful, though it's not their fault and they can dance very well.'

I asked if a late starter, an adult, could become a good dancer.

'It would be hard work but she could become very good, but she would not become a top dancer. Her body would not be supple enough and if there was no 'dance blood' in her she would never be top class. If she was not pretty it would be no good — people want to see pretty dancers. We dance so close to the people they can see us very well. They want expert dancers and pretty dancers with fair skin. It is very hard to get to the top. Ksatrias have a very strong spirit and perhaps we succeed because of that. We dance together with the gods, and get more spirit from that.

'Sometimes westerners try to learn Balinese dancing. Mostly they try for only a short time, though it would take three years to become a good dancer. We had a ballet dancer from San Francisco here and she learned very well but the cultural connection was missing. Besides, it's very hard to change from one style of dancing to another. When I dance disco the classical moves keep getting in the way. Western dancers learn to reach high, while we keep low. Their legs are straight, ours are bent. We turn our toes up, they point theirs out. I've tried to dance their way and it's very painful. Another problem is that to be a good dancer you must work with musicians, work together with them. You can't learn to dance to recorded music.'

I asked how the Peliatan dances were organised. 'We have a

group within the village. Here everyone is an artist and this is a partnership to produce shows. Income from the dances goes first to pay all the expenses, and what is left is shared. The musicians get a minimum of from 500 to 1,000 rupiahs and the dancers get from 1,500 to 2,500 rupiahs. If anything is left over it is distributed equally to all of us.'

Did she feel that dancing for tourists diminished Balinese culture?

'The shorter dances for tourists are not true Balinese culture. The movements are the same but the dances are not complete. If you want to see the real Balinese dances you must stay in the villages. But despite the tourists our culture remains the same.'

Any complaints?

'Only one. When we finish dancing all we want to do is get out of our costumes. We are so tightly wrapped that breathing is difficult and also we are tired. But tourists with cameras ask us to pose this way and that way. In a way I like this because it means the tourists have enjoyed seeing us dancing but we really are very tired. Also, they say they will send us pictures but they very rarely do.'

Tourists' interest in posed pictures of the dancers, in addition to shots of them in action, is understandable because the costumes are often superb creations of gold-leafed sarongs, gilt sashes and draperies, intensely decorated leather collars and aprons, jewellery and ornate floral headdresses which may include even burning incense. As performing groups become more prosperous costumes become more splendid. The trap of tawdriness is generally avoided.

In Ubud and Peliatan one is surrounded by dancers, by dance classes, by preparations for performances, and there are shows almost every night somewhere nearby. Sunday morning at the Mudraswara Foundation in Ubud offers entrancing sights of small girls in everyday dress learning the classical movements — and how to concentrate. One night in the same hotel I saw an example of the concentration a dancer needs. A large praying mantis fluttered through the hanging decorations during a performance and fell to the stage. Moments later a dancer had occasion to kneel, and she did so right on top of it. I am sure I heard the crunch through the music. The dancer never flinched. 'She wouldn't know anything about it,' Ratih said when I told her about the incident. 'She would have been concentrating on the music.'

Balinese dancing is often said to be descended from, or at least related to, Indian but the connection seems tenuous. The Indian poet and philosopher Rabindranath Tagore once commented that 'Lord Siva gave his dance to Indonesia and left India with his ashes', but some scholars today will not accept even that. It is 'highly exaggerated' to assert that Indonesian dances originated in India, writes Professor Prijono Winduwinoto, one of Indonesia's foremost students of such matters. Others claim that the deities and heroes of the Indian Ramayana and Mahabharata epics from which many dance and drama stories have sprung have long since been transformed into Indonesians.

One study counted 32 'mudras,' or specific hand and finger movements, in Indian dancing. In classical dancing in Thailand, Cambodia and Laos only nine are to be found. In Java seven remain. In Bali, only one or two. As mentioned in the previous chapter, there is a theory that the hand movements in Balinese dancing stem from priestly gestures, just as Balinese music by one theory stems from the sound of his bell.

Whatever the origins, Indian or local, there is no doubt about the complexity of the result. No fewer than 30 names have been listed for feet and leg movements, 16 for those of the arms, 19 for those of the hands and fingers, 14 for the trunk, 20 for the neck and shoulders, 16 for facial expressions. All these must coincide exactly with the musical accent, and this can be achieved only by training so thorough that the music 'enters' the pupil, that gesture and accent become one.

These standards remain, and some people claim that the professional teaching now available in government colleges means that Bali today has more good dancers than ever before. What has changed is the audience. Originally all dancing, all music, all drama was for the entertainment of the gods during their occasional descent to various temples. Since the gods were both demanding and fickle, performances had to be both excellent and varied.

This tradition eventually was adjusted to meet the demands of aristocratic houses which claimed to be, if not actually divine, at least descended from the gods. With the decline of the aristocratic houses after the Dutch conquest of Bali, the tradition moved to the villages and became in effect a form of folk art, absorbing new vigour as a result. It is from this, perhaps, as much as from the need to find new ways to entertain the gods, that Balinese dancing derives its enthusiasm for experimentation and change.

Professor Prijono, commenting on differences between Balinese dancing and that of Java, where the aristocratic tradition continues, says that the Balinese is more dynamic, gay, lively, fast moving, exuberant and violent. Dancers use all parts of the body, including eyes moving with incredible swiftness, to express inner feelings. Javanese dancing is much more restrained. The Balinese, he says, is more 'complete'.

This is the dancing which has been enthralling tourists ever since their first encounter. The first commercial performances were probably staged in the Bali Hotel in Denpasar in the 1930s. The legong became almost a routine event but faced competition from new dances which kept cropping up whenever villagers felt like trying something different. One dancer, Mario, became famous for his kebyar, a virtuoso, flamboyant solo performance in a cross-legged position, and also as a peerless example of the Balinese dancer's detachment. Writers at the time commented that they failed to recognise the quiet young man they met by day as the brilliant dancer they had seen the night before. Indeed, he did not recognise himself — when shown his own photograph he exclaimed, 'That man is a good dancer,' then was amazed to find it was of himself. The reason is simple: Good performers are possessed by their roles, serving only as vehicles for dances which can change even their appearance.

Covarrubias lists no fewer than 17 dances and dance-dramas as being performed in the 1930s. One of them was the gambuh, 'the classic technique for dramatic performances' which in the 1960s became the target of an official rescue operation. It was then in serious decline, which was worrying because mastery of the gambuh was equivalent to being able to dance all the Balinese dances. Since then it has in fact been saved, but only in a technical and scholarly way because the Balinese in general are not much disposed to antiquarian efforts.

Covarrubias' list includes also the janger, 'a modern musical comedy with many foreign elements'. He says it was adapted from a Malay operetta. Another version is that it derived from a song sung by girl coffee pickers with boys joining in. In those days the janger lived a double life, a restrained version for tourists, another apparently a parody of the tourists — the boys wore outlandish European attire and false or painted moustaches — with elements of the kecak tossed in, wild and amazing. It swept the island and every village had its own version. Covarrubias called it an interesting example of the Balinese love of novelty which enables them constantly to create new styles and inject new life into their culture while yet preserving its Balinese character.

The janger is important also as an exception to a Balinese rule. Bali has no harvest dances, no erotic mating dances, no folk dances in which the whole village takes part. Its dances are 'show dances' rather than 'social dances'. The janger, with boys and girls taking part in a free-wheeling manner and with singing as well, broke with this pattern. That may be why it was such a hit and why performances remain popular to this day.

In general the stage today is ruled by performances which, though perhaps new in detail, belong to a great tradition. This does not mean that all dances are of religious or magical origin, a point sometimes made so the versions which tourists see can be called 'profane'. Some are of secular (a much fairer word than 'profane') origin, relating stories not connected with religion, dealing with everyday matters, existing purely for their own magnificent and graceful movements. Some encompass both roles. The pendet, for example, is part of a ritual to pay respect to the gods and also now a dance of welcome.

After the 30s came the Japanese, and a different, more forceful kind of audience. Bali became a resort for Japanese soldiers and performers came under pressure to vary their programmes. Some dances which resulted became popular with the Balinese themselves, and some, such as the prembon, the candrametu and the wiranata are still performed for tourists today — most of them doubtless thinking they are seeing something from ancient Bali.

This flux was accompanied by an inevitable drift away from old standards. The gods may have been fickle in demanding variety in the shows staged to entertain them, but at least they knew good from bad and had a certain patience. Tourist audiences by contrast could be ignorant and impatient and the Balinese were in no way loth to cut corners, shorten their programmes, include some gimmickry, and cash in. Tourists who had visited Bali in earlier times were horrified and pretended that the fault was not partly theirs. This phase could have been prevented only by preventing tourists from landing in Bali.

But the news is not necessarily bad. Two things have happened, in addition to an economic upsurge which has given the Balinese more scope for indulging their cultural interests. First, KOKAR, the conservatory of music and dancing, and ASTI, the academy of Balinese dance and drama, both in Denpasar, are producing both performers and teachers enough to arrest the technical decline and to offer hope that standards will rise again. Second, competition has set in. Bali today has perhaps 40 legong groups, 30 kecak, 20 barong (about which more shortly) and many others. They are competing for audiences. The contest which the Bualu kecak dancers won is another kind of incentive.

There will be no return to long-gone days of only dedicated community performances to honour the gods, but that does not mean that superb performances must vanish from the Balinese scene. Many that are on offer are superb, and the fortunate traveller can well find non-commercial dances and dramas, if he is in the right place at the right time.

While I was in Bali two Americans walking along the beach from Kuta found themselves the only foreigners at a janger performance which lasted till 2 a.m. Two nights later I returned to the village with them, and we were the only outsiders at a legong. Near Ubud I chanced upon week-long temple celebration which included a sacred baris dance, a sacred mask dance, a janger, a dance drama, a kecak and a shadow play. All performances were free, and it is a measure of Balinese acceptance of tourists that the best seats were reserved for them.

For the less fortunate the commercial offerings are not to be derided. I have mentioned the kecak and the legong, and there are more. Consider the barong, which has been helpfully described as 'the most familiar and the most obscure figure in Balinese dance drama'. Traditionally the barong, a fantastic mask which resembles that of the Chinese dancing lion also-of unknown origin, defends villages from witchcraft, disease and death. It is a mask 'increased to superhuman proportions', with one man wearing it and working its jaws, another forming the beast's back and hind legs beneath a shaggy cloth.

The Bali Museum in Denpasar has a fine collection of these masks. The barong vies endlessly with Rangda, an historical figure who lives on in Balinese lore as the most dangerous of all witches (see the chapter on History). Their eternal duel appeals to the Balinese love of theatre and is featured in various performances.

In one, followers of the barong attack Rangda with drawn krisses, or daggers. Rangda overcomes them with magic and they fall to the ground, trembling and twitching. The barong comes to revive them. The men rise to their feet and with savage shouts begin to thrust their krisses into their own bare breasts. They struggle

'Kris dancers' during a performance for tourists.

fiercely against attempts to disarm them and might go into convulsive seizures and have to be carried into the temple for reviving rituals. Jane Belo, who recorded such performances nearly 50 years ago, wrote that they were an exorcism of evil, relieving dancers and onlookers alike of their anxieties.

Even as she was involved in her studies, however, change was afoot. Some of the ever enterprising Balinese were merging a barong dance with other dance forms — and adding a playful monkey for light relief. In 1936 they put on a performance in the village of Denjalan, in Batubulan just outside Denpasar. And Denjalan in Batubulan is until this day the place where thousands of tourists see today's version of the barong dance. It has not been a continuous performance since 1936, of course, because Bali has been through too many vicissitudes since then. But its managers told me early in 1984 that it had been performed for tourists virtually every morning for 12 years, which surely sets a record of some kind.

Denjalan (its name means 'near the road' as Denpasar means 'near the market') seemed almost deserted when I arrived, though much traffic raced along the highway it faces. Slowly men began appearing, wearing sarongs, batik shirts, head-cloths, drifting slowly towards an airy, thatched hall with bamboo seats. Ticket sellers collected 1,500 rupiahs per visitor and distributed publicity sheets in English, French, Dutch, German, Italian, Spanish and Japanese. The Balinese men I had seen outside turned out to be gamelan musicians; they began warming up. Each had a kamboja flower behind his right ear. Busloads of tourists, Indonesian as well as foreign, arrived and the hall filled rapidly.

A low brick stage in the pit of the hall backed on to a split gateway, as is found in most temples, the entrance and exit for all performers. There was much decoration with flowers and greenery. The barong appeared, posing in the gateway, then ambling on stage, amiable and a little stupid. A monkey almost as splendidly costumed as the barong followed and engaged in what would be called horseplay if that were not so clearly the wrong word.

Three villains entered and attacked the barong and the monkey. All retreated. Two pretty girls performed a pretty dance. And then the pace picked up and action became continuous, the gamelan beating every switch with ever-changing tempo and mood. I tried keeping count of the performers: Two men in the barong, one monkey, two dancing girls, a prince, a servant, another prince, an old woman, a woman in great and vocal distress who wound up tied to a tree at stage-side, various monsters, the barong coming and going, the monkey, several more villains, and then a busy passage with which I could not cope. But I did note eleven men bare to the waist, flourishing krisses, and a man dressed in white as a priest. Altogether more than 40, plus more than 20 in the gamelan, plus who knew how many backstage and out front collecting and counting the money.

This abundance of people staged 90 turbulent minutes of comedy, drama, action, farce, pathos and a 'trance' scene with men trying to stab themselves. It was fast and slick throughout and it had the tourists enthralled. It was, in this sense, very professional. This quality of excellence made more surprising still my discoveries as I gossiped with the performers around a roadside drinks stall later. All the performers, all the helpers, about 80 people, lived in two banjars, or village wards, with an adult population of only 120. No one was brought in from outside, yet the community managed to present the show, day after day, the year round except for one day off each Balinese year, at Nyepi, when no one stirs from home.

Virtually all the performers and helpers had other work, mainly growing rice. Their daily routine was to go to the fields at daylight, before 5 am, and return home about 8am to prepare for the show at 9. Later in the day they returned to the fields. The four women in the cast were all housewives — or, as it was put, people who prepared temple offerings. Two of the men I talked to had scars on their chests from years of pressure from their kris points during the trance scene. One of the two pretty girls who appeared early in the show moved straight from dancing to trying to sell postcards to tourists. Then she rushed home to feed her seven-month-old baby. I remembered a senior police officer in Denpasar, who came from Borneo, telling me how impressed he had been to find that Balinese performers always remained modest.

I asked how much the performers and musicians earned from their daily presentations. Figures were hard to pin down but seemed to range between 10,000 and 20,000 rupiahs a month — 'Only enough for coffee and cigarettes,' a man said, only half joking. The rest went to expenses and banjar funds. One expense they did not have was any form of teacher or director. Not even the dancers needed to study: 'We grow up knowing how,' one said.

It has been commented that the Batubulan barong performance has moved away from its sacred origins and is now 'profane', and that its performers have lost faith in themselves and become 'mere theatrical actors'. Perhaps, but that word 'mere' seems unduly harsh. And as for losing faith, who knows?

The trance dance

What a visitor to Bali will not see, unless he is extraordinarily fortunate, is a trance dance. If he does, if he is absolutely sure of what he has seen, he will be free to say he has been witness to one of the island's deepest mysteries. This does not mean he has joined the throng at Bone (pronounced Bona), near Gianyar, for its three times a week programme of kecak, fire dance and trance dance.

The trip is worth making. The kecak, at least the one I saw, is vigorous and exciting, as it should be, and the fire dance enthralling. It is a one-man act, with its performer in a fanciful costume of grass and other foliage. The only illumination, except when tourists make the night bright with camera flashes, is from a bonfire of burning coconut husks. The dancer cavorts back and forth, rather as if he were riding a horse, then kicks the bonfire asunder. Then, as tourists gasp, he prances repeatedly through the burning embers, stamping on them with his bare feet. Eventually he is dragged forcibly from the arena, attended to by a priest, sprinkled with holy water and left sitting alone as the audience files out, displaying his unburnt feet in the light of kerosene lamps.

Perhaps the priest is not really a priest, or the water really holy; but though firewalking is widespread in Asia I have never seen it well explained. Claiming that people who habitually go barefooted have such thick soles that they can withstand fire does not allow for those firewalkers who have shoe-protected feet as tender as those of any western city dweller; and suggesting a hoax without explaining it is just lazy. I found the Bone act intriguing.

The trance dance which comes between the kecak and the fire dance I found more worrying than intriguing. It had two little girls in identical costumes, their eyes firmly closed, going through gentle, identical dance movements. Chanting men and women behind them provided a chorus. Three times the girls fell to the ground, each time to the right, each time in precisely the same manner. Twice women, presumably their mothers, came forward to set them back on their feet. The girls' eyes never flickered, which was a feat in itself. After falling for the third time they were led away and revived.

Were they really in a trance? I have met no one who believed so, and not just because organising an authentic trance dance three times a week would involve great strain. It is more that a real trance dance, a real communion with the gods, is something too valuable to waste on tourists. What we saw was something like a sanghyang dance, which in its best known form involves heavenly nymphs coming down to inhabit two girls who have not yet reached sexual maturity. The girls are put into a trance by the use of incense and choral singing and then do a dance similar to the legong, but slower and gentler. They become temporarily divine. In Bali almost anything is possible but were those little girls, eyes tightly closed, really gods dancing before us?

Jane Belo, who spent several years in Bali during the 1930s and made a particular study of trance dances, described the Balinese in these terms: '[They] are a people whose everyday behaviour is measured, controlled, graceful, tranquil. Emotion is not easily expressed. Dignity and an adherence to the rules of decorum are customary. At the same time they show a susceptibility and a facility for going into states of trance, states in which there is an altered consciousness, and behaviour springing from a deeper level of the personality is manifested.' If this should happen during a temple ceremony, they were believed to have been entered by a god, a heavenly nymph or a demon.

The kris-wielding warriors of the barong dance described earlier represent a staged example of such possession. Real occasions also exist, as when a traveller near Klungkung in 1984 found a temple seething with kris-wielding dancers, all entranced, some drawing blood.

McPhee provides an earlier example. He is describing a temple ceremony which has been going on all night. It is now near dawn and a priestess is dancing frantically, kris in hand. The music becomes heavy, hypnotic, violent:

'All at once there was a commotion in the gamelan. One after another the musicians grew rigid, and fell with a crash over jangling keys. Youths and men rose panting, eyes staring as though answering some dreadful summons. Sarongs rolled to their loins, they stepped like somnambulists out into the centre of the court, krises high, bodies tense, until, with a sudden thrust of the blade against his chest, each threw himself into a frenzy.

'With wild stabbing motions they attacked themselves. I wondered at the strange resistance which kept the blade from entering the flesh, for I thought they must surely kill themselves. One by one they collapsed shuddering and sobbing to the ground, to lie with outstretched arms, flexing their backs, thighs braced, writhing in spasms both tortured and ecstatic.

'In the early light the white form of the barong was now clearly visible. It stood at one end of the courtyard staring and motionless, but now two men entered beneath the body to bring it to life. . . . Bodies relaxed; the sobbing died away. One by one the boys awoke or were awakened by the priest. They looked about, rose, and silently walked away.'

Belo said that men involved in such paroxysms later reported an overwhelming feeling of anger, 'of a sort which is not customary for Balinese not in a trance state to experience or express'. The whole performance was an exorcism of the powers of evil, and it relieved the anxieties of performers and onlookers alike.

As for child trance dancers, they were typically two little girls chosen for their ability to go into a 'disassociated' state and then to dance. It was believed that their dancing was proof that a god had entered them because they had not previously been taught to dance. Villagers would form a 'club' around them to manage the ceremonies they would be involved in, which were usually to bring benefit to or ward off danger from the village.

During their ceremonies the girls would dance with eyes closed, as if asleep, at times standing balanced on men's shoulders, in no way supported, bending backwards and forwards without falling. An old photograph shows precisely this, and there are accounts of how the men — who keep their arms by their sides and do not grasp the girls' feet or calves — find themselves directed here and there in ways they cannot explain.

The girls' performances stopped when they reached puberty. According to Belo, they showed no signs of being neurotic or psychotic either before or after being inducted as trance dancers. They were able to dance every night for a month if the village required it. 'It is easy to see how the child dancers embodied for the attendant audience the idea of the pure and godlike,' Belo commented.

But at Bone, for busloads of tourists? Belo also commented, 50 years ago, that it was difficult to distinguish between acting and a genuine trance because the Balinese show what she called a great talent for dramatisation. Perhaps that was what we saw: Sheer talent.

The shadow play

Most Balinese performances involve many people but there is one which involves extraordinary, almost solo presentations. It is the shadow play, or wayang kulit, and an attempt to describe it runs immediately into a deficiency in the English language.

What should we call the man who wields the puppets which cast the shadows which depict the action? The only word in English is 'puppeteer' and that is far from adequate. It does not begin to cope with the talents which a Balinese practitioner must possess to pursue his craft.

First, he must be dexterous, able to bring his show (wayang) to life by manipulating decorated leather (kulit) puppets. He must cause them to spring at each other when necessary, to gesture when necesary, to stand calmly (stuck into a banana tree trunk) if that is what the story calls for.

Second, he must have an encyclopaedic knowledge of Ramayana, Mahabharata and Balinese folk stories. He would not prosper around the villages with only one or two stories in his repertoire, no matter how good, no matter how well done.

Third, he must have a considerable knowledge not only of his stories but also of their separate characters, so he can present them consistently to audiences almost as well informed on such matters as he is.

Fourth, he must be a linguist, using old Javanese, or Kawi, for narrative and for the voices of his principal characters and then Balinese (in its various forms) and Indonesian for lesser characters. These characters provide translations for people who do not know Kawi. About a third of a typical performance is in Kawi, the rest usually in Balinese.

Fifth, he must be of good voice to render impressively the introductions, explanations, narratives, dialogue, songs and classical quotations which his play demands, always in the appropriate language, style and accent.

Sixth, he must be creative and knowledgeable about local, district, regional and national matters, since nothing so lifts a show as a timely and clever reference to some current affair.

Seventh, he must have musical knowledge as well, so he can conduct his small orchestra, not with his hands, since they are busy, but with a wooden knocker held between the first two toes of his right foot. He uses it to signal starts, stops, tempo and mood with sharp raps on the box he stores his puppets in between shows.

And reference should be made also to his ability to remain seated, crosslegged, without a break, throughout his performance, and performances may go on all night.

Puppeteer? The word, the only word, is dalang, and a chance to see one in action is not to be missed. A night show is better than a day one. By day the Balinese dalang works without a screen and his audience sees his puppets directly. By night the puppets are manipulated between a lamp or flare which casts sharp and enlarged shadows on a cloth screen, and the effect can be magical. An hour or so is enough because visitors to Bali are not expected to know the languages being used.

Even that hour may be difficult to get, however, because the dalang in Bali is a dying breed. So much is expected of him and so much competition from other entertainments comes his way that this is not surprising. In the 1930s there were perhaps 1,000 of his kind. Now they are few and fast becoming fewer.

Painting

ali's best known export, if one chooses to overlook such intangibles as a reputation for beauty and culture and a glamorous image in the world, is its paintings. They are distinctive, cheap and portable and the numbers on display in homes around the world are beyond calculation. One cannot say that all visitors to Bali take paintings away with them but a high proportion do; and have been doing so for decades; and there is a healthy commercial trade as well which sees them being shipped out in bales.

Typically these paintings are colourful and exuberant depictions of everyday village life. A street or market scene in the foreground shows people engaged in all manner of activities; there may be a temple in the middle distance with people at prayer or in procession; and beyond that a vista of ricefields with still more people cultivating, planting, harvesting; with mountains — possibly Gunung Agung — in the distance. Or the picture may show a cremation, or a close-up, as it were, of a harvesting scene, or a jungle glade complete with wildlife, or cockfighting. Or perhaps the theme is mythological, with awesome monsters and splendid heroes.

The possibilities go on and on, yet they are united by a distinctive style. Paintings are colourful (but oddly, despite the dominating greenness of the Balinese countryside, rarely predominately green). They contain an immense amount of detail, often with each leaf on each tree carefully shaped and shaded. Their human figures are so precise that commentators again and again have remarked on Balinese artists' instinctive and accurate knowledge of human anatomy. They are crowded, as if the artists are reluctant to let any part of their canvasses escape close attention. Any one of these works, in any gallery anywhere, would stand out instantly as Balinese.

Now, it would be pleasant to be able to write that these paintings follow a kind of grand tradition, that the Balinese have long been artists of note, that to have one of their paintings is to possess a direct link with an ancient culture. It is not so. Balinese paintings even in the older forms which grace galleries and museums are largely a product of recent times. A really old work of art is rare. Once again we have entered a cultural field marked more by change than by adherence to old ways, more by the Balinese desire to create anew than to continue along customary paths.

All they need is a catalyst, some event or person to link ability with opportunity, and off they go in an exciting new direction. As recently as the early 1960s, an artist named Ari Smit found himself cast in this role and he still looks back on the consequences with a kind of astonishment. Smit, from Holland, a prisoner of the Japanese on the 'death railway' in Thailand during World War II, an Indonesian citizen since 1950, was one day sketching a landscape in the fields near Ubud. A 12-year-old village boy guarding a flock of ducks nearby watched him and then began drawing houses and people in the sand. Smit, who now lives in Sanur, later wrote of the events which followed:

'I asked him whether he would like to draw on paper and afterwards use colours. We had to ask permission from his father. His father was not willing because the boy was his only son — and who would guard the ducks? But [later] it was agreed that I should teach the boy, and the father borrowed some money from me to hire a duck guardian. I never taught the boy but I encouraged him to draw and paint everything I could think of.

'The technique he applied was in the main course of Balinese painting, based on a firm outline, very graphic in the way that the design fully covers a given sheet of paper, and finally richly decorated in gay colours. . . . With youngsters it seemed only natural to encourage them in whatever they wanted to paint, and, as everywhere else in the world, they painted their own environment.

'[Because] in Bali children are in so many instances given the responsibility of an adult, they show in accomplishing their duties a greater care and discipline and a general behaviour that arises from pride and skill in work. . . . The duck guardian, who became a painter and at the age of 13 could buy a cow for his father with the money he earned from his paintings, introduced a nephew, and then another relative. Parents looked for talent and in three years the group consisted of 25 boys.' More joined later, and the group came to number about 40.

These boys were to become famous as Bali's 'child artists', 'young artists', and later as 'peasant painters'. The third title was used by a Malaysian architect, Lim Chong Keat, when in 1970 he organised exhibitions of their work in Singapore and Kuala Lumpur. In his introduction to the exhibition catalogue he described the art movement which resulted from Ari Smit's casual intervention as 'perhaps the most fascinating and brilliant example of peasant art to be found in the world today'.

Smit, Lim continued, was the catalyst who unlocked the boys' native talent, leading them to produce 'clumsy' paintings which nonetheless were vivid and spontaneous. The complexity of their subjects did not daunt them. On the contrary, their intimate awareness of the complexity of village life helped them produce paintings which combined the hustle and bustle into rich and colourful compositions which captured the spirit of daily living.

Not the least, perhaps the most important, of Smit's contributions were his gifts of paper and paints to boys who could not afford them — and who made their own brushes from bamboo. Their village, Penestanan, was very poor, but this changed rapidly as tourists began snapping up the boys' paintings in huge numbers.

That boy guarding his father's ducks and sketching in the sand as Ari Smit worked was named Nyoman Cakra. He still lives in Penestanan. I went to see him, and found a man far removed from that urchin of more than 20 years before. His purchase of a cow (for 12,000 rupiahs) for his father was just a first step on the road to his much more prosperous situation today. In 1978 he was able to rebuild the family home into a substantial dwelling, he has some rice fields of his own, when I saw him he had an exhibition of paintings on in one of the big hotels in Sanur, and he is a man of substance in his community.

Yet totally and engagingly in touch with that community. When I visited him his wife and three of his five children were with him on his porch — and so were women sewing and making offerings, a man at work on a big landscape, and two dogs and a cat. A hen

Rice Harvest, by Dewa Nyoman Djati, 1977.

and chickens scratched for food in the garden. Visitors came to talk to Cakra, leader of the village's music group, about their programme. He is sturdy, stocky, open-faced, dignified, and perfectly willing to admit that if he had not met Ari Smit he would still be a more or less impoverished rice farmer.

Cakra sells paintings today for an average price around 30,000 rupiahs, though that can double if dealers are involved. The price is low by any international standards, and this low level is a reflection of a besetting problem. As the young artists or peasant painters or whatever they may be called became famous, imitators and dealers turned their creativity into a vast commercial industry. Everywhere he goes in Bali the visitor is confronted with 'galleries', shops, stalls, roadside hawkers selling paintings. The great majority of them follow the style developed by Cakra and his companions in Penestanan.

It is hard not to be disillusioned by the degradation involved. Many artists are undoubtedly controlled, exploited, by dealers. It is also not to be doubted that some dealers commission work as if from a factory, having work which sells well not only copied but even traced, and then copied by relays of women and children, perhaps with each one adding one colour. At times it is a process not much removed from the painting by numbers which some western hobbyists indulge in. It is all very sad but, given that so many tourists buy totally without discrimination, unavoidable.

This does not mean that good work is not available. It does mean that one must look carefully for the jewels, or at least the honest metal amid all the dross, and that can be hard work. Probably the best advice that can be given to any visitor intent on taking away a good example of Balinese art is to take time, to seek opinions from dealers and guides, and in the end let instinct guide. Time and care will not necessarily lead to a masterpiece but it can well lead to a work which will hang comfortably for years as a reminder of a special field of Asian creativity.

Ari Smit's adventure with Cakra and his friends highlighted once again this remarkable talent. Smit found that an astonishingly high proportion of the boys in Penestanan could turn out reasonable drawings. A similar proportion no doubt could have carved wood or stone, or become musicians. Where the western child is often reluctant to try his hand at creative pursuits, his Balinese counterpart grows up in a world which assumes he will do so, and lets him try. The western child is generally assumed to be incapable unless he proves otherwise. The Balinese is assumed to be able to carve, or paint, or play music, or dance, and accordingly is never reluctant to try. Talent is encouraged to flower. Traditional Bali therefore literally had no need for words to express such ideas as 'art' and 'artist', since everyone was potentially an artist. Today's sometimes unfortunate treatment of art with mass-production methods seems in an odd way consistent with this historical legacy.

Traditionally Balinese artists were anonymous craftsman — just as the great majority of them are today — and they used whatever methods seemed appropriate for the result they wanted — just as they do today. They worked primarily as sculptors in stone or wood. Painting even until the first third of this century was almost entirely confined to colouring strips of cloth for house and temple decorations during festivals, or cloth panels for use as curtains or wall hangings in palaces, folded and put away when not in use. Subjects were virtually always mythological and literary, very rarely contemporary and of daily life. There were also painted flags but they deteriorated with every exposure to the weather and in any case were little used once the aristocratic houses lost most of their power. In 1930, when Covarrubias arrived in Bali, painting was little in evidence as a living art.

What had been practised until then was painting of the kind I came across in a crumbling palace in Amlapura. I was poking around amid decrepit pavilions when I looked upwards, and found a porch ceiling covered with obviously old and badly damaged paintings. I worked out that they purported to show some of the punishments that wrongdoers would suffer in the next world, but the paintings were in such poor condition, flaking and fading, that not much could be accurately deciphered. It seemed to me that that half-collapsed porch, let alone its decorations, would not survive much longer.

Later in Klungkung, I found that the ceilings of the Kerta Gosha, a much-photographed and often-described old courthouse, featured almost identical paintings, but with many more of them and in much better condition. One can see people being boiled and beaten, torn and crushed, rended apart by monstrous animals. It is these scenes that have made the Kerta Gosha famous, but torments for the departed occupy only only one tier among several showing different levels between hell and heaven. There are also engaging renderings of daily life, with market scenes, cooking, cock-fighting, dancing, a gamelan orchestra (playing beneath kerosene lamps), and some decorous, well-covered love-making.

The visitor should take note not only of the subject of these paintings but also of the style — and then take transport four kilometres or so towards the sea, to the village of Kamasan. There is nothing here externally to catch the eye, but it is a village which looms large in the minds of all students of the history of Balinese painting. It is the only village in Bali where the old style of painting survives.

In a single household there — and there are more like it — I found silversmiths turning old Dutch coins into the silver bowls in which women carry offerings to temples; brass-smiths turning empty artillery cartridges (spirited away from army practice ranges) into vases decorated with Ramayana themes; and men and women at work on paintings in the style of the Kerta Gosha. I found also why some of the Kerta Gosha paintings look fresh: Kamasan artists in recent years had been given the job of restoring them.

They work on a thin, unbleached cotton cloth which has been filled, as it were, with a rice paste coating until an even, matt surface has been obtained. This seems to have the effect of dulling even bright colours laid on it and the result, to use a good Indonesian word, is 'antik', especially as the artists continue to observe some antique conventions.

Heads are usually shown in three-quarter profile. Refined young men are clean-shaven or have simple moustaches and coarser characters have bushy moustaches. There is a clear progression from the straight and thin noses of high-born aristocrats, through the wider and rounder ones of common people, to the snouts of animals and demons. Perhaps most engaging of all is the difference between the eyes of refined men and refined women. In men the lower lid is a straight line, the upper lid curving down on to it, while in women the upper lid is straight and the lower lid an upwards curve. This gives men a direct and masculine look, women a downward and demure one. Another convention holds that right is good and left is evil — but from the viewpoint of a person behind the picture, not in front of it. There seems to be a connection here with the shadow play, where the same convention is observed — from the point of view of the dalang, from behind the screen.

Nyoman Agotini, a school teacher who does 'antik' painting in her home in Kamasan in her spare time, showed me some of her work and some by other members of her family. I was much taken by a blue Arjuna, a romantic mythological hero. She told me she does not copy but thinks about a Ramayana story and then sets out to depict it. The story and the style are old but the imagination is original. The paintings that result have an engaging charm, especially if one learns a little about the characters and stories they represent.

They can be folded and are easy to carry, and do not cost much — say 5,000 rupiahs for a child's first effort, 20,000 for a good, fine work, 60,000 for a largish one. Mostly they are not signed, which is another direct link with days when producing such work was a matter of everyday craftsmanship. That the painters of the past

Conventional eyes, from an 'antik' Kamasan painting.

appear always to have been commoners working for aristocrats points in the same direction.

Because such paintings set out directly to illustrate an event or a personality, they have been described as 'coloured drawings', and this description can still be applied to most Balinese art. It almost always sets out to be specific and illustrative, very rarely indirect and allusive. The major difference between the traditional and modern styles is that the traditional dealt with another world, the modern deals with this.

Now I come to a problem. There was little or no modern Balinese art when Covarrubias arrived in 1930, and very little traditional. The change to today's effusiveness came swiftly and powerfully, and there is no doubt that a substantial factor was exposure to outside ideas and people. Ari Smit was just one in a series of artists from outside Bali who set this change in train and kept it going — but it would be foolish to claim that they alone caused it.

John Darling, an Australian film-maker and student of Balinese art who has lived in Ubud for many years, rejects as 'a kind of artistic colonialism' any notions that the Balinese leapt from mediaeval to modern through the intervention of foreigners. The new art sprang up in some parts of Bali where foreigners were present, in others where they were not, and many questions about the whole process remain unanswered, Darling writes.

He does so in a recent book on Walter Spies, a German artist who was the most prominent of the foreigners involved in the process. The role of Spies and of other foreigners has been much written about, but always by other foreigners, while little has been recorded about the role of the Balinese themselves. This is a perennial problem of Asian history. The men and women who carried colonial flags were always eager — and had the education, the means and the leisure — to record their side of complicated stories while the Asian side as often as not was lost. My problem now is to present Spies in such detail as his extraordinary life demands without at the same time suggesting that he alone wrought enormous change upon the Balinese art scene.

Walter Spies was born in Moscow in 1895 of wealthy German parents and grew up in the cultural hothouse of the last years of Czarist Russia. During World War I he was interned in a camp near the Urals, and spent time with the Tartars there. Eventually he was able to return to Germany where he began making a name for himself as a painter and musician. Then, for reasons still not clear but possibly connected with his homosexuality, he went to Indonesia, then the Dutch East Indies.

In the early 1920s he was in Bandung, in West Java, playing the piano in a cinema. A few months later he was in Jogjakarta, in Central Java, teaching music to European children. The Sultan of Jogjakarta made him manager of his European orchestra. He learned to play gamelan instruments. In 1925 he visited Bali, experienced 'an explosion of delight and wonder', and moved there two years later.

Spies settled in Ubud where a leading gentry family, the Sukawatis, in 1928 gave him land and material to build a house at a point where two rivers flow together. A kind of Camelot in Bali resulted. His house (now part of the Tjampuhan Hotel, with his room preserved) became a focus for foreign visitors, including Covarrubias and his wife, Colin McPhee, Vicki Baum and others whose names dot the pages of this book. It was during this time that Spies invented the kecak dance for a German film company, as mentioned earlier.

He became much involved in efforts to preserve Balinese artefacts and played a prominent role in the foundation of the Bali Museum in Denpasar, which was designed partly to collect items which would otherwise have been sold to tourists. He was its first curator when it opened in 1932, which indicates high standing with Dutch officials.

Equally important, Spies was much involved in the formation of an artists' organisation, Pita Maha, which scrutinised members' work, registered the best and endeavoured to ensure that standards were kept high despite commercial pressures. Another foreign artist, Rudolf Bonnet, was equally important in this organisation. In 1934, as a measure of the impact of such activity, a senior Dutch official reported what he called an astonishing renaissance in painting in Bali and the development of a revolutionary new style. Spies, he said, was the decisive influence. All the time Spies was carrying on with his own painting, developing a style of bright pastoral landscapes interspersed with gloomy patches of jungle or dense undergrowth. And he was pursuing his music as well, to such good effect that in 1938 he 'owned' two gamelans.

Then his life fell apart. A colonial government campaign against homosexuals, in line with the law in Holland, saw him arrested and imprisoned in Surabaya for eight months. A few months later, in May, 1940, when Germany invaded Holland, he was back behind bars again, this time as an enemy alien. The Dutch put him and other prisoners on a ship bound for Sri Lanka. The ship was sunk by the Japanese off the Sumatra coast in January, 1942, and Spies was drowned.

Today his name is still well known. The Art Centre in Denpasar includes a memorial to him where reproductions of some of his paintings are on show, and in Ubud men with memories of pre-war days continue to speak of him with great respect. Spies' name crops up again and again. He is even credited with a hand in developing Bali's distinctive style of elongated wood-carving. It resulted, the story goes, when Spies asked a craftsman to make two carvings from a long piece of fine wood. The craftsman said later the spirit of the wood was so strong that he was unable to cut it in two, and so made one long, thin statue.

But it would be foolish to pretend that there were not other people at least as important as Spies in Bali's creative life during the 1930s. The important and talented members of the Sukawati family who gave him powerful support may in fact have been happy to use him in their dealings with the Dutch colonial rulers. And there were also Balinese artists of remarkable stature in their own right.

Consider Gusti Nyoman Lempad. He was a master craftsman, designing and building monumental gates, carving temple and palace decorations, making barong masks and cremation towers, when Spies arrived. Spies gave him a piece of paper — and for the next 50 years Lempad produced a stream of pen-and-ink drawings which were always clear, strong, independent, and never an imitation of anything European. He died in 1978, reputedly over 100 years old.

Nor are other Balinese artists who came to prominence in the 1930s to be regarded as mere imitators, and Indonesian art historians now give them full credit for their achievements. Any good catalogue of Balinese artists contains the names of numerous men (but rarely women) of considerable talent, and their number is growing all the time. I could attempt to list some of them here but it would be an arbitrary list, either unfair to many or so long as to be meaningless.

What then are we to make of Spies? Undoubtedly he had great talent — but we must allow also that he was fortunate in his place and time, until the final disasters closed in. Bali for much of the 1930s was a kind of paradise for Europeans whose backgrounds of wealth and culture gave them entree to the highest levels of both Balinese and Dutch colonial life, and Spies was such a one. There is no doubt that he contributed much to the Balinese, but as for his influence on Balinese art — that, in John Darling's phrase, is a jungle of conjecture. Certainly Spies alone could not have triggered the astonishing creative outburst of his time.

Bonnet, who at one stage in the 1930s rejected an American order for 90 wood carvings because he feared it would lead to mass production, was not as exotic a figure as Spies but is beginning to loom larger in artistic history. He appears to have been just as active as Spies in organising the Bali Museum, with Dutch officials and scholars also prominent, and in setting up the Pita Maha. He worked as closely as Spies did with the Sukawati family, especially

Drawing by Gusti Nyoman Lempad.

Cokorda Gde Agung Sukawati, and with Lempad and other leading artists.

He is remembered mainly for a more recent development, however. After spending World War II as a prisoner of the Japanese, he returned to Ubud and joined enthusiastically with Cokorda Gde Agung Sukawati in planning what is now the Puri Lukisan, the Palace of Paintings, Ubud's art gallery, which was opened in 1956. Two years later he had to leave Indonesia — many foreigners have had problems with Indonesia's immigration department — only to return in 1972 to carry on working for the gallery.

Six years later he returned to his native Holland for a visit, only to die there in 1978. In his will he said his ashes must be returned to Bali. They were, in a parcel through the mail, eventually to be included in the offerings at Cokorda Gde Agung's cremation in 1979, and later scattered on the sea. Since then Bonnet's memory has been much honoured by the Indonesian government and a foundation created in his name. The Puri Lukisan is his outstanding memorial.

Spies, Bonnet and Covarrubias, an artist as well as a writer, were of course not the only foreign painters on the scene in the

1930s. Another was Theo Meier, Swiss, who found when he landed in Bali in 1936 after a visit to Tahiti that 'a delirium laid hold of him' which persisted until his death in 1982. He married twice in Bali, lost many works when the Japanese looted his studio in Sanur, and received President Sukarno in his home in Iseh, in the foothills of Gunung Agung. In 1957 he moved to Thailand but visited Bali frequently for the rest of his life.

Then there was A.J. Le Meyeur de Merpres, who spent 32 years in Bali, who died in his native Brussels in 1958 at the age of 78, and whose home in Sanur is open to the public. His widow, Polok, lived there until her death in July, 1985; some fortunate visitors were able to compare this gracious old lady with the many paintings of her as a young woman which adorn the gallery.

The postwar crop of artists includes Han Snel, one of the impressive number of Dutch conscript soldiers who declined to fight against the new republic of Indonesia, and deserted. He has lived in Bali since 1950 and is married to a Balinese, Made Siti, who manages one of Ubud's better hostelries for him while he carries on painting. Since the late 1950s, Antonio Mario Blanco, a Manila-born Spaniard, has made Bali his home, also in Ubud, with his Balinese wife and their four children. Blanco is colourful, running with frantic energy around his gallery as he talks about his art, his picture frames, his philosophy, his sex life, his conception of the universe. Donald Friend, Australian, arrived in Bali in 1966 and spent most of his time there until 1977, when he returned home.

But there is no suggestion now that foreign artists are notably important on the Balinese art scene. Anything they can do the Balinese, and the Indonesians from other islands who have come to Bali, can do as well or better. This extends even to re-creating in modern form an ancient form of co-operation. At Pengosekan, a couple of kilometres from Ubud, for example, two brothers have set up an artists' community which produces some fine work while sharing resources and profits 'on the village principle'.

The communal principle extends, as an example, to four men working simultaneously on one painting, combining their skills 'because in Bali artists work not for themselves but for the gods'. They also work for profit, yet there is said to be no contradiction so long as artists remain ready to stop doing commercial work to help with decorations for a temple festival or a cremation. Religion, culture and customs remain properly linked. The 34 members seem content with the arrangement, which at least spares them the need to hawk their wares around the streets, or to submit to autocratic dealers. 'It can be very difficult,' one said, speaking from experience. 'Some painters make only 1,000 rupiahs a day; they can make 1,500 working as building labourers — or as house painters.'

Good paintings are to be found anywhere in Bali's tourist belt, if one searches carefully, but a beginning to understanding can come only from a visit to Ubud. All manner of studios where artists can be seen at work are dotted through the town and the surrounding villages. The Pengosekan community alone is instructive, and a visit to Lempad's old home in Ubud's main street must be rewarding even if little of his original work, now deservedly expensive, is to be seen. Being in Ubud is itself an education.

But still more benefit comes from visiting two institutions in particular. One is the Puri Lukisan, where Bonnet spent so much time, perhaps the only noteworthy collection of paintings in the world housed in a thatched building with ricefields outside. A stroll through its display of old works, mainly on mythological themes, helps make sense of the modern paintings on sale up and down the main street.

Then there is the Neka Museum, best reached by walking the mile or so from Ubud on a cool, damp morning so one arrives with a properly open-minded attitude. The 'museum' ('gallery' would be better) has four display rooms set apart in an elegant garden. One

Inside the Pengosekan artists' community.

room is for outstanding Balinese artists, including Lempad. One is for other Indonesian artists who have worked in Bali. One concentrates on Spies, Bonnet and Ari Smit. And one features other foreign painters such as Meier, Snel, Blanco and Friend. These displays alone are more than enough to justify the walk from Ubud, or the visit to Ubud.

There is also the possibility of a bonus. The name 'Neka' is from Wayan Suteja Neka, an eager and exuberant Balinese, the son of a noted sculptor and Pita Maha member, who has done much to educate the world about the art of his island. He possesses an endless fund of information about his subject, and is honest to the point of admitting into his museum work he does not like, purely for the sake of completeness. He is fascinated by his subject, just as from time to time others have been fascinated by him.

Theo Meier asked Neka to pose for a portrait, and later praised him as 'an extremely dynamic man who instead of giving vent to his energy — in Balinese fashion — in cockfighting has taken to pictures, classical and modern'. Because Neka is dynamic he is always busy, running his gallery in Ubud and other ventures, but often not too busy to talk to his visitors. From such an occasion can come still greater insight.

The main message, always, is of Balinese eagerness to produce rich, natural paintings interesting in themselves yet consistent with tradition. Ari Smit and others believe that their style amounts to a rediscovery of an old one — with the difference that the old one was expressed not in painting but in carved panels. This accounts for the depth without perspective, for the careful outlining of each element in the painting, for the full use of all the space available. At times an artist will use three lines of different weight to create just one line, just as a carver does when he cuts deeper and deeper into wood or stone.

Perhaps therefore the best way to start understanding Balinese painting is to look at the stone panels which adorn so many temples and homes. At the beginning of this chapter I remarked that Balinese painting as we know it today does not follow in the footsteps of any grand tradition. Perhaps that was wrong. Perhaps there is a grand tradition, but the medium has changed from stone to canvas.

Carving

n the previous chapter I mentioned that carving in stone is part of the Balinese grand tradition, in some cases these days converted into painting on paper or canvas. Carving remains a primary art, however, as alive today as it ever was.

One reason for this is geological, as I began to realise when I saw reddish stones piled up in hardware shops. They turned out to be farmers' sharpening stones, whetstones, imported from Lombok and Java. Bali does not produce any hard stone of its own. Temples and statuary are made mostly of volcanic deposit, 'paras', so soft one can work it with a penknife. In the north more durable but still soft sandstone is also used. As a result carvings age rapidly and can look ancient within a few decades. The need to repair and replace degenerating stonework has kept carving a living art. Today many temples have squared-off stones in prominent places waiting for the local sculptors to get around to them.

One effect of this continual process of renewal is continual opportunity for new ideas to creep in. To see an example of this I went to Kubutambahan, about 20 kilometres east of Singaraja, in search of a temple carving of a man on a bicycle. As I did so I had the grace to feel that my quest was a little foolish, leading nowhere, teaching nothing, merely Eurocentric. My consolation was that I was not alone. Visitors stream to this temple, and have done so since drawings of the carving were published in Europe early this century.

It is on the left side of the temple as you face it, and finding it is worth the touch of conscience. The carving, just over a metre high, is engaging, and so is its story. The panel appears to show a Balinese but in fact it originated as a portrait of a wandering Dutch artist, W.O.J. Nieuwenkamp (1875-1950). Visiting Bali in 1904, he was much impressed — and he impressed the Balinese with the bicycle he rode. They recorded him in stone as recognisably European. But when the temple needed restoration after an earthquake Nieuwenkamp become Balinese, with a flowered sarong, and his bicycle emerged as an impossible machine with floral wheels.

Nieuwenkamp probably sympathised with the changes because he loved Bali, 'the most wonderful land I know'. After a second visit he published two books about Bali and Lombok, and today he is much honoured among the cognoscenti as one of the first outsiders to appreciate the island — a Dutch guidebook calls him 'the first flower child'.

A couple of days later, following a guidebook's advice, I went looking for more such modern creations. The book said that a temple in Jagaraga, only a few kilometres from Kubutambahan, had a carving of Dutchmen in a car being held up by a man with a gun. In Jagaraga men thatching a temple roof referred me to another further up the road. I walked on, searching each temple I came to.

The first yielded a carved panel of a man holding an antique pistol and a seated European facing a man holding a hoe. The second temple had three phallic images side by side. The third was locked.The fourth yielded two men, possibly Dutch, wearing jackets and trousers and with guns and a dog, threatening a monkey up a tree. Its gateway carried a 1933 date. The fifth temple, though a passer-by strongly recommended it, yielded nothing of the exotica I was looking for. Then a foodstall owner at the gate told me the temple I was looking for was back at Jagaraga, by this time several kilometres away.

Too hot and tired to plod all the way back, I caught a bemo — and the driver dropped me a few metres from where I had begun my search. The carved panels I had been looking for were right across the road, fully visible. Earlier in the day I had ridden right past them.

The panels showed, from left to right and ignoring breaks for decorations and doorways: A man on a bicycle with undecorated wheels; aircraft with cowering figures beneath them; a European fishing; a Balinese flying a kite; two men paddling a canoe; a house with a European seated in the porch, apparently smoking a cigar; a car almost a metre high, with four doors, canvas roof, open sides,

Many Balinese craftsmen cannot resist opportunities to change things. The bicycle carving at Kubutambahan originally depicted a European, the artist Nieuwenkamp (left, from an old drawing). But restoration after an earthquake changed him into a Balinese riding a bicyle with splendidly floral wheels. — Photograph by Peter Assmann.

long-haired driver, two passengers in the back seat, one with a neat, pointed beard; and another car, two-door, roof folded down, with two Europeans in it being held up by a man with a pistol.

About dusk the same day I happened to visit another famous temple, at Sangsit, near Kubutambahan. Dedicated to the rice goddess, it is so lavishly decorated that I counted more than 50 collectors' items, as it were, on one side of one gateway, not including decorative floral pieces. The other side of the same gateway had another 50. The whole ebullient mass of faces and figures contrasted oddly with the tiny doors they embraced and sheltered.

None of these figures is an object of worship. As mentioned earlier, Balinese gods are invisible and the function of temple carvings is purely decorative. In north Bali, perhaps because the sandstone used there lasts longer, temple sculpture is much more exuberant than in the south.

This does not mean carving is confined to temples. On the contrary, it is to be found everywhere. Countless homes have carved panels and statues in their gardens and living rooms. In the Bali Museum there is even a carved chopping block. In Tabanan town a set of traffic lights is buried deep in brick and stone pillars carved in the shape of a very narrow temple. So much is carved that one is in danger, after a time, of not seeing it at all.

When first in Bali, I was fascinated to see more than 20 men from Gianyar at work on what were to become pillars in a new government building, cutting through paper patterns into the wood beneath. They worked rapidly and precisely, changing chisels and gouges (15,000 rupiahs for a set) surprisingly often. They were so good at their work, so fast, that they made the job look easy. These were tradesmen in a field which at its upper levels has artists of astonishing skill. I heard one apparently fine work criticised because the hair on a girl's head was not perfectly incised. In the Art Centre in Denpasar I was so taken with a wood carving of Hanuman, the monkey god of the Ramayana, that I had to touch it (despite warning notices) to assure myself its lifelike fur was just wood. All good galleries have spectacular pieces, often not for sale, of such intricacy that it is impossible to imagine the sculptor's thoughts before he began work. The story that artists meditate on a piece of wood, and then release the shape that they see waiting inside, makes much sense.

As well as growing up in an environment which helps talent develop, Balinese carvers enjoy a purely physical aid which gives them an advantage over most of those of us who would copy them. We westerners use only our two hands and are thus deprived of much of the holding and sensory equipment which the Balinese employ. Using a vice to hold the wood and standing at a bench involve a remoteness from the task quite foreign to the Balinese carver with his work lying in his lap or clasped between calves and feet. (Also, we use wooden handles on our chisels. Not good, a carver said. For good work there must be continuity between fingers, steel and wood.)

How efficient as craftsmen the Balinese can be I realised when I came across a workshop, or studio, or gallery, in Mas, on the way to Ubud, which had just completed an order for 50 masks, lifesize, complete with wooden spectacle frames, of Bruno Kreisky, the Austrian Chancellor. All seemed to me to be absolutely identical. Why anyone should want 50 Kreisky masks I never learned.

In another porch in the same building (workmen do not need workshops here; any covered area will do), I found carvers making identical Buddhist masks to fill an order from Japan. Two men not on the order were making rhinoceroses, roughing them out from baulks of timber (imported from other Indonesian islands) without so much as a drawing to go by. Children were making ducks. These workers were either on wages or expecting to earn perhaps 25 percent of the eventual sale price. The general picture is of lowly paid artisans at the bottom, overcharged tourists at the top, and a confusion of dealers, agents, guides and drivers in between, as everywhere else in the world.

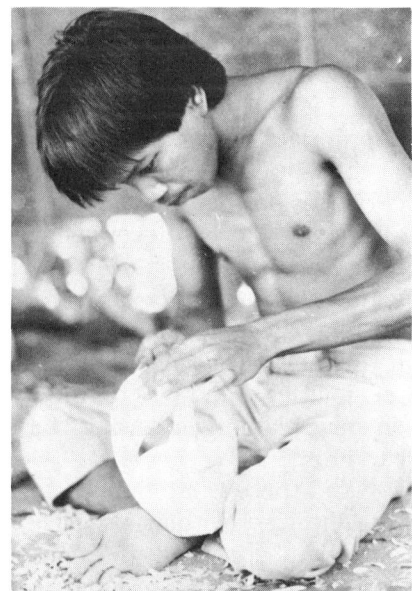

Two mask-makers of Mas at work.

The top of the woodcarvers' tree is making masks for sacred or semi-sacred use, like the barong mask or the masks worn by performers in some other dances. At this level work goes on in a religious and traditional haze, bound about by indefinable forces. The carver may from time to time visit a temple where ancient masks are kept, not so much to see as to breathe inspiration from them. At its highest levels mask making demands identification with the personality being depicted, which can involve not only skill but also scholarly knowledge, ability as a performer and a faculty for introspection and meditation as well. The result should be a mask so powerful that whoever wears it becomes the mask and acts accordingly.

The method involved in such creativity is fittingly elaborate right from the apparently casual, slow, indirect process of picking the right piece of wood to start with. Usually it comes from a member of the balsam family. Carving is similarly a matter of not trying too hard, of letting inspiration rather than concentration guide the knife. Eventually the mask is sandpapered, 'lived with' as it hangs on a wall for weeks or months, coloured with perhaps 30 coats of paint, and perhaps fitted with mother-of-pearl teeth or actual pig's fangs. It is a complicated, almost other-wordly process, and the longer one remains involved in it, even as a shopper wandering around the galleries, the more fascinating the best masks become. Salesmen help this process. They are often eager to don masks and to act the appropriate personality. The best actors sell many masks.

The latest vehicle the Balinese have found for their skill as carvers is pottery, in a new ceramic research station between Kuta and Sanur. Bali has never been noted for its pottery, though a village near Kapal, just north of Denpasar, produces engaging primitive ware. The new station is an attempt to create a new product, a new avenue for employment, a new means of earning foreign exchange. It probably eventually will do so. But I was less intrigued by such possibilities than I was to find that the young men carving patterns on new plates were using the same tools and methods as wood carvers.

And there is another engaging detail as well. Pottery can last for centuries. Nothing else the Balinese have ever carved — except the Pejeng gong with the face featured on the cover of this book — has survived for so long. The various woods the Balinese use, ebony, hibiscus, coffee tree, sandalwood, balsam, and so on, will endure only by freakish conditions of dry air and being left alone. The stonework, as mentioned, is not as durable as it looks. Our world far, far into the future may have only tomorrow's ceramics to tell of Bali's remarkable sculptural talent.

History

ne day I asked a woman who lives near a temple of great antiquity if she knew how old it was. The question surprised her. 'It was here before I was born,' she said. 'My mother says it was here even before she was born.' Variations on this theme occurred so frequently that I came to feel that fascination with history has no great role in Balinese life, except perhaps among the gentry with status to maintain. This attitude, if it is so, has much to commend it but a book of this kind must still pay homage to those processes of the past which made Bali what it is today.

The most important of these were migration and filtration. In prehistoric times wave upon wave of people drifted through southeast Asia, usually from west to east. Some waves were presumably a result of some other people enlarging their territory, perhaps as far away as China, triggering a ripple effect as the people they displaced moved into the terrritory of others, and so on.

Migration is never a clear-cut process. There is always a blurring along the boundaries and a filtering effect as people of different cultures collide, merge or recoil from each other. Some elements vanish, some are adapted, some survive more or less unchanged to await identification thousands of years later as evidence that certain people moved by certain routes. Balinese culture is a compendium of such surviving elements, massively adapted. Those who reached Bali from other islands would have been determined partly by accident, partly by the history of other peoples, largely by geography. The importance in Bali's history of the island's rugged coastline, surrounding coral reefs and streaming tidal currents is never to be minimised. The tourist beaches conceal a much harsher reality.

At first, during those millenia in which stone-age people crossed from island to island on their way from Asia to as far as Polynesia in the most primitive craft imaginable, Bali's marine defences would have filtered out all except the more fortunate and the more courageous. The first people on Bali presumably staggered ashore through the surf by accident of wind or current, to begin contending with tigers for mastery of the island. Later, once Bali was populated and its people were believed to be tough and fierce, navigators had still more reason to give the island a wide berth — shipwreck meant death or slavery.

The first Balinese were probably hunters and gatherers, perhaps with the dogs which today appear to be essential in every home inserting themselves into the system at that time. A knowledge of gardening and of how to rear animals, especially pigs, would have followed, and about 2,000 years ago the Balinese learned how to grow rice. The social disciplines of rice farming would have played a big role in shaping the Balinese way of life.

As if the island's rugged surroundings were not enough to keep it free from an excess of visitors, the chance circumstance that Bali's best farmland is in the south also helped. As trade between the islands of what is now Indonesia developed, the Java Sea became something of a businessman's lake. Routes between Java, Borneo, Sulawesi (the Celebes) and Maluku (the Moluccas) were much travelled but there was little incentive for any trader to call at Bali's barren and unproductive north coast. The south coast, where opportunities awaited, faced directly on to the Indian Ocean, a much more difficult proposition.

All this did not protect Bali from arrivals but it did filter their numbers down to absorbable levels. The Balinese rarely felt threatened and were able to look on newcomers more as curiosities than as dangerous, to be indulged for whatever novelties, religious as well as material, that they might bring with them. The intensely fertile part of their well protected home was to become what Geertz has described as 'a forcing house for a singular civilisation'.

Away to the west Sumatra and Java began learning about Indian religions. Traders and perhaps scholars and priests arrived with ideas which seemed considerable advances on the animisms of the day. Particularly successful was the notion of the god-king. Rulers who otherwise had to rely on guile or brute force to retain their thrones learned quickly that a touch of religious justification could work wonders. This and many other Indian ideas filtered slowly through to Bali, though often much changed on the way. Inevitably these ideas travelled by way of Java, where the rise and fall of considerable civilisations produced shock waves of varying intensity which frequently embraced events in Bali as well.

Scholars have contrived to learn much about the island's early history from ancient inscriptions, and have firmly identified a Balinese king, Udayana, as ruling at least part of the island, probably around Gianyar, about 1000 AD. Bali's largest university today is named after him. Udayana and his queen, a Javanese princess, had a son, Airlangga or Erlangga, who was sent to Java for education. The times were turbulent, the emperor of Java was overthrown and Airlangga eventually took his place. In the course of rebuilding the empire Airlangga included Bali in his domain, creating a political and cultural link which endured for more than 300 years.

Airlangga is important in history but his mother, Mahendradatta, is much more famous in Balinese lore. Folk belief has it that her husband exiled her into the jungle for practising black magic. When her husband died and she became a widow, a rangda, she conspired to destroy Airlangga's kingdom by magic, reputedly because Airlangga had failed to persuade her husband not to take a second wife. Before Mahendradatta was vanquished by superior magic, she had caused great distress among the Balinese.

This episode is frequently recalled today. There are dance dramas which depict the struggle between Airlangga and Rangda (now with a capital R, as it were) and the barong dance is in fact based on the lion-like barong and Rangda contending endlessly for supremacy. The famous, or infamous, queen-turned-witch is said to be buried in a sanctuary near Kutri in Gianyar, where a weather-beaten statue depicts her as an Indian goddess of death. Her reputation lives on in a widespread belief in witchcraft and the need to take precautions against it.

The empire that Airlangga patched together was not easy to rule. Bali proved fractious time and time again, with rulers feuding among themselves and with the Javanese. In the 14th Century, Gajah Mada, Prime Minister of the great Majapahit empire, brought Bali into a domain which included also Sumatra and much of Borneo. Six hundred years later Indonesians honour him as a national hero, as the man who first united their nation, and that is why the main street in Denpasar is named after him.

But no empire lasts for ever. In the 15th Century, Majapahit was weakened by feuds within its own ruling class, the arrival of European merchant adventurers began to cut into its trading revenues, and early in the 16th Century it vanished. As all this was happening, Islam was spreading ever eastwards from Sumatra, where it had found its first beachhead in southeast Asia. Islam preached an egalitarianism which many Javanese aristocrats found distasteful, and it also tended to create trading communities where commoners could prosper. The contrast with the old concept of the god-king was so marked that when it became clear that Mataram, emerging as successor to Majapahit, would be strongly influenced by Islam an exodus to Bali began.

Thousands of Majapahit priests, nobles, soldiers, artists and artisans fled from Java to give fresh impetus to the Balinese culture. By this time Bali's centre of political gravity had moved from Gianyar, site of the oldest kingdoms, to Gelgel, near present-day Klungkung. Here a brilliant court developed, fuelled by the influx of talent from Java, which long maintained a kind of prestige leadership over all others in Bali.

A name to conjure with from this period is Batu Renggong, who became ruler of Gelgel, or Dewa Agung, about 1550. He not only brought all the Balinese kingdoms under his control but also began extending Balinese control west into Java and east to the islands of Lombok and Sumbawa. His time was one of prosperity and Gelgel became a major cultural centre. Ideas imported from Java which had filtered down to the villages were adapted to the creation of new art forms. Geertz's 'forcing house for a singular civilisation' was in full production.

Batu Rengggong's son and grandson were unable to maintain his successes, losing both overseas territories and status. They moved their court a few kilometres from Gelgel (where today virtually nothing remains) to Klungkung, as if to escape from ill fortune, but even that failed to improve matters. As the authority of the Dewa Agung declined, new kingdoms emerged, of which seven survive to this day as administrative regencies: Badung, Bangli, Buleleng, Gianyar, Negara, Karangasem and Tabanan. And Klungkung is still there, the eighth, still professing a vague kind of supremacy over the rest.

The power which had been centred in Klungkung moved first to Buleleng, where the capital and port now known as Singaraja became Bali's first important trading centre, attracting Chinese, Arab, European and other ships. Karangasem's turn came next, spurred on by military adventures in Lombok which were to lend endless complexity to Balinese life.

Nor was that the only endless complexity. Early in the 19th Century, to quote Hanna's Bali Profile, 'the patterns of Balinese power and politics were becoming almost incomprehensible even to the Balinese'. States feuded, fought, entered into alliances, betrayed each other and ran for cover in a perpetually changing drama sufficient to bewilder any observer. Only one element was more or less constant — the growing influence of the Europeans, especially the Dutch.

The Europeans

About 40 years before Batu Renggong became Dewa Agung in Gelgel, Portuguese mariners were seeking instant fortunes in Sumatra and Malaya. Thirty years before, Ferdinand Magellan had died in the Philippines after crossing the Pacific from east to west. Other navigators began filling in the gaps and soon an island named 'Java Minor' began appearing on the charts immediately to the east of 'Java Major'. It was under this name that Bali, if it was Bali, was introduced to the western world, but only as a name; it seems that for many years no western adventurer actually went ashore.

From the middle of the 16th Century onwards, however, landings were frequent and 'Java Minor' gave way on the maps to various spellings of the word Bali, usually 'Bally'. Sir Francis Drake, sailing around the world, paid a visit in 1580. Five years later a Portuguese attempt to open a trading station on Bali came to nothing when a ship from Malacca was wrecked off Bukit. Only five men survived, to be well enough treated, being given homes and wives, but not permitted to return home.

The next arrivals were Dutchmen who have become the stuff of a legend which is solemnly recited each year to thousands of tourists, and which often finds its way into print as well. The legend is that when the first Dutch ship reached Bali in 1597 the entire crew jumped ship, and it took the captain two years to round them up again. But it was not quite like that, though one part of the true story shows that Bali indeed made a powerful impression: The Dutch

Sometimes Balinese kings were drawn by fanciful beasts . .

commander was so taken by its beauty that he wanted to call it Jonck Hollandt — Young Holland.

The commander was Cornelis de Houtman and he arrived with three ships and 89 men, the survivors of 249 who had left Holland on a trading venture up to that stage marked by mutiny, murder, piracy and practically no business success. Even so, there was no mass desertion; only two men contrived not to be aboard when the ships sailed for Holland less than two months, not two years, after arriving. They settled in Gelgel, married Balinese wives and learned the Balinese language. One of them was of much assistance to the next Dutch expedition to reach Bali three years later, and eventually returned to Holland. What became of the other man is not known. The Dutch expedition also found a survivor of the Portuguese wreck about 15 years earlier, who said he was content to remain in Bali with his Balinese wife and two children.

More important than all this was the process of education which began at that time. The captain of one of de Houtman's ships wrote a substantial report about Bali, introducing it to the west, and the

. . sometimes carried by men — Two 17th Century European renderings.

Dewa Agung, inspired by a chart of the world that the Dutch gave him, demanded and was given his first lesson in world geography. It was the first stage in a relationship between the Balinese and the Dutch which was to last 350 years.

At first it was a very diffident relationship, with Dutch East India Company officials in Java remaining aloof while less elevated personages engaged in slave and opium trading. The Balinese were in great demand as slaves, the men for their dexterity and courage and the women for their beauty and artistic skills. Thousands were shipped to Batavia (now Jakarta) and even to French Mauritius. This trade was carried on by arrangement with Bali's own rulers, who enjoyed traditional rights as slavers. In return they received opium, which was easy to sell either to the Balinese gentry or to Chinese and other traders who smuggled it to other parts of the Indies, in defiance of Dutch attempts to impose a monopoly.

Just as diffident was the relationship between the Dutch and the Balinese when the Balinese went to war, usually with each other, and sought support. Normally, at least for the first two hundred years or so, the Dutch chose not to get involved, confining their activity to driving Balinese armies back from Java. The reasons for this restraint were complicated, usually involving preoccupations elsewhere in the Indies, but the result was simple: For 200 years, all through the 1600s and the 1700s, the Balinese were largely left alone.

The 1800s were different, initially because of a man who probably never heard of Bali — Napoleon Bonaparte. Napoleon led the French to victory over the Dutch in Europe. As a result the French took over all Dutch colonies, including those in the East Indies, and this brought them into conflict with the English in Asia. To forestall the French, the English seized Java, only to have to hand it back to the Dutch as part of the package of diplomatic settlements which followed Napoleon's final defeat.

During this episode, English, French and Dutch officers all came to see Bali as a strategic island well placed on the great-circle shipping route between Europe and east Asia, and between Asia and Australia. A contest developed for the affections of the various Balinese rulers. In 1814 a British military mission visited the island briefly, and a year later Stamford Raffles, the Englishman who was later to found Singapore, also sailed in. Later his widow Sophia would write that the Balinese were not so numerous as a nation as to be dangerous to the English, 'and yet sufficiently numerous to be in the highest degree useful'. This interest alarmed the Dutch, who tried all the harder to reserve the island for themselves. They knew Raffles was looking for one to colonise and worried that he would pick Bali. By the time he selected Singapore in 1819, the Dutch were committed to negotiations with the Balinese rulers which were to continue through many tortuous decades.

The frustrations of the whole tedious business caused the Dutch missions which arrived so often from Java to become increasingly impatient. The Balinese responded by being increasingly intractable and the inevitable result was a series of colonial wars. The first was in 1846, when the Dutch sent a military expedition to help three truculent rulers see the light of western reason. It achieved success, winning a battle for the town of Buleleng and exacting a treaty of submission from the north coast Balinese.

Celebration was premature, however. Truculence continued and two years later the Dutch felt obliged to go to war once more. This time a young prince, now a hero of Balinese history, named Gusti Ktut Jilantik showed how well he had learned the lessons of the first conflict. The Dutch did well at first, but when they pursued the Balinese to the small town of Jagaraga, behind Buleleng, they were quickly in trouble. Brilliantly led by Jilantik, the Balinese trapped the Dutch force, broke its discipline, forced a retreat and then turned the retreat into a rout. Balinese losses were heavy, about 2,000 men dead to the Dutch force's 264, but the victory was impressive. Its main result was to make a third war inevitable.

It began a year later. This time the fighting was confused, widespread and prolonged, marked by fluctuating fortunes. Casualties included both the Dutch General and Jilantik, and when the two sides at last agreed to discuss peace it was more from exhaustion than from clearcut victory or defeat. Both sides had learned expensive lessons and both were reluctant in the future to embark on courses which might lead to further conflict.

Yet there could be no return to the previous cool and distant relationship between the Balinese and the Dutch. The three wars, in 1846, 1848 and 1849, were a watershed in Bali's affairs. Inevitably, the Dutch, with their arms, their money, their growing control throughout the archipelago, came to enjoy ever-increasing influence in Bali. The island was about to embark on more than a century of increasingly rapid change.

Five years later Buleleng came under direct Dutch control, and step by step this control spread throughout the island over the next half century. Political authority moved steadily, kingdom by kingdom, from the rulers to Dutch colonial officers, some of whom became serious and sympathetic students of Balinese culture. It was a process not without stress, however, and some powerful dramas remained to be played out.

Meanwhile more and more ships began to show up in the seas around Bali. The island became a popular point for buying provisions. In 1780 a British ship, the Tartar Galley, paid $2 a head for bullocks and $1 a head for pigs, and offered cutlery and opium for lesser purchases. The East India Directory of 1843, a book of sailing instructions, said Bali was a good place to get fresh water, bullocks, hogs, poultry, rice, pumpkins, sugarcane and plantains though 'the chief of Bally Town sometimes makes a demand of two muskets as a kind of port dues'. All manner of ships routinely called for supplies and some merchants began looking for trading opportunities in Bali and its nearby islands.

Outstanding among the merchants was a Dane, Mads Lange, who did well in Lombok, became deeply involved in wars there,

Mads Lange — adventurer, trader, Kuta pioneer, and great-great-grandfather of a king.

eventually found himself on a losing side, and in 1839 moved to Kuta, in south Bali near Denpasar. He opened a trading 'factory' there, made so much money that soon he had a fleet of more than ten ships trading as far afield as Singapore and China, and played an important role as well in dealings between the Dutch and the Balinese rulers.

In a way Lange can be considered just another of the dozens of Europeans who during that age carved little empires for themselves in as many corners of southeast Asia. James Brooke, the first 'white rajah' of Sarawak, was another and more could be found on various islands and up various rivers. But Lange had a touch of style which most of the others lacked, a flair for grand living, politics and adventure as well as for making a fortune, and he became famous throughout the Indies.

Lange died in 1856 at the age of 49, just as he was planning to return to Denmark. He and his brother Hans, who died two years later, were both buried in Kuta. Their grave is to be found in a Chinese cemetery near 'Gang Tuan Langa' or 'Mr Lange's Lane', the only street in Bali named after a foreigner. These are not all that remains, however. The family name has survived in a remarkable manner, to such effect that the installation of a new king in Malaysia in 1984 made headlines on the other side of the world, in the Danish town of Odense.

Lange had three children, one of them a son who died while in school in Singapore. Another son, Emil, whose mother was Balinese, also went to school in Singapore and later moved to Sarawak where he became secretary to Rajah Brooke. He married there and fathered a large family. His descendants all eventually left Sarawak and settled mainly in Singapore where no fewer than thirteen Langes are listed in the 1984 telephone book. Other descendants are scattered across the world from England to Australia.

Mads Lange's third child was a daughter, her mother Chinese, named Cecilia. She too went to school in Singapore, where she eventually met and married Sultan Abu Bakar of Johor, ruler of the southernmost state in peninsular Malaysia. She had two children, a daughter who married the Sultan of Pahang, another Malaysian state, and a son, Ibrahim, who succeeded his father as Sultan of Johor in 1895 and ruled until his death in 1959. Nor was he merely long-lived; he was an energetic, shrewd, determined ruler — and he was grandfather of Sultan Mahmood, the present ruler of Johor who in 1984 became also Malaysia's Yang Dipertuan Agung, or Paramount Ruler. That was when a Danish newspaper published its report about a hometown boy making good, four generations later. It is to be wondered how much of the vigour of this line of succession is to be attributed to that remarkable Dane who more than a century earlier had made a name for himself in Bali.

A frenzy of death

But this is to run more than a century ahead of our story. While men like Mads Lange found Bali generally congenial, the Dutch who attended to political matters faced still more trouble. They had two more battles to fight, in 1858 and 1868, the southern kingdoms continued to feud among themselves, and a bitter war against the Dutch on the neighbouring island of Lombok in the 1890s is not to be separated from the history of Bali itself.

Finally, the turn of this century found old-world Bali engaged in a desperate, doomed attempt to stem the tide of change. The buildup to this last-ditch stand was long and complicated but the actual trigger was an old issue of contention between the Balinese and the

Dutch: the looting of ships wrecked on the reefs which encircle the island.

The Balinese kings regarded wrecks as their property while the Dutch, drawing on a completely different maritime and legal tradition, insisted that wrecks remained the property of their original owners. Since wrecks around Bali were frequent, the point arose frequently, usually with angry feelings on both sides. In 1904 a ship from Banjarmasin in Borneo was wrecked near Sanur and was looted. Its Chinese owner demanded compensation and the Dutch presented a bill to the Raja of Badung on his behalf.

The ruler refused to pay and won support from two other rulers, who were all eager, even desperate, to stop the erosion of their powers and privileges. The Dutch, under great pressure from commercial interests to bring an end to such defiance, sent yet another military expedition. Their troops marched to the palace in Denpasar, expecting to encounter only token resistance from a much inferior force. What they actually encountered shocked them, rang around the world and made a permanent impression on their colonial administration.

A procession emerged from the palace gates, led by the raja in a palanquin carried by four bearers. He was dressed in white, laden with jewellery, and carried an ornate kris, or wavy-bladed dagger. His entire household followed — wives, children, ministers, priests, servants, all wearing their jewellery, all dressed in white. There was no sound.

A hundred metres or so from the Dutch soldiers the procession stopped. The raja stepped to the ground, gave a signal, and a priest stabbed him in the heart. Immediately a frenzy of killing began with some of the Balinese killing themselves and each other and others hurling themselves suicidally at the soldiers, who were forced to open fire in self-defence. More and more people poured from the palace to join the carnage. A similar frenzy of death broke out at another palace in the same town later the same day.

Thus did the Dutch encounter the rite of puputan, or mass ritual suicide. Nor was it their only encounter. A bitter little war in Klungkung ended similarly two years later. In Hanna's words, 'after 600 years of rule in Bali, the lineal descendants of the Majapahit emperors were decimated, the ritualistic victims of relentless Western intrusion'. More private suicides occurred as dignitaries in other parts of Bali chose death as a superior solution to their problems with the Dutch. The puputan participants are much honoured in Bali today, especially by a memorial near the Bali Museum in Denpasar which shows men, women and children marching to their deaths.

These grisly events had a vast impact on public opinion back in Holland and on official attitudes, and it can even be argued that the deaths in Denpasar and Klungkung were not in vain. They helped the Dutch into a process of soul-searching about what they were doing in their colonies and led to major policy changes. In Bali's case, this saw their administration assume the style of a trusteeship which tried to balance modernisation with the need to protect Bali's unique culture. Not all Balinese will agree today that the Dutch succeeded in this, but they might allow that the survival of their culture owes much to the puputans of 1906 and 1908.

Up to this time colonial exploitation had largely bypassed Bali, concentrating on Java and Sumatra. Very little land in Bali had been handed over for plantations and few of the big Dutch companies had bothered even to set up offices in Bali. From now on they would find it much more difficult to do so. No more plantation development was permitted and the Balinese were thus spared the near-slavery lives of plantation workers. Trading companies which would have followed in the wake of plantation development found little reason to show interest in Bali. The large Dutch enclaves which appeared in many other towns in the Indies found only small counterparts in Bali.

At the same time the colonial administration discouraged the arrival of foreigners — including Christian missionaries, though this led frequently to political pressure at high levels and to an occasional concession. The preachers who were allowed in were never present in numbers enough to threaten the Balinese religion. All this the administration backed up with a dedication to learning more about the Balinese way of life, which led to brilliant scholars producing literally libraries of work.

The period also saw a major development in Balinese artistic life. I mentioned earlier that the courtly life of the Gelgel era developed new forms, but they were not the forms we know today. These were to arise from another historical development, the decline of the courts until they could no longer afford their traditional role as patrons of the arts. This role moved to the villages, to the world of the commoners.

Music is a case in point. The courtly music of old Bali was styled on the Javanese, elegant and refined and sweet. When it moved out of the palaces into the villages, almost literally from indoors to outdoors, it became louder, faster, infinitely more robust. Much the same process was to be repeated with other art forms as the native Balinese genius threw aside high-caste restraints and developed folkish styles of its own.

An indirect chronicler of this era of change in Bali was the German novelist Vicki Baum, whose A Tale of Bali about the puputan of 1906 is based on a manuscript given her by a Dr Fabius who had lived many years on the island. Here is a passage in which Pak, a rice farmer, considers what he has been told about Dutchmen:

'It was said that the white men were tall as giants and tremendously stout and strong. Their eyes were without colour but they could see quite well, although they moved about like blind men, as stiffly and clumsily as figures of stone. It was uncertain . . . whether they had souls and whether any part of the divine nature dwelt in them as it did in every creature in Bali. . . . They were clever and powerful beyond measure, probably because they had fair skins like many of the gods. . . . On [their coins] was stamped the picture of a long-nosed, full-breasted but not unpleasant looking goddess.'

Writing in the 1930s, Vicki Baum concluded that the Dutch deserved high credit for their administration of Bali over the previous 30 years. 'Scarcely anywhere in the world are natives free to live their own lives under white rule so happily and with so little interference and change as in Bali,' she said; 'and I would like to believe with Dr Fabius that the self-sacrifice of so many Balinese at that time [of the puputans] had a deep significance, since it impressed on the Dutch the need for ruling this proud and gentle island people as considerately as they have done, and so kept Bali the paradise it is today.'

Other writers of the 1930s echoed this view and we have been handed down a picture of life so idyllic that those enjoying it would have liked it to continue for ever. Of course, it was never like that, except for small numbers of fortunate people. No matter how benign the colonial administration might have been it was still a colonial one, with all the inequities and prejudices that this involved. It could not last, and would have failed eventually even if the Japanese had not sailed in during World War II.

They did, forcibly but without opposition, in February, 1942, taking Bali as a base for their invasion of Java a week later. Three hard years followed, with food and medical shortages growing steadily worse and the island's transport system grinding to a standstill. As the beaten Japanese departed the Dutch endeavoured to return. It was a vain hope because the independent republic of Indonesia had been proclaimed and would eventually prevail, but it was a hope which was to shed much blood.

Some of it was shed near Tabanan in November, 1946, when a Dutch force trapped a party of almost 100 Balinese guerrillas led by Colonel Gusti Ngurah Rai, only 29 years old. Earlier Ngurah Rai had written to a Dutch officer: 'We people of Bali want only our freedom and for the Dutch to leave Bali. We are prepared to fight until our wishes are achieved.' Fight he and his men did, to the death, in an episode reminiscent of the puputan in Denpasar 40 years earlier.

The spot, named Margarana, is now a heroes' cemetery for 1,372 men and women who died during the fighting in Bali, some Muslim and Christian but most Balinist, as indicated by the swastikas on their memorial stones (not gravestones, because their bodies were cremated). A high level military ceremony is held there each year, and the hero of that 1946 battle is remembered also in the name of Ngurah Rai airport near Denpasar, the only one in Bali.

In an attempt not to lose their entire Indies empire, the Dutch then included Bali in a 'Republic of East Indonesia' which they sponsored as a rival to the revolutionary republic based in Java. For political reasons they also devoted much effort to restoring Bali's broken-down economy, winning many friends among the Balinese in the process. About all that this achieved in the long run, however, was a degree of suspicion between Denpasar and Jakarta when Bali was eventually incorporated in the new Indonesian republic in 1950. Jakarta thought that too many people in Bali had co-operated too easily with the Dutch and Bali came quickly to resent the incompetence, arrogance and corruption of the Jakarta administration. Much more trouble lay ahead.

The wrath of the gods

When the centenary of the Krakatau, or Krakatoa, volcanic catastrophe was celebrated — as it were — in 1983, some scholars drew attention to the eruption's impact on political events. It had direct effects on a long-simmering religious and political revolt in West Java, on a war between the Dutch and the Acinese in northwest Sumatra, and on relations between Dutch colonial rulers and their masters back in Holland.

One effect was military. Fighters on either side in the Aceh war thought the explosions they heard were made by enemy cannon fire. Another effect was political. So many thousands of people were in distress that relief operations — or the lack of them — became an instant issue. A third effect involved popular attitudes to the fact that the disaster had taken place, with many people believing it signalled divine anger. Long after the eruption had ended and long after the survivors had rebuilt their lives, the political and religious reverberations continued.

In recent years an American film-maker gave a rather rubbishy production a title which put Krakatau east of Java instead of in the straits to the west. What lies to the east of Java, of course, is Bali, which has had volcanic and other disasters of its own. As with Krakatau a century ago, Bali's most recent eruption can be linked with subsequent political events, including a massacre and a change of government.

It is natural that volcanoes should figure strongly in Balinese life. Without them the island would not be so fertile because its soils are enriched by minerals discharged during eruptions. Without them Bali would be a much poorer island, much less cultivated, much less productive, much less cultured — and the price the Balinese pay for this bounty is the perpetual threat and occasional reality of eruption. No wonder that volcanoes are regarded with religious awe, and that Gunung Agung is seen to stand at the centre of a cosmic universe, directly beneath a many-tiered heaven.

In the early 1960s, when President Sukarno was ruling in Jakarta, even the normally exuberant Balinese had been reduced to a melancholy condition. Here is part of Hanna's description of those years:

'A clique of Sukarnoists, civilian and military, more of them Javanese than Balinese, dominated the island, competing vigorously with one another for power and wealth. They exercised administrative authority mainly to reward themselves and their friends and to punish their enemies, a category of persons which came to include many of the island's leading citizens. Their offices were packed with badly trained and badly paid bureaucrats who demanded bribes before performing even the most routine services. After having been one of the best administered regions in the archipelago in the late colonial period, Bali became one of the worst neglected and most exploited provinces of the new republic [of Indonesia].'

Political parties competed recklessly for influence, corruption ran riot, a blackmarket flourished, roads decayed and were not repaired, transport began grinding to a standstill and the great majority of the Balinese — while a few became rich — fell into poverty not much removed from that they had known during the Japanese occupation years. Some believed that because President Sukarno had a Balinese mother (and a Javanese father) they could look to him for help, but they soon learned this was not so.

On the contrary, he exploited Bali just as any colonialist or entrepreneur might have wanted to. When he came to Bali, usually with a large party of officials and cronies, it was to command special dance performances, to call for, admire and take home — often without payment — the finest works of art, to treat the island as his own. On a hilltop above the sacred spring and temple at Tampaksiring he turned a former Dutch resthouse into a palace from which he could look down on the separate bathing places for men and women. Any women who took his fancy would be virtually kidnapped to the palace above.

As I mentioned earlier, one had a daughter as a result, who today runs a small handcraft shop in Tampaksiring. That she is the daughter of a former president seems not to have made her life any easier. Hanna says that advance parties of soldiers used to shoot pigs and dogs in the village streets so that fastidious Muslim visitors would not be offended by the sight of them. 'Most Balinese preferred pigs and dogs to state visitors,' Hanna comments.

Late in 1962 preparations began for Eka Dasa Rudra, the most sacred of all Balinese festivals, at Besakih, the mother temple on the slopes of Gunung Agung. Why it was decided to revive the festival, in theory held every 100 Balinese years but in practice not observed for several centuries, is not clear. Premonitions of approaching disaster and evidence of divine displeasure in the form of a plague of rats in 1962 were involved. So, it seems, were political interests eager to get any public credit they could by any means. It was to be literally a distraction from hard times. On the other hand, some religious leaders argued that the time was not ripe, that the event should be postponed or even cancelled, even that the calculations had been done wrongly and that the date set was 15 years too early.

In the end President Sukarno took a hand. He announced that he would attend, and that left no room for further argument. Eka Dasa Rudra was to go ahead as a kind of command performance, starting on March 8, 1963. A conference of foreign travel agents, called to help promote Indonesia's then pathetic tourist industry, would be brought to Bali for the climax. No one expected that this mishmash of religious organisation, civilian interference and meddling from Jakarta would produce anything except a fiasco. What they got was a disaster.

On February 18, Gunung Agung began emitting smoke and ash and minor earthquakes were felt. The religious authorities wanted to call off the festival but were overruled. The festival began on schedule — but with the mountainside coated with ash, with smoke swirling around, and with Sukarno absent. Here is part of Hanna's description:

'On March 12, while the ceremonies still continued, Mt Agung began to throw out mud and rock. On March 17 great rivers of molten lava were pouring down the mountainside. Flames leaped higher and higher into the sky; smoke and volcanic ash blotted out the sun and darkened the countryside. The Besakih temple complex, situated on a sharp ridge and bracketed by deep valleys through which the lava flowed, escaped the main line of destruction. But it was covered deep in hot ash; the palm fibre thatch of the shrines was set ablaze, as were some of the wooden superstructures. The main sanctuaries themselves were miraculously spared, but the very first casualty was [an] ornamental gateway built to honour Sukarno.

'By then not only Bali but the whole of the nation was aware that Mt Agung had terminated the ceremonies which Sukarno had ordered. Javanese as well as Balinese interpreted this as a divine judgement upon the Sukarno regime. Not only the island of Bali but the eastern end of Java, including the city of Surabaya, was darkened at midday by dense clouds of smoke and ash such as no one could remember ever having experienced before.'

Thousands died. According to Howard Palfrey Jones, the American ambassador in Jakarta, the first victims perished 'on a sunny day in February'. In his book Indonesia — The Possible Dream, he says that on that day 800 men, women and children were kneeling in prayer in the Besakih temple when a rumbling sound came from within the great mountain. Jones continues: 'The people on their knees prayed harder. Did this mean the god was angry? Or was he simply acknowledging their gifts? The rumbling became a fiercer roar, and they knew the answer. And then came the explosion that rocked the earth beneath them as though the world were coming to an end. As they looked tongues of fiery red lava licked out of the huge mouth above them. The tongues grew longer and longer until they became great rivers of fire, pouring down the mountain toward them. The people had time to escape, but no one moved. . . .'

I have not been able to find confirmation of this account but it could derive from a tragedy described in Anna Mathews' book, The Night of Purnama. She and her photographer husband lived near Gunung Agung throughout the eruption and her book is an engrossing, disturbing account of what happened. She relates a story told by a boy ordered by his father, a priest, to go down the mountain to safety.

The boy departed just before dawn, amid explosions and earthquakes, but hid among trees and watched as his father and the villagers, men, women and children, dressed in their best and assembled in the temple. There they lay together in family groups and covered themselves with sheets of white cotton, signifying purity. The priest prayed and rang his bell . . . until 'the lava leapt the temple wall and blanketed them. Not even a baby cried. The lamps disappeared in the uprush of poisonous black smoke, and the boy knew they were dead when the bell stopped ringing'. Ten days later the Mathews climbed to the village and calculated that the lava over that temple, still hot and steaming, was between 40 and 50 metres deep.

But the world came only slowly to learn that Bali had been struck by disaster. The first substantial messages finding their way through Indonesia's then chaotic communications reached the Singapore Straits Times on March 21 and appeared in the next morning's newspaper, ten days after the eruption began.

They described earthquakes, clouds of smoke from the volcano, Denpasar radio appealing for volunteers, Surabaya in darkness shortly after noon, ash falling on Jakarta. Thousands of people were reported to be streaming away from the volcano while stones 'as big as houses' rained down on the eastern town of Amlapura. A bus with 70 bodies had reached Klungkung.

The following day the newspaper said that police had estimated the dead at 1,100, aircraft had reported lava flows on all sides of the volcano, and President Sukarno had proclaimed a national disaster. A day later the death toll was put at 1,500 and 50,000 people were said to be homeless. The police had put up roadblocks to prevent refugees returning home to look for relatives.

A report by an American journalist who reached Singapore on March 26 said that all the white cloth in the Klungkung hospital has been used for wrapping bodies, and that a five-year-old girl who died of burns while he was there had been wrapped in purple and white striped material, rolled in a coconut mat and carried away for burial.

The worst hit area, he said, was northeast of the volcano, where 75,000 people were trapped between the lava and the sea. Rocks as big as footballs were being hurled five miles and the lava flow at times was faster than people could run. He had heard reports that 700 people had been found dead in a temple; another that 200 had died in a mosque. Everything within five miles of the volcano was blackened and the crater was still belching smoke. The island had become a hellhole for thousands who had lost their families, their possessions, their means of livelihood.

Inevitably, also, reports began emerging about scandals — about officials who did nothing, about how the conference of travel agents was flown in on military planes while the Indonesian Red Cross was crying out for transport, about how the same agents were lavishly entertained in Denpasar while refugees were starving only 40 miles away. One reporter wrote about the constant bafflement he and his colleagues felt at officials who smiled broadly while they read out the latest casualty figures.

These figures kept on climbing. Before the end of March they were put at 11,000 dead, 77,000 refugees, another 30,000 awaiting rescue, 350,000 people out of work and destitute. A fifth of Bali had been laid waste. The 200 earlier reported to have died in a mosque turned out to be 45. They had taken shelter there and when a river of hot water attacked the building had climbed into the ceiling, only to fall one by one into the flood as the building disintegrated. Only one person survived, though he lost his entire family; he is still living in Amlapura.

The March figures were probably too high, however. A report to the Indonesian Parliament in May put the death toll at 1,584 and the number of refugees at 78,000. Later that month perhaps another 100 people died when Gunung Agung erupted again, and buried the north coast road beneath 18 inches of sand and gravel. An informed guess years later was that about 2,000 people had died.

Anna Mathews' book about the disaster, from the viewpoint of a person dangerously close to the events it describes, can have no equal as an account of a major eruption in progress and for a picture of a Balinese community under stress. It contains also a remarkable pointer to the growing disorder which was shortly to embrace all of Indonesia. When Mrs Mathews and her husband left Bali, she chanced to leave a copy of the manuscript of her book with friends in Surabaya. All other copies she deposited in the British embassy in Jakarta — which was shortly after looted during troubles connected with the formation of Malaysia. All copies of her book were lost, except for the one in Surabaya. The looting of the embassy was harbinger of another disaster to come.

In Amlapura I asked people to tell me about that traumatic time 20 years before. Here are two accounts which resulted:
'Small earthquakes woke us up about 2 am. I looked out and saw the mountain apparently on fire. We fled to the temple ground and camped there for three months, as long as the quakes continued. At first there was dust and sand falling on us. The river was in flood with hot water and the bridges were broken. We were all very frightened. There were heavy quakes for two nights and the eruption lasted a month.

'Amlapura was cut off for two days. The river in flood carried big trees and big stones. The lava in Subangan [an Amlapura suburb] was four metres deep. There is still a house there with its former second floor now serving as its first floor. On the evening of the fourth day the flood destroyed a mosque at Subangan with 40 or 50 people inside. There was one survivor but he lost his entire family.

'Help came from the United Nations and from other countries but most of it never got here; it was eaten up by government officials. After three months so many people had left that Amlapura was a ghost town. We went to Lombok.'

The second account came from a man who had been a child at the time:
'Before the eruption there was a grumbling sound from the mountain, and just before the eruption, before daylight, a sharp earthquake. We were sleeping. We ran outside. About 9 am the big eruption began, and everyone was very frightened with many people weeping and praying. They were not worried about saving their possessions but only about their children and themselves. The sound like boiling water from the mountain was very loud and the ground was trembling. After the eruption there was dust and sand everywhere. People covered their heads against it. There was heavy rain as well. The mountain kept erupting and we children were excited to see the fire falling. We were not frightened — it was too interesting.

'Refugees from the mountain villages came pouring into Amlapura. The river was so full of debris that it blocked itself and

Gunung Agung today, sleeping quietly.

flooded the area around it with hot water — hot, like this coffee, too hot to touch.

'We stayed two months in a tent. No rocks were thrown as far as Amlapura, so it was safe, but there were many earthquakes and also whirlwinds stirring up the dust. My parents I remember were very worried but I was happy because there was so much to see.

'Later there were many political problems. The Communist Party was very active. The government sent rice, sarongs, milk, medicines, canned food, doctors, soldiers, and there was much work for everyone to open up roads and repair bridges. Difficulties continued for months. Schools were closed for two or three months and the electricity was off for three years.

'According to the people the gods were angry with us and the eruption was the result of his anger. There were many ceremonies and sacrifices, even with live animals being thrown into the volcano crater.'

Then came 1965. The island was strung taut, humming like a hawser about to break. People were angry with the politicians and their followers who had broken with the old ways, fearful that the gods who had sent fire and wrath upon them would do so again. If that hawser were to break, who knew what damage its lashing ends might cause. And break it did.

Trouble began with a coup attempt in Jakarta. A conspiracy of communists, Sukarnoists and others made their move on the night of September 30. Their successes endured for only a matter of hours but during those hours they kidnapped, tortured and murdered five army generals and a lieutenant they mistook for another general. That night has gone into Indonesian history, and the national consciousness, as Gestapu, from the initials and first syllables of words meaning the September 30 Incident.

As news of the murders spread through the islands, fury against the communists in particular was unrestrained. The result was a massacre. At times the army led, at times the people acted spontaneously. The full story of events throughout Indonesia has never been, never will be told. It is enough that the most horrifying stories imaginable are probably true.

In Bali, trouble was slow to arrive, though there was never much doubt that it would, eventually, so tense was the atmosphere. October and November passed without major incident. But in December a clash between the army and communists in the west of Bali triggered, in one correspondent's words, 'a frenzy of savagery'. Whole villages, including children, took part in an island-wide witchhunt for communists, he wrote. They were slashed and clubbed and chopped to death. Whole villages which had embraced communism were wiped out and 'night after night the sky flared red over Bali as villages went up in flames, and thousands of communists, or people said to be communists, were hunted down and killed'. In the end General Suharto, the new focus of power in Jakarta who would soon take over from Sukarno as President, had to send paratroops to Bali to restore order.

The correspondent, John Hughes, of the Christian Science Monitor, who collected his information after the event, quoted 'knowledgeable sources' as saying that 40,000 people died in two weeks, and said other estimates ran as high as 80,000. The London Economist collected information from a team of Indonesian graduates and calculated that perhaps a million people died in Indonesia, 100,000 of them in Bali. This is the highest estimate published and has not been generally accepted.

Nor are even the lower estimates necessarily given credence. Arnold Brackman, a journalist on the spot who later wrote a book entitled The Communist Collapse in Indonesia, said in it that virtually all non-communist and non-Indonesian correspondents in the area in 1965 and 1966 were sceptical about the massacre figures. An almost total lack of photographs, films and eyewitness accounts makes even speculation, let alone calculation, difficult. There is agreement, nonetheless, that many people disappeared and were probably murdered. An Associated Press journalist in Bali a few months after what was generally described as a massacre concluded that there had been no mass murder but that in every other village one or two people had been slain. (Since Bali has hundreds of villages, this would still amount to a massacre.) Descriptions of villages in flames are also queried: 'There was no need,' I was told.

What is not in doubt is that the communists of Bali paid dearly for their policies. In retrospect, these can be seen to have been extremely dangerous, even suicidal. While in Java and Sumatra the communists had been extremely careful not to criticise Islam, in Bali they had derided religious and cultural traditions and mocked temple observances. 'The communists' fatal mistake had been to try to impose an alien ideology crudely and harshly upon an island in a state of perpetual enchantment with its own mystique,' Hughes wrote. Nor is there any doubt that the Balinese in general looked on the events of 1965 and 1966 as a kind of purification, an end to pollution, a purging of evil. So much had gone wrong, including the Gunung Agung disaster, that only a return to the old ways, a rejection of the communists, could bring salvation. More, salvation need not be just abstract, but personal and physical as well. One does not seek discussion of what happened in 1965 and 1966 but the subject crops up from time to time, and then one frequently hears the sentiment expressed that if the communists had not died, the speakers would have. It was a matter of survival.

Meanwhile the damage that Gunung Agung had wrought lay all around. The closing years of the Sukarno regime, the early ones of Suharto's, were not times when an area of desolation at the lonelier end of one of Indonesia's lesser islands was a matter for urgent national attention. The political scene in Jakarta was confused, the administrative machine was decrepit, the economy was a shambles. Crucial issues far more demanding than Bali's jousted for urgent attention.

Slowly the new administration gained in confidence, skill and resources, and eventually some small share of all of these was available for rehabilitation of the devastated area. Slowly work picked up speed and began to show results. The visitor today finds little to remind him of the eruption of 20 years before. So much has been achieved, indeed, that late in 1983 President Suharto visited the mountain to mark Indonesia's annual Reforestation Day, to view the greening of a desert.

Lower down the slopes, farms and villages have been re-created. The diligence of the farmers and the irrepressible fertility of the Balinese soil — even richer now as the volcanic ash sinks in — have worked a miracle. The traveller by road east from Denpasar to Amlapura, and then west along Bali's north coast, sees fields, plantations, gardens, thriving villages.

Dr Ir Gusti Made Tantera, the head of Bali's Forest Service, told me that a big tree-planting campaign on Gunung Agung's upper slopes was basic to Bali's overall forest management. First priority is to ensure that forests exist to conserve rainwater for irrigation; second is to produce some timber if that does not conflict with the first aim; and the third priority is to serve a social function. Work on Gunung Agung will serve all three causes.

As befits an island where the remarkable never ceases to happen, Bali has a unique tree which may help make the task easier. A mountain casuarina native to Bali and nearby islands has turned out to be so well adapted to volcanic conditions that it can survive severe burning. 'It lives where others die,' Dr Tantera said. It grows in poor soils, it traps nitrogen from the air to make those soils more fertile, it is attractive, and it grows up to 25 metres high. Scientists are looking hard at this casuarina and it may be planted on a large scale, along with the pines and eucalypts now being grown. This is typical of Bali. Disaster leads to regeneration. The wounds of the 1960s are mostly healed and even the scars are disappearing.

No more Nyomans

n London in 1964, Tarquin Olivier, son of the famous actor Sir Laurence Olivier, published an account of recent travels in southeast Asia. He had visited Bali and there had met a girl whom he identifies in the book as 'Sri', then about 16. 'Sri had asked me to her family's compound for dinner that evening,' he wrote. 'I thought of the tilt of her nose and upper lip, her black slanting eyes and her hair which was silky and blue-black, folded within itself so that it hung down the back of her head in two loops. I had known her for two weeks. . . .'

Her family made him welcome, though it was not normally done for Balinese girls to have anything to do with foreigners, or even other Indonesians. Perhaps they knew he would be leaving soon, not staying long enough to be a nuisance. That evening at dinner, 'Sri was looking lovely with a red hibiscus behind her ear and tiny gold earrings. A long strip of scarlet cloth was wound round and round her body. Her shoulders were bare and her skin mellow in the glow of the oil-lamp. . . .'

Later they sat together and held hands. 'In Bali,' Sri said, 'we have a custom when it rains. We cut a banana leaf and hold it over our heads to keep dry. And when it stops raining we throw the banana leaf away.'

'So I have read,' Olivier replied, knowing what she was about to say but not wanting to spoil the beauty of it. His narrative continues:

'I hope,' she hesitated and looked down at our hands, 'you will not treat me as your banana leaf.'

The next day they took two bicycles and food and headed out into the countryside. At one stage Sri pretended to be Javanese, speaking Indonesian to drink-stall girls because she did not want them to know she was Balinese. 'My family understands me,' she said, 'but anyone else would be very upset to know a Balinese girl goes alone with a European.'

They spent much time looking for a place where they could be alone but even in forest groves people intruded, passing through on their way to sundry local destinations. A deserted temple was no use because 'the demon faces' made Sri nervous. But at last, paradise! They found a grassy glade with birds and butterflies — and, it turned out, 'among the leaves about thirty boyish faces, grinning monstrously'.

Olivier concluded, when writing about this episode, that stories of fulfilled frolics in Bali were false, but he could not, he said, entirely blame the writers: 'A mere breath of Balinese air is sufficient to provoke the wildest, most passionate imagery.'

In Ubud I met the woman who had so fascinated young Olivier twenty years before, happily married, the mother of five children, successful in business, and still a beauty. Olivier visits her from time to time from his home in Hongkong.

Just as 'Sri' is not much changed, the Balinese in general still disapprove of women fraternising with foreigners, as uncounted numbers of male tourists have discovered to their chagrin. Girls are often beautiful, friendly and charming, but untouchable. There are exceptions, of course, as there are with virtually everything in Bali, but in general Balinese women are not available to visitors for casual liaisons. The women who are come from Java or other parts of Indonesia.

'I dare not go to the beach with my husband's European friends,' 'Sri' told me, 'because if I did people would think I was a prostitute. Balinese boys can go with foreign girls but not our girls with foreign men.'

This story of Olivier's brief tropical idyll is worth relating for its own sake and as an example of Balinese morality in practice. I have included it here also, however, for the sidelight it throws upon one of the most urgent problems which faces the Balinese today. Twenty years ago this young couple found their part of the lush

Balinese countryside heavily populated. Since then the population has doubled.

Because the island is tiny beside Java and far fewer people are involved, its problems have not received the same international attention but its population pressure is almost as serious — more serious if you allow for the island's high proportion of mountainous terrain. Java in 1980 had 91 million people, 690 of them to the square kilometre. In the same year Bali had just under 2.5 million people, 460 to the square kilometre. The Indonesia-wide figure was 77 to the square kilometre. Bali's farming areas are among the most densely populated regions in the world.

Until about the year 1900, Hanna writes in his Bali Profile, the island's agricultural economy was able to support the masses of the Balinese people in such rustic affluence that they enjoyed the plenty and the leisure to indulge themselves fully in the elaborate and costly ceremonialism which is the island's most distinctive characteristic. It enabled the creation of palaces, courts and temples richly ornamented with works of astonishing artistry or craftsmanship, because the land was, and is, astonishingly fertile and its farmers were, and are, astonishingly skilful, 'the envy even of the industrious Javanese'.

But population growth was about to explode. As deaths from disease and in war decreased, and as a kind of stability encouraged people to have more children, effects were startling. By 1930 Bali had 1.1 million people and pressure on farm land was mounting, with holdings becoming smaller and smaller. A generation later in 1954, despite the depredations of the Japanese occupation and Indonesia's war of independence against the Dutch, there were 1.5 million Balinese. In 1961 the population was almost 1.8 million, in 1971 it was 2.1 million, and in 1980, at the time of the latest census, it was — as stated above —just under 2.5 million. In the early 1980s projections indicated that by the year 2000 Bali would have a virtually unsupportable 4.4 million people.

Part of the answer to this critical problem lies in improving the local economy, and this is happening with better agriculture, tourism and some industry. Part of the answer lies with 'transmigration', the Indonesian government's programme to move millions of people from Java and Bali to the emptier islands. This has already resulted in complete Balinese communities existing today in Sulawesi (the Celebes), Kalimantan (Borneo) and Sumatra.

More important than either of these, however, must be birth

control, so I went to see Dr I. B. Astawa, head of the island's family planning organisation. His modern, Balinese-style office is in Renon, the government complex on the outskirts of Denpasar, not far from the Governor's headquarters. As one makes the rounds of such offices in Bali, in Indonesia generally, one becomes accustomed to meeting elderly, at least middle-aged men (never women) because the system makes much of seniority. Dr Astawa turned out to be young, in his mid-30s, alert and bearded. The change from the norm which he represented to me carried over to his family planning

There are fewer children now — but what excellent children they are. Boys dressed for a temple festival — Picture by Bob Lienhardt.

programme. Bali's is different from all others in Indonesia and may be unique in the world.

The principal difference is that it is conducted by men among men. Eighty percent of Astawa's field workers are male. This makes sense because they work entirely through the banjars, those all-pervading village groups. 'The key to the success of our programme was inviting the participation of the community through community leaders,' Astawa said. 'We've spread the family planning ideal through our very strong traditional community organisations.' It helps also that Bali has a tradition of male 'midwives', or 'midhusbands', who in the early 1980s were attending to more than half of all births. Women were coming to prefer the trained women workers in government health centres but the transition was a slow one.

Family planning in Indonesia got seriously under way in 1970, having been held up earlier by President Sukarno's opposition, by inefficiency, by the time it took the administration to get over turbulent political events in 1965 and 1966, and by the hyperinflation which followed. A national organisation was created and Java and Bali were the first target areas.

At that time Bali had an annual birthrate of 4.5 per 1,000 people and a 2.6 percent population growth rate. A survey found that the average Balinese woman would have 5.9 children. Six years later this last figure had been brought down to 3.8. By 1980 the island's growth rate, calculated from census results, was down from 2.6 percent in 1970 to 1.69 percent. This was Indonesia's second lowest provincial rate, improved upon only in Jogjakarta in Central Java. The all-Indonesia figure was 2.34 percent.

'According to feedback from Jakarta,' Astawa said, referring to his national head office, which does all the statistical work, '69 percent of all eligible couples in Bali are using family planning methods' — IUDs 70 percent, pills 15 percent and condoms 5 percent, and there is also a 7 percent sterilisation rate among women. No incentives are offered. The Indonesia-wide figure for couples using family planning methods is 45 percent.

Astawa explained how this had been achieved. 'We train the leaders of the banjars during three-day courses, persuading them of the need for family limitation for their own sakes and for the sake of the nation. The most important argument is the economic one. We tell them to tell their people that they can afford small families but that big ones would keep them in poverty.'

In addition there is a field worker for every 10,000 people, operating out of 150 clinics all over the island. The message gets through. A problem other provinces (and countries) have had from shortages of women doctors has not arisen; male doctors do the IUD insertions. 'We began with them because we had no choice,' Astawa continued, 'and had no difficulties, but now we're training government midwives to do this work.'

Curiously, however, the Balinese traditional ways which have been so helpful have lately also produced a complication. At first the campaign promoted families of three children but lately it has reduced this ideal size to two. Posters throughout Bali show a family of four, mother, father and two children, and the slogan Catur Warga, or Four Citizens, instead of the earlier Panca Warga, Five Citizens.

(The words Catur and Panca are from Sanskrit, and are distinct, of a higher class, as it were, from the usual Indonesian words for these numbers. Catur has entered standard Indonesian as the word for chess, and Panca as the first part of Pancasila, the state ideology which sets out five principles of belief. A four-faced statue looking down the four streets of a main intersection in Denpasar is known as Caturmuka — Four Faces, naturally.)

This drop from five to four produced a problem. The traditional Balinese naming system allows for three 'planned' children, Wayan or Putu or Gde (or Gede), Made and Nyoman. The name Ktut (or K'tut or Ketut), for the fourth and by some patterns for subsequent children, implies 'unplanned'. 'Our ancestors saw the ideal number of children as three,' Astawa said. 'Now we must change this attitude — no more Nyomans. We also have to persuade them that girls are as good as boys, so they do not keep on trying until they produce a son.'

The campaign is widening in other ways. Since 1980 it has promoted good nutrition as well as birth control, on the reasonable grounds that if people are to be persuaded to have fewer children they must keep alive those they do have. Astawa's workers are also teaching such money-earning skills as embroidery and sewing, and even helping women get credit to buy materials, so they spend time not employed tending children to good purpose. Family planning will also enable women to take some of the jobs that tourism is creating.

Eventually, through the family planning campaign, education, the spread of wage labour, better health and social change generally, the population of Bali will stabilise at around 3.2 million. As I mentioned earlier, in the mid-1970s a total of 4.4 million by the year 2000 had been forecast.

The prospect of pressure eased by more than a million is in itself encouragement for the government to try harder to cope with the additional people. In the meantime, Astawa notes that on his frequent visits to even the most remote villages he finds people better fed, better dressed, healthier, and in the case of children of primary school age attending smaller classes. Much of this must stem from the family planning campaign.

Better Living

r Astawa is not alone in considering that the Balinese in general are better off today than they were, say, ten years ago. Everyone I spoke to agreed that the island is more prosperous now than it was and that the benefits of prosperity have filtered down through the whole population. This does not mean that the great majority of the Balinese are not extremely poor by any western standards. Every country has poverty in some degree, according to its own definition, and by any definition Indonesia is a poor country. But Bali is today one of the more prosperous parts of Indonesia and its growth rate is sufficient to offer all Balinese steadily improving standards.

Initially this view was merely the compounded result of many general conversations. Then it was given firmer shape during an extended session with Drs D.M. Wedagama, head of the Bali Development Planning Organisation, and his senior officers. The organisation's task, Wedagama said, is to help plan development and evaluate results. Its special interests are agriculture, 'tourism based on Balinese culture', and industry and handcrafts; and its strategy is based on principles of equity between districts, economic growth and stabilisation.

The briefing involved some figures, daunting as figures always are but interesting all the same. Bali's annual income per person was 16,000 rupiahs in 1969 and 147,000 rupiahs ten years later. Then in three years it almost doubled: 1980 — 198,000 rupiahs; 1981 — 240,000 rupiahs; and 1982 — 263,000 rupiahs, or about US$425, against less than $100 less than ten years before. Over the same three years the inflation rate was 16 percent, 9.1 percent and 9.8 percent.

(The inflation rate figures are slightly lower than those for Indonesia as a whole. The country has been much plagued by this problem, and the Jakarta government has had to devote extraordinary effort towards achieving financial stability. In 1966, when General Suharto took over from President Sukarno, the rate was 640 percent. It was brought down to 10 percent in 1969 and 3 percent in 1971, but was sent soaring again by the two 'oil shocks' of the mid-1970s and by a devaluation in 1978.)

Bali's real growth over the period from 1975 to 1982, year by year, was as follows, in percentages: 11.35, 7.47, 9.23, 17.79, 17.81, 14.7, and 12.92, for an annual gain of 12.92 percent. This is impressive by any standards, especially for an overcrowded island in one of Asia's poorer nations, even allowing for a low starting point.

Nor was this entirely a matter of a tourist boom. Gains in agriculture were so substantial that Bali, despite population pressure, has regained its old status as a rice exporter, shipping out 90,000 tonnes a year. Earlier the Governor had told me that rice output was up to ten tonnes per hectare, against a 'traditional' two tonnes.

There is also diversification away from agriculture, as is to be expected with tourism racing ahead. In 1975, Wedagama said, agriculture produced 47 percent of Bali's gross domestic product. In 1981 the figure was down to 41 percent. Similarly, a census in 1971 showed 66 percent of Balinese to be engaged in agriculture. By 1980 the figure was down to 50 percent. When allowance is made for population growth this may not be so impressive because there is virtually no scope for agriculture to take in more hands. 'Employment in agriculture is saturated,' I was told. It does show people are finding jobs elsewhere, however. An indication of how extensively they are doing so was provided by a survey which showed a 35 percent change in occupation among workers within the previous five years; and 52 percent of those changes had involved switching from agriculture to other occupations.

Growth figures alone do not necessarily mean better living for all. They could simply mean the rich are getting richer. A World Bank rule of thumb to deal with this problem is that the lowest 40 percent of a population should receive more than 17 percent of gross domestic product. In Bali they receive 23 percent, 'so equity is good and distribution is improving'.

As for the old, universal difficulty which sees people giving up more or less sufficient livelihoods in the countryside to move to poor and precarious livelihoods in the towns, 'the quality of life in the mountain villages is now better than it is in the towns'. And overall, 'Bali has one of the best qualities of life in Indonesia' — a detail born out by migration to the island from other parts of Indonesia, particularly Java. The arrival of these migrants is something the government of Bali must accept as part of the price of comparative success. (One attempt was made to persuade me that migration from Java was a renewal of the exodus from Java of 400 years ago, with people coming to Bali to renew their religious roots; but the overwhelming force is surely economic.)

One does not have to accept that everything development planners do is right and good, or that their processes are always greeted with enthusiasm, to appreciate results when they arrive. The considerable increase in rice production, for instance, has been achieved at the cost of considerable dispute with farmers who would prefer to grow tastier, lower-yielding and higher-priced varieties rather than the high-yielding varieties the government promotes. Problems have arisen from the greater use of fertilisers and pesticides. Government intervention in farming at times has threatened damage to traditional rural institutions. In this sort of debate one encounters

Despite acute population pressure, Bali is again exporting rice.

more grey areas than black and white ones. The figures which result are meaningless unless they are accompanied by the appearance of improved well-being in the homes and in the fields.

But when the high-sounding maxims that emerge from planning offices are matched by visible progress, and when the plans themselves are level-headed, then it is hard not to take them seriously. When Wedagama pointed out on a map just where Bali's economic prospects lie and will be concentrated it was impossible not to accept that results will follow. Ten years ago perhaps one would have had substantial reservations, but now it is reasonable to accept that results will follow in some degree.

'Our strategy is to ensure that all eight regencies grow harmoniously in all fields,' he said, 'and that we achieve even growth between the rural and urban sectors. Therefore projects are spread all over Bali.' Projects under way include coffee and coconut replanting (replacing old trees with more productive ones), a great swathe of vinyards in villages along the comparatively arid north-west coast, fisheries development, the promotion of small industries. Everywhere the encouragement of tourism. And everywhere close attention to agriculture, to help Bali grow more rice, coffee, coconuts, fruit, vegetables, cattle, pigs.

In Ubud I was given an illustration of what wage labour can mean to village people. One can entertain a picture of happy peasants living entirely self-sufficient lives, growing all their own food and bartering their surpluses for goods they cannot produce themselves. But such an ideal remains for most people unsatisfying. What they want is money coming into the house. An enterprising Ubud woman set up a wig-making factory (using imported blond and brown hair as Balinese hair, though rich and glossy, was considered too coarse), with her workers painstakingly stitching each hair into position. From one point of view they are exploited, working hard and making derisory sums. But the factory is a cheerful place, an extension of home and village life, and the purchases the women make casts light on the rural reality.

Overwhelmingly their first interest, as soon as they had their own cash in hand, was soap, shampoo and small cosmetic items. Food, subsistence, was not the problem; the problem was keeping clean and attractive. Bathing in the irrigation canals is all very well, and doing what one can with homemade herbal soaps and unguents is all very well; but the common picture of women sitting together to pluck lice from each other's heads is not so, and that represents reality for millions of people. Eventually, sooner rather than later, they will expect better rewards and if they do not get them a kind of exploitation will become obvious; but this first phase is the start of a useful transition.

That wig factory is a tiny example of industrialisation. Much larger is the garment industry of Denpasar, Sanur and Kuta, which in December, 1983, comprised 151 establishments and employed nearly 7,000 people, mostly women. In that year exports were worth US$5.8 million, against $4.2 million the previous year. Comparable figures for coffee, a traditional and highly regarded Balinese export, were $4.1 million and $3.2 million.

The garment business began with travellers buying Balinese products and shipping them off to their home countries. From such unsophisticated beginnings it has grown rapidly, but at the expense of Balinese creativeness. Exports today typically are designed in other countries and Bali's only role has been to supply cheap and nimble-fingered female labour. The chain runs down from overseas designer and buyer, to the scores of foreigners contriving to remain in Bali to work in this business, to factory owners (Indonesians, many of them Chinese Indonesians, but rarely Balinese), to Balinese workers. The whole business gets a lift from the Made in Bali labels which result but in fact the Balinese component could be have been added in virtually any other cheap labour country. If the economy of Bali keeps on growing as rapidly as it has in recent years, rising wages will perhaps persuade the industry to move on.

Some pressure on wages in Bali is already apparent. Towards the end of 1983 the Indonesian Workers Federation said that wages in Bali averaged 1,000 rupiahs a day, the same as in Jakarta and East Java. By contrast the figure for Central Java was 600 rupiahs a day and for West Java and North Sumatra 700 a day. It is no accident that most migrants to Bali come from Central Java, one of the poorest and most densely populated regions in Indonesia.

The garment industry involved virtually no planning initiative but the government is not leaving growth to such unreliable processes. Wedagama gave examples of longer-range work. A new port is operating at Celukanbawang, on the north-west coast, as an alternative to the notoriously exposed Singaraja, where the port is now a shadow of its former self. A 1983 guidebook advised me to go there to hear the fascinating tales of sailors from all over the archipelago but when I went there to do so there was only one tiny boat in port, unloading dried anchovies. 'Singaraja is finished,' a worker exclaimed rather disgustedly, and the beach is more a scene of browsing goats than of commerce. Not that Celukanbawang was much more active when I called — only one ship and a couple of coasters, the new jetty and port buildings almost deserted under the sun, and an optimistic bar nearby locked and its bright paint fading.

Every offshore area of coral reefs has been explored for its tourist potential and an area right at the western end of the island is being turned into a marine park. Buffalo racing has been revived as a tourist attraction. Considerable effort is going into creating rural industries outside the Denpasar-Sanur-Kuta area, to try to stem the population drift in that direction.

Part of Bali which has received special attention is the 45,000-population island of Penida, between Bali and Lombok. Traditionally it was inhabited by demons, historically it has in fact been inhabited largely by exiles from a remorseless social and religious system. Penida, like the Bukit peninsula in the south of Bali, is a huge coral outcrop from the seabed with very shallow soil and rapid water run-off and as a result is arid and unproductive. An imaginative development programme will see this rather sinister territory become greener.

Electricity is another field of enterprise. The island now generates about 80 MW — and this is to be raised to 250 by the year 2000. If necessary this will be done by burning more oil, but two fascinating other options have been raised. New Zealand engineers working on an aid project have determined a considerable potential for thermal power, using undergound heat. And Dutch and Indonesian engineers are at work on a heat conversion process on the northeast coast, using differences in the temperatures of surface and deep seawater.

The idea is to use warm (30 deg) surface seawater to evaporate ammmonia, which has a low boiling point, into a vapour which will drive a turbine to generate electricity. Then cold (8 deg) seawater from 500 metres down offshore is used to condense the ammonia back into liquid. Then more warm water will turn it back into vapour again, and so on. The plant is being built at Bondalem, near Tejakula, and should be producing by the end of 1985. Gross output will be 160 kilowatts, of which 60 will be used to run the plant. The idea is neither new nor unique to Bali but it gains a little zest when matched with the Balinese notion that only trouble resides in the depths of the ocean.

About half of Bali's villages have electricity already, more than half the population is familiar with the upside-down switches (up for on, down for off) the Indonesians inherited from the Dutch, and there is considerable awareness of the effect electricity can have on life. When the Governor, perhaps tempting fate a little, asked villagers systematically what they wanted, they asked for sealed roads, electricity and water. Wedagama said it was hoped to have almost all villages supplied with electricity within five or six years. The economics are not entirely good because incomes are not suffiently high to ensure heavy enough usage for substantial revenue; but the social benefits would be considerable.

Telephones provide an illustration of the Balinese situation. They are not common and sometimes finding one can involve considerable effort. Ubud, for instance, is an important tourist centre but as far as I could determine it has only two or three telephones. None of the hotels I stayed in had one; I suspect an artist who has lived there for years has one because I heard something like a phone ringing while I was in his gallery; and perhaps one or two senior government people have them. But the usual course when you need to make a call is to go to Denpasar, 25 kilometers away.

There is rapid growth, however. A home I visited had a collection of Bali phone books covering five years. The 1979 directory had only 22 pages, was printed in large type and listed fewer than 2500 phones. The 1980 book had 27 pages. The 1981 book switched to a smaller type and had a separate page and a half for government offices and more than 4000 entries. The 1982 book continued this process with more pages and about 6000 entries; and had yellow pages as well. The telephoned word was beginning to get around the island.

More, the quality was good. When you could find a phone you normally did not have any cause for complaint, whether calling from Kuta to Denpasar to check an airline detail, or Jakarta or any other Indonesian city by the country's own Palapa satellite, or calling London or New York by one of the international ones. And telex machines were also cropping up in likely and unlikely places. The world was catching up with Bali.

None of this means that you might not encounter some small problems when you eventually get through on your telephone to other parts of Bali. Installing telephones is much easier than learning how to use them. But then, the traumas that can result are universal, liable to happen anywhere. In this sense too Bali is catching up with the world.

Better Health

 arly in 1984 an Australian current affairs television programme presented a devastating picture of health hazards awaiting tourists in Bali. The food and water are dangerous, the monkeys bite, the roads are perilous, and if one were so unfortunate as to have to go to hospital, then the future was black indeed, it said.

Reaction came quickly, with the defence claiming that Bali had been the victim of an inaccurate piece of television reporting. Qantas, Australia's airline, and Garuda, Indonesia's, who make much out of the Bali traffic, led the response, with support from people who love Bali or who stood to lose money if its popularity were diminished. In the process the actual health picture in Bali was usefully illuminated. The programme shown in Australia had given the impression that many tourists are bitten by monkeys. In fact this is rare. It gave the impression that one victim the reporters did find had cut short her visit because she was unhappy about the medical attention she had been given. In fact, according to the Qantas-Garuda response, she was booked to fly back the day after she was bitten, and travelled accordingly.

The airlines also said the programme gave the impression that tourists who had to go to hospital were admitted to the public ward in the Denpasar hospital, which was illustrated. They said it did not mention that tourists are automatically admitted to the first class ward, or that an airconditioned VIP wing is available for Aust$3.75

a day.

The programme had reported that a child's death from dehydration resulted from inadequate hospital treatment. In fact, said the airlines, she had been ill for 36 hours before being taken to hospital and died less than half an hour later. The programme featured the victim of an accident — five years before — who complained that doctors had 'drilled holes in his head', implying they had not known their business, whereas the airlines said this was conventional treatment for relieving pressure on the brain.

The programme's message that Bali is dangerous included details of total tourist deaths but did not mention that half of them arose from traffic accidents, overwhelmingly the result of dangerous riding on rented motorcycles. Nor did it mention that the death rate among tourists (admittedly a generally youthful and generally healthy group) was lower than that for an Australian community of similar size.

When the two airlines had finished dealing with such details, the main message was that tourists should not expect to find the health standards and facilities of developed countries when travelling in undeveloped ones. Nor should the Indonesian government be expected to provide high-class treatment for tourists while its own people can expect only such facilities as a poor country can provide. 'Discriminatory practices — one set of services for tourists and rich indigenes — is as much anathema to the Indonesians as it would be to anti-colonial egalitarian Australia,' wrote Max Harris, a columnist for the newspaper The Australian. And, 'a Royal Melbourne [Hospital] seems an essential for l00,000 Australians passing through, but it's a long way off in the order of priorities of the Balinese.'

And since Bali does not have a Royal Melbourne or its equivalent, tourists should use commonsense. Airline advice is that they should get anti-cholera and anti-typhoid injections before they travel, get medical advice about malaria, eat and drink with caution and discretion — and confine motorcycle riding to those with experience who can do so safely. 'Do you know what I call some of the Australians I see riding bikes around the island?' a senior policeman commented to me. 'I call them temporary Australians.'

Shortly before this little Australian fuss about health care for tourists broke out, I interviewed Dr A. Y. Iksan, chief of the Bali provincial health department's planning unit. He is from Central Java, has been 15 years in Bali, likes it, and plans to retire there. 'During my time here I've seen big changes,' he said. 'Now we have got to the stage where we have 81 health centres in Bali, each one with a doctor, so the people in each sub-district have access to medical care. There are also 300 sub-centres, each one headed by a paramedic.'

The island's primary health problems are parasitic diseases and gastroenteritis. Malaria has been controlled but not eliminated, though its incidence is among the lowest in Indonesia. Cholera occurs occasionally but has not been reported in recent years in the tourist areas of Kuta and Sanur. Bali (and the chain of islands to the east) is free from rabies, which is just as well because the island is plagued with miserable dogs.

Expectation of life for Indonesia as a whole is about 53 years and is probably higher in Bali though figures do not exist, largely because the age of many older people cannot be determined. Indonesia's infant mortality rate is 98 per 1,000. In Bali's urban areas it is probably about 70 and in the rural areas about 80, and falling. It should come down dramatically when immunisation programmes for all babies get under way within the next two or three years.

Bali has fewer nutritional problems than the rest of Indonesia and water quality is above the Indonesian average. PVC piping, much cheaper than iron, enables the government to install water systems in areas which would otherwise have to wait for years. About 52 percent of the rural population has 'protected' (but not treated) water, with walls around wells and springs to keep them clean. Piped water to villages means that thousands of people no longer have to carry water long distances.

Dr Iksan said stories about the reinfection rate — catching a new ailment — at the Denpasar hospital being abnormally high were not true, and thought it was probably the same as in other parts of Indonesia. But the hospital could be under strain as more and more people resort to the government's medical service instead of relying on their traditional healers.

During my time in Bali there was some sensitivity to complaints about the Denpasar hospital, in the suburb of Sanglah, presumably because the reinfection rate was such a subject of gossip among tourists and foreigners living in Bali. Perhaps because of this, a hospital spokesman told a Bali Post reporter that during 1983 a total of 347 tourists had sought medical help and 64 had been admitted, but only one had died. Another twelve had died outside the hospital but figured in its statistics because their bodies had been brought to the morgue. The spokesman said they were traffic accident or drowning victims or people who had committed suicide. In Dr Iksan's words, 'tourists figure in the health statistics more as accident cases than as disease victims.'

Most tourists who go to the Denpasar hospital would be intent on not spending much money. Others would seek private medical treatment. One who did, a West Australian who cut his leg when he fell into a drain, later wrote to a newspaper praising the attention he had been given. His doctor had given a local anaesthetic, stitched the wound, and examined the results three times over the next few days. Later the Australian consulted his own doctor in Perth, who said all was well and no further treatment was needed. The Australian doctor's bill for this advice came to Aust$11.50. The Bali doctor's bill (not including prescription items) for treatment and follow-up examinations had been $20.

I also asked Dr Iksan about the mental health of the Balinese, a much conjectured point because of their intricate culture. He said psychiatrists had told him the Balinese have a balanced way of life which permits the release of pent-up emotions through customary activity. He thought there were fewer mental cases, proportionate to population, than elsewhere in Indonesia. Other commentators have concluded that rituals have the effect of releasing fears and tensions and freeing the Balinese from fear of their gods and demons.

Later I had a chance to check this with a man with special knowledge. Bali's only mental hospital is in the small town of Bangli and is headed by Dr Denny Thong, originally from Sumatra. His is the hospital which Bill Dalton's Indonesia Handbook, one of the most successful tourist guides to Indonesia, describes in these terms: 'If you freak out on mushrooms you're sent to the psyche-hospital in Bangli, where they still use 18th Century methods such as the infamous "water treatment".'

Here is Dr Thong's response: 'The primitive methods rumoured about may have been true in older times before the advent of modern treatment, but since I became director of this hospital in 1967 we have never used them. Treatment in the mental hospital is far from perfect, but we do our utmost with our available means and manpower to provide treatment as humane as possible.'

This is surely much more humane than traditional Balinese practice. Though various forms of harmless insanity are tolerated in the villages, the fate of a person who becomes aggressive is grim. Traditionally he has been confined permanently in stocks. Old documents tell precisely how this is to be done and give the practice a kind of legitimacy. In 1983 alone sixtynine people, mostly in remote villages, were released from such captivity and brought to Bangli for treatment.

The hospital itself belies the sinister implication of Dalton's comment. It is open and airy and staffed by male and female nurses in neat white uniforms. There is provision for restraint, as there is in every mental hospital in the world, but the main impression is one of freedom. 'Ninety percent of our patients are free to come and go. Right now [it was mid-morning] most of them are out meeting their friends around Bangli. Only very few, the aggressive ones, are restrained,' Dr Thong said.

When I asked him to comment on Dr Iksan's remark that Bali possibly had fewer mental cases, proportionate to population, than other parts of Indonesia, he said that numbers could not be used to prove the matter either way. Some Indonesian societies are more willing than others to consign their mental cases to hospitals. In Bali's case they have traditionally been accepted in the community, 'not chucked out'.

But times are changing. 'This mental hospital, just by existing, disrupts the old order,' Dr Thong said. It represents rules which determine who is mentally healthy and who is not, which did not exist before. And so does a chain of twentytwo outpatient clinics which has been set up around Bali to deal not only with psychotics and other mental cases but — it has turned out — with marital and even school problems as well. Attendances are now up around 25,000 a year. The trained nurses who run them administer drugs according to doctors' orders, offer sympathetic hearings to people with complaints, and alert visiting doctors to serious cases. No stigma attaches to visiting the clinics, Dr Thong said, and they have turned out to fulfill a social need as well as a medical one. Bali is the only province in Indonesia to have such clinics.

Although all this represents a substantial change from the old order, it is an essential one, a necessary part of Bali's efforts to cope with modern pressures. 'There is much stress within families. Before all was in a state of equilibrium, with very strict rules and with emotional outlets through trances, music, cockfighting, drinking. Now the pace of change is so great that these traditional ways may not be enough.

'For example, not long ago there was never any fighting over inheritance. Now it's a big issue, especially when land is involved because land is valuable. Even the banjars are under stress, though they are still very effective. Now we have families trying to dump their unwanted relatives upon us. We are doing what we can to retain or restore family unity, even to the extent of admitting whole families when just one member is being treated. The new ward we are building is designed according to strict Balinese rules, to help people feel at home.'

Some foreign tourists are admitted to the Bangli hospital, and not just for the overdoses of magic mushrooms that Dalton mentions. 'Usually it turns out that they had a mental problem at home,' Dr Thong said. 'They come to Bali looking for a solution but the problem is within themselves. They are just running away from their own dissatisfactions.'

Then there are drugs. By some definitions Bali has no problem at all, by contrast with the drug-blighted world in general. Only one hundred addicts have been listed. But the pressures that produce addiction in other parts of the world are beginning to operate in Bali as well and usage is beginning to descend from the tourist world down to the schools.

'In the past people used to be happy with their chickens and ducks and regular lives,' the doctor explained. 'But now they want motorcycles. It's the same pattern everywhere, in the mountain villages as well as in Kuta. Some people will not be able to get what they want and will turn to drugs. The problem will get worse.'

Bali's Wildlife

An island as crowded with people as Bali is would seem to offer little scope for wildlife; but there is life in the forests and seas; and there is also the beginning of awareness that it needs help. Depending on how one approaches the subject, the picture is either encouraging or depressing. This chapter begins with the good news, ends with the bad.

The good news is the Bali Barat [West Bali] Wildlife Reserve, at the arid western tip of the island, so close to Java that Gilimanuk, where the ferries berth, is an enclave within its embrace. The reserve is in business, as it were. This is by contrast with events in Indonesia's disastrous 1960s. Then, with administration in a shambles, poverty verging on desperation and remote areas vulnerable to any kind of despoliation, West Bali had a bad time.

Fishermen from Java and Madura landed at will to cut firewood and create any other havoc that took their fancy. Settlers moved in. Hunters had free rein. But now, in the word used by Dr Ir Gusti Made Tantera, head of Bali's Forest Service, the wildlife park is 'secure'. Settlers are being 'transmigrated' out to other parts of Indonesia, destruction has been much reduced and a management plan is starting to take effect. There is every hope that this 'environment' will be saved.

This development comes far too late to save the Bali tiger, the smallest of the eight sub-species of this great cat but large enough to leave behind stories about how dangerous it was. Once it was considered fairly common but uncontrolled hunting after World War I played havoc. In the mid-1930s an international wildlife commission predicted its coming extinction, and in fact the last known Bali tiger was shot in 1937.

Nonetheless other animals have survived, and the wildlife preserve will provide wild cattle, deer, mousedeer, leopard cats, civets and macagues with a permanent refuge. Another benefactor will be the Bali starling, Leucopsar rothschildi, a mainly white bird about nine inches long with a startling blue flash around its eyes, the only bird found only in Bali. A mere two hundred survive in the wild — there may be more than that in zoos around the world — and the bird is listed by international treaty as endangered. A large cage behind the wildlife reserve's headquarters at Teluk Terima when I was there contained two of the starlings, for study of their habits, and splendid creatures they are.

However, a view of these birds behind wire netting was not good enough for an amateur ornithologist from Canada I met about the same time. He wanted to see them in the wild. Twice he made the two-hour bus trip from Singaraja for day visits, without success. A week later, two days before leaving Bali, he made another journey from Kuta, more than four hours away, arriving at Teluk Terima after dark. The next day a guide showed him a tree used for observing the starlings and the two men sat there for hours, hot and thirsty.

Time was against them because the Canadian had to return to Kuta that evening and public transport in Bali closes down early. Minutes before calling off his venture, however, two of the birds appeared only 100 metres away and he was able to watch them for several minutes. When I saw him in Kuta much later that night, after he had spent more than four hours getting back, he was surely the happiest man in Bali, which he rated one of the best bird-watching places he had ever visited.

Another happy man I met at the park, but one with a different time scale, was Bastian van Helvoort, an ornithologist on a World Wildlife Organisation assignment to do what he can to help the Bali government develop the reserve and save the starling. He is confident this can be done, though helping the bird may call for some police work to stop trapping. It may also be necessary to provide water supplies and even nesting boxes for birds who normally nest in holes made in tree trunks by other birds.

There is much work to be done, not just for the starlings but for

The Bali tiger, though the smallest of its kind, was much feared. Here is one, in an old drawing, threatening a palm-wine collector. The tiger's spots represent artistic licence; real ones had stripes.

all animals in the reserve. Sufficient guards must be given enough equipment, including boats, to prevent firewood cutters landing. At present they have radios which merely let them report back to base that they can see the cutters but can do nothing about them. Six hundred hectares of coconut palms, one of the few commercial ventures of this size in an island which early set itself against such enterprises, and some man-made teak, eucalyptus and other plantations must be allowed to revert to jungle. Roads through the park must be policed to prevent more damage.

Fortunately the reserve has one asset, in addition to rare and beautiful birds, which gives it also the economic point that governments tend to look for. In addition to nearly 20,000 hectares of different kinds of forest and mangrove swamp, it has 6,600 hectares of coral reef and marine waters, ideal for snorkelling and scuba diving. The coral and its life are superb and the deeper waters abound with creatures, including a toothless whale shark up to ten metres long. Whales and dolphins often pass through on their way to and from the Bali Straits between Bali and Java. Mooring buoys have been installed so boats do not need to use anchors which could damage the coral. Tourists coming to visit this aspect of the park, and to visit Nusa Menjangan where deer graze and which is totally surrounded by coral reefs, will help give the entire reserve the fame and flair it needs to survive and prosper.

Adjoining the reserve is a much larger area marked on some maps as the Bali Barat National Park. This title is premature. According to Dr Tantera, it is still a proposal: 'Everyone must agree first.' But they have already agreed that exploitation of its 50,000 hectares of forest extending far along Bali's central mountain chain, stopped about 1980, is not to be resumed; and that the Forest Service is to manage some buffer areas around the edges. Campaigning for the park goes on.

That this area of forest has survived is remarkable. More than a century ago Alfred Russel Wallace, the English naturalist, wrote of a countryside so highly cultivated as to leave not much room for indigenous vegetation. Since then population pressure has grown enormously but Bali still manages to be home to no fewer than 200 species of birds and 32 species of mammals -- some of them inevitably ingredients in one of Wallace's major discoveries. The line between Bali and Lombok which he proposed as dividing mainly Asian and mainly Australian species, and which is now known as the Wallace Line, has its origins in his visit to this region in the 1850s.

In his book The Malay Archipelago, published in London in 1869, he described how various animals were found both on the Asian mainland and in various islands of the Indies, as far as Bali. On the other hand, the islands from Lombok onwards had no apes, monkeys, tigers or other cats, wolves, bears, hyenas, deer, antelopes, sheep, oxen, elephants, horses, squirrels or rabbits: 'None in short of those familiar types of quadruped which are met with in every other part of the world. Instead of these [Australia] has marsupials only, kangaroos and oppossums, wombats and the duck-billed platypus. In birds it is almost as peculiar. . . .'

The Bali starling — will it go the way of the tiger?

Nowhere was this great contrast more abrupt, Wallace wrote, than between Bali and Lombok, where the two regions are in closest proximity. 'The strait is here fifteen miles wide, so that we may pass in two hours from one great division of the earth to another, differing as essentially in their animal life as Europe does from America.' And so Wallace developed his theory that during past ice ages the sea level between various islands had fallen far enough for animals to move from the mainland -- but the deeper trench between Bali and Lombok prevented them going further.

Yet it was almost an accidental discovery. Had Wallace been able to get a ship direct from Singapore to Sulawesi he would never have visited Bali and Lombok, 'and should have missed some of the most important discoveries of my whole expedition to the East'. The Wallace Line is certainly among them but Wallace today is deservedly better known for having arrived at a theory of the origin of species by natural selection, without knowing that Charles Darwin had reached virtually the same conclusion at virtually the same time. It is tempting to think that Bali had at least a small hand in it.

But back to conservation, without which this story would be saddening rather than engaging. Some of the methods which Dr Tantera and his officers of the Forest Service are using to protect and reclaim forest are ingenious. For example, they are interplanting villagers' illegal coffee plantations on the mountain slopes with durian trees, resulting in fruit and eventually in timber. 'If we work together, if the people have things explained to them, then they will accept the need. But if we confront them, the effect will be worse than the problem in the first place,' Dr Tantera said. While I was in Bali Governor Mantra said in a speech to mark Indonesia's National Reforestation Day that about 39,000 hectares of land had to be reconverted to forest to produce an 'ideal' 30 percent for the whole island, against the present 22 percent.

(The Indonesian word for reforestation is 'reboasasi'. Thereby there seems to hang a tale, or at least a speculation, about another of the many links between European and south Asian languages. A powerful figure in Balinese mythology is Bhoma, Son of the Earth, a god often associated with vegetation (and featured on the back of cremation towers). The Dutch word for tree is 'boom', from the same root that gave English its 'boom' and 'beam'. The French 'bois' also comes to mind. It was from Dutch that Indonesia derived 'reboasasi', which I like to think closes a neat circle with 'Bhoma'.)

Perhaps the task of preserving forests is made easier by Balinese sympathy for nature. For whatever reasons, the island is dotted with what appear to be reserves which over the centuries have gained a kind of religious air. The tiny 'monkey forest' near Ubud is one. A superb grove of tall, straight trees at Sangeh is another (but the official leaflet which says the trees are nutmegs is wrong; they are dipterocarps, and the mistake arises from confusion between words with similar sounds but different meanings in Balinese and Indonesian). Tiny, more or less sanctified groves are to be found throughout Bali, not always in association with a temple.

Not all elements of conservation are ancient, however. A pleasant long walk, or an easy bike or bemo ride, from Ubud is the 'heronry' of the village of Petulu. When I arrived there about 4.30 one afternoon and asked about the birds, I was told that they would arrive at 5.00. They did, precisely, the empty sky above the coconut palms suddenly filled with large white birds wheeling in from the surrounding ricefields. They landed rather clumsily on the palm fronds and settled down for the night, safe from disturbance by the villagers below. 'How many are there?' I asked. 'Thirty thousand,' I was told, with a touch of precision unusual in Bali.

Village custom is that the birds must not be disturbed — so long as they stay up in their trees. Any which fall or fly to earth may be caught and eaten. 'Are they good to eat?' I asked. 'Very, very good,' was the reply, making still more remarkable the villagers' acceptance of the way their home has become a kind of sanctuary. Even more remarkable is the fact that this role is a new one, the birds for some reason having taken to the village as recently as 1966. Their arrival followed a sacrificial ceremony — a village-level version of Eka Dasa Rudra — asking for blessings and protection after the killing of communists early that year. A big banyan tree burst into flower and perhaps it was this which attracted the birds. But I was told most villagers preferred to remember their arrival as a sign of divine goodwill. My Canadian ornithologist friend was able to identify the birds: Cattle egrets, plumed egrets and some Javan pond herons.

Another sight frequently shown to tourists could also perhaps be termed a wildlife sanctuary, though to me it was more like a nightmare. It is a bat cave, Goa Lawa near Padangbai, a horror story of squalling, squabbling, smelly long-nosed fruit-bats fighting for space, squeaking and scrabbling for clawholds on the rockface. The smell is revolting. A large python lives in a crevice nearby, emerging slowly once in a while, picking up a bat and oozing glacially back. It probably has not had to move fast in years. Assuming it is not nauseated by batmeat, it is in snake heaven.

The existence of sanctuaries does not mean that animal life is generally sacred. If it were, there would be no need for sanctuaries. There is little of the respect for animal life one finds in India, though Bali is so often said to be Hindu. Cruelty and neglect are common, most dogs live miserable lives, and sacrifices to the gods can override all other considerations. A protected grey and silver eagle was among the creatures killed during the Eka Dasa Rudra ceremony on

Gunung Agung as recently as 1979. Wildlife officials argued with the priests in an attempt to save the bird but in the end failed.

Economic rather than religious pressure has caused much destruction, not only to the forests but also to coral reefs around the coast. Virtually every reef has been damaged by fishing with explosives and by mining. Along part of the southeast coast, around Candidasa, destruction is so serious that the reef no longer protects the shore, which is being lost at the rate of two or three metres a year. Despite official protestations that action is being taken, the reef at Candidasa at every low tide sees men, women and children using crowbars to prise blocks of coral loose and baskets to carry them ashore.

The coral is sold to kiln operators who turn it into 'kapur', lime which is used as mortar. One can sympathise to a degree with the government's predicament — endlessly repeated throughout the developing world — because if it applies its own law strictly families will lose their livelihoods. In this case, in addition, an essential material is involved. It is moving on both counts, to provide new livelihoods and an alternative source of mortar, but in the meantime the destruction continues, with the loss of both land and tourist attractions resulting.

That is by way of being bad news, but the really bad which I signalled at the beginning of this chapter involves sea turtles. Here the picture is of almost unbelievable destruction. Awareness did not spring upon me instantly but grew gradually through a series of events.

One was seeing, in the distance, from a bus as it drove past, a turtle upside down in a village street with men clustered around. One was looking in vain for turtles from a lookout over the sea where, my guide said, it had 'always' been possible to see them. One was finding three huge ones in a muddy drain which I crossed on my way to a beach festival near Gianyar, tethered by ropes through their flippers, with children jumping on and off their backs. One was noticing the extraordinary number of dead and stuffed turtles being offered to tourists. One was realising that publicity which presented a 'turtle island' as a breeding ground was deliberately deceptive, designed to conceal from tourists the fact that the turtles there were being held only for slaughter. All this involved an endangered creature at the centre of a world-wide conservation programme.

There is a small turtle hatching programme in Bali, run by the

Fisheries Service, but it is small and not very successful. In 1982 it collected and tried to hatch only 3640 eggs, succeeded with fewer than a third of them, and had most of the hatchlings die anyway. I knew a little about this subject, having recently visited Malaysian and Sri Lankan hatcheries where much higher success rates are regularly achieved. In Bali not even a l00 percent success rate would begin to compensate for the rate of destruction.

Here are some figures. In 1981, the Balinese killed and ate 21,000 turtles. In 1982, 23,000. Up till October, 1983, with two major festivals marked by feasting to come in the next two months, 18,000. The demand for turtle meat is so great that Bali imports supplies from Kalimantan, Sulawesi and the chain of Indonesian islands reaching away to the east. Areas with mainly Muslim populations are important suppliers because Muslims will not eat turtles.

But the Balinese do, with gusto. 'Lovely for sate,' a passer-by told me when I was looking at those pathetic creatures tethered in that muddy drain near Gianyar, referring to meat skewered and barbecued over charcoal. Historically turtles were eaten mainly during religious feasts and a kind of balance between supply and demand existed; there were more turtles in the sea around Bali and fewer Balinese to hunt them. But an improving economy, a larger population, a market for turtleshell products and more efficient hunting methods have changed that. And so has another aspect of tourism — some of the hotels offer turtle meat and turtle soup to their guests.

All seven species of sea turtle, five of which are found in Indonesia, are protected under CITES, the Convention on International Trade in Endangered Species, to which Indonesia is a signatory. But the Bali slaughter does not involve international trade and in fact there is no Indonesian law against it. It is an issue on which the Bali government treads cautiously because of the turtle's entrenched position in Balinese tradition. Indonesia's Nature Conservation Agency wants to make catching and trading in turtles illegal but it seems to have no prospect of short-term success. In the meantime the killing goes on.

Two days before leaving Bali I was told that most turtles eaten in the Denpasar district were slaughtered at Pegok, a village on the edge of town. 'I used to like eating turtle meat until I went there,' my informant said. 'But not now. It was so sad.' Late that night, after midnight, I went to Pegok. Two butchers' shops, more like shacks, were working. In one 16 turtles were waiting, in the other

22. They ranged in size from less than a metre long to nearly two metres. All had their front flippers tied together in front of their beaks, which rendered them helpless because a turtle needs all four legs to lift his bulk off the ground for movement. They were not penned but lay strewn on the concrete floor around the killing blocks where they would eventually die.

When? Not necessarily that night, or even that week. 'They'll stay alive like this for more than a month,' one of the butchers told me proudly. The killing rate depended on demand, normally a dozen or so a night but before a festival as many as 40 would die. They do so upside down on the blocks, and continue moving long after their stomach plate has been cut away and their intestines exposed. A shell which had been virtually emptied of its contents still had its hind legs and tail attached — and they were still moving.

The owner of one of the two butcheries defended his business on grounds that the Balinese need turtle meat for ceremonial feasts and because of the number of people dependant on working with turtleshell for their livelihoods. 'They can't ban it — it's too important,' he said. I had no ground for argument with him, any more than I would argue with any slaughterhouse worker anywhere in the world for doing what he does. The fault is not his. But after that exposure to charnel sights and smells I needed my long walk through deserted streets back into Denpasar to settle my stomach. And to come to hope that even if the provincial government does not ban turtle killing it will at least demand more humane slaughter. It was all a far, far cry from the work going into saving the Bali starling, Leucopsar rothschildi, away in the forests of the west.

Tourists in Quarantine

n his invaluable Bali Profile, Hanna lifts back from limbo the name of Bali's first tourist. He was Heer H. van Kol, a member of the Dutch Parliament, who in 1902 came of his own accord, at his own expense, just to see and to learn as much as he could. On his return to Holland he published a book, Out of Our Colonies. Most of its 826 pages dealt with Java and Sumatra but van Kol found room also for 123 pages about Bali, including an account of how each visitor must have a special passport. Hanna describes these as great four-fold documents on heavy paper impressively inscribed in Dutch and Balinese and even more impressively sealed. Getting one could consume many days, if not many weeks or months.

Travellers also needed interpreters, servants, porters, ponies and camping equipment, and whatever would be needed to live in lodgings which were always stifling, filthy, vermin-ridden and stained with betel-chew spittle. Well equipped, van Kol, always with a senior Dutch official at his side, toured the island, interviewed dignitaries and collected an impressive amount of information on all aspects of life. In the end he decided that his country's performance in Bali was not all that bad, and encouraged all concerned to 'proceed with this beautiful task in a spirit of dedication and selflessness'.

Perhaps van Kol's description was too dour for many people to want to follow him as tourists to Bali. Perhaps getting passports was too difficult. Perhaps living in stifling and verminous lodgings did not appeal. In any event it was to be another 30 years before anything like a tourist industry began, and then only in a small way. A Dutch shipping company began bringing in tourists by sea, the Bali Hotel in Denpasar was opened, liners on world cruises occasionally dropped in — and that was about all. Bali was becoming famous but remained remote, and was to remain so for nearly another half century.

The 1940s, 50s and 60s slid by with many political and economic changes but without any great influx of visitors. Facilities were few, times were often turbulent and tourism was fairly low-key not only in Indonesia but throughout much of the world. In 1964 — the year after Gunung Agung erupted — the whole of Indonesia had fewer than 36,000 visitors. In 1965, the figure was below 30,000, many of whom would have been businessmen using tourist visas, and many would not have come if they had anticipated the turmoil the year's closing months would produce. In 1966 the total was below 20,000, of whom only 2,150 got as far as Bali.

However, 1966 was also the year the 300-room Bali Beach Hotel was opened, an ugly square block looming amid the coconut palms of Sanur as a kind of warning of the flood which was about to begin. The new government in Jakarta, swinging Indonesia through a 180-degree foreign policy switch and avid for foreign exchange by any means, opened its doors wide. The Bali airport was enlarged and by 1968 much bigger planes were arriving much more often. In that year 5,000 people flew to Bali; the following year, 10,000; in 1970, 23,000.

And so on. In 1978 there were 133,000 arrivals, in 1981, 158,000. French and Japanese consultants calculated that by 1990 the figure would be up to around 700,000 a year. These figures relate only to foreigners arriving in Bali and not to Indonesia's own domestic tourists, who are beginning to flow about their country in impressive numbers. More people arrive in Bali by ferry than come in by air and in 1982 domestic tourists occupied more than a third of rooms rented out in the better hotels. So, make allowance for Indonesian visitors, be conservative, strike a balance, and assume that Bali is on its way to entertaining a million visitors a year.

Of the foreign visitors, it is likely that the largest group will continue to be Australians, as at present. In 1982 there were 65,000 of them (with 6,000 more women than men), against 32,000 from the whole of Europe, 30,000 from Japan, 16,000 from north

America. No other group was significant though most of the world's countries figure in the statistics to some degree. At the time of writing it seemed that 1983's final figures would be about eight percent above the previous year's.

When these tourists arrive they mostly know little about Bali, some nothing at all. Some are surprised to learn they are in Indonesia. If they want to learn about this place they have spent so much to visit, and not just sit in a bar or on a bus, they must rely heavily on their guides. I visited perhaps the most famous guide of all, Njoman Oka, and quickly learned why he is so well known. He is so deeply versed in the lore and history of his island that he spends time as a missionary for Balinism in Bali's own villages, telling people about their own religion. He is fluent in English, French, German and Dutch. And he is totally charming. Visiting him in his home in Denpasar — when I could find him, for though he is over 70 and 'retired' he leads an active life — was always enlightening and enjoyable.

Sometimes he reminisces. Before World War II he spent seven months as a secretary to Margaret Mead, translating for her and writing down every word spoken in religious ceremonies. He taught two American boys in Sanur to speak Balinese. After the Japanese occupation, during Indonesia's war of independence against the Dutch, he was imprisoned for guerrilla activity. One day Dutch military policemen fetched him from prison and he thought he was being taken for execution. Instead they drove to the Bali Hotel, where the American boys' mother, 'a Mrs Mason from Pasadena', was waiting for him. A few months later he was released, he thinks because of Mrs Mason's efforts on his behalf.

Njoman Oka worked as a clerk in the Bali Hotel, became a headmaster in Tabanan, became a member of that regency's ruling council, and then head of the council; 'but I didn't like it and was happy to quit later'. In 1956, he and some friends took over a Dutch travel office, and as its manager he found himself occasionally escorting visitors around Bali. He enjoyed it, and did it more and more often. 'My mission sacre,' he says, 'was to help people see Bali off the beaten track.'

One of his clients in 1968 was an associate editor of the National Geographic Magazine in the United States. Oka spent 40 days with him showing him as much of little-known Bali as he could, frequently leaving the hotel at 3 am so as to be in a village in time for early morning photography before the light hardened. Two years later Oka received a big envelope with contents informing him he had been elected a life member of the National Geographic Society. His client of those days is now the society's president.

Another 'client' was Queen Elizabeth of Great Britain, who visited Bali with Prince Philip, her husband, in 1974. Oka sat between them in the back seat of a Cadillac for a day's touring. 'The road all the way was lined with children waving flags and cheering,' he recalls. 'Some of them recognised me and called out in surprise, 'Hey, Pak Oka!' Throughout the tour, from 10 am to 9 pm, the Queen said nothing, just smiled from time to time 'so I knew she was listening' as Philip and Oka kept up a lively conversation.

I mention all this to indicate that Njoman Oka, as an expert guide, is qualified to comment on today's exponents of the art. What does he think of them? 'I'm disappointed by their lack of knowledge, language and dedication,' he told me. 'A good guide will persuade people to be interested in what they are shown. A poor one may only answer questions. Also, their knowledge of other languages is poor. The training courses for guides have English as a subject but it is easy to study a language in a classroom for years and still not know how to use it.'

As a result some guides cannot communicate effectively, the visitors they are escorting lose interest and fail to ask questions, and their tour becomes depressed. Oka says this is a serious problem for an island which has made tourism a major industry, especially as it is an island which cries out for explanation — everything one sees has a fascinating explanation to it. A traveller with a good guide derives much more from his tour than one who does without; but the one who does without is spared the frustrations of a visitor burdened with an inadequate guide.

I asked Drs Ngurah Ketu, director of the Government Tourism Office in Bali, about this. He agreed there was a problem but did not think it was as serious as Njoman Oka had said it was. There are some excellent guides and a government training school is at work improving the skills of the others. A grading system for the island's 500 licensed guides is being prepared, so that tourists will know the quality they are getting and so the guides themselves will try to improve, to reach a higher level.

The language problem is serious but as one moves around the island one hears Balinese guides discoursing in English, French, German, Japanese, with their listeners apparently taking in every word. Some tourists even accuse their guides of talking too much, and some

The Ubud Post comments on one of tourism's universal traits.

Balinese say some guides get their facts wrong — which is not surprising when so many different versions of the facts exist.

The quality of guiding is only one of Ketu's concerns. When I saw him he was just back from helping run a course for the owners and managers of small hotels. He is involved in everything which might help Bali remain popular — from trying to prevent overcharging to the awesome problem of the effects that tourism might be having on Bali's culture. Awesome, but in his view not impossible. It does bear thinking about, and can be seen in fact as a problem rather like that of feeding the right amount of water into Bali's irrigation systems.

Too much water or too little, and there will be no crop. Too much control or too little, and the tourist industry could lose momentum. Just the right amount, and all will be well; and this right amount of control could in fact turn out to be quite small since Bali is adept at adjusting to change. 'There has always been change,' Ketu said. 'We believe in the process of change. We must ensure only that change is steered a little by our philosophy and by the art and industry of our people. We can leave much of the process of adjustment to the people themselves, and the government's role is to provide those cultural aids which the people cannot create by themselves. This means setting up colleges so our arts are professionally taught, setting up competitions so standards are kept high, setting up art festivals so our people can see that their creativity is appreciated.

'We believe we can retain the uniqueness of our culture,' Ketu continued. 'Culture and art are part of the spiritual makeup of all Balinese. It causes them to "vibrate" as a family, and to produce a friendly and helpful atmosphere. The Balinese people themselves, and not the things they make or the dances they perform, are our biggest tourist asset.'

To this asset must be added a stroke of good fortune. Despite population pressure the Balinese had left an infertile part of the island, the barren Bukit peninsula at its southern tip, largely unpopulated. Today, entirely by chance, Denpasar, the airport and the two tourist centres of Sanur and Kuta are all adjacent to Bukit. Part of Bukit named Nusa Dua is where the tourist hordes of the future will spend their nights. A 350-hectare stretch of land at Nusa Dua (Two Islands, from two nearby islets) with an excellent lagoon and beach is the hub of present development. Engagingly, this is not entirely a new process, as an inscription found nearby tells of a VIP visit in the year 916 AD, making Nusa Dua a 1,000-year-old resort. More recently the Bukit peninsula was a hunting preserve for royalty, presumably as animals driven south by cultivation took shelter there.

Today the government-owned Bali Tourist Development Corporation is preparing hotel sites and building infrastructure — potable water to World Health Organisation standards from deep wells, electricity, telephones, a sewerage system, golf course, fire brigade, clinic and perhaps later an expensive medical centre as well. Some hotels are already in business, most notably the luxurious Nusa Dua Hotel opened in 1983. Its 450 rooms include two presidential suites with their own swimming pools and bullet-proof windows. Its palace-style decor includes literally thousands of statues, other carvings and paintings. It is a showpiece of Balinese creativity.

This and other hotels within the enclave will present the tourist industry at its glossiest. All hotels will be four-star or five-star, by 1990 they will offer about 2,700 rooms — as many as Sanur and Kuta together — and they will charge rates equivalent to about US$100 a night at today's value. It will be a marvellous asset with which to woo the world's wealthy, and even moderately well-off. Its customers will be the kind of people who spend more in a day than many of today's visitors spend in a week.

Nusa Dua in full operation will heighten an effect which is already apparent and which people who love Bali can only applaud: The quarantining of the tourist. Already it is clear that visitors have

A tourist beset by women selling batik tablecloths.

less impact on Bali than their gross — at times very gross — numbers suggest. The great majority spend their nights in the Denpasar-Sanur-Kuta-Nusa Dua region. They have to. There are very few hotels anywhere else on the island and the number of travellers who slip out to stay in losmens, or lodging houses, elsewhere is relatively insignificant.

In 1982 Bali's office of Indonesia's directorate-general of tourism classified 24 hotels as worth 'star' grading, and all of them were in Sanur, Kuta and Denpasar. Nearly 2,000 of their 2,763 rooms were in Sanur. Most of the hotels to come will be in Nusa Dua. The same organisation in the same statistical report listed 157 restaurants (both in and outside hotels) with places for 10,000 people. No fewer than 132 of these with places for nearly 8500 people were in Badung regency, the same area. The unseen business of segregating tourists, of quarantining them, is very efficient.

More, the great majority of tourists do not just spend their nights in this region. They spend most of their days there too, mostly on beaches or in bars, or watching dance performances or shopping. When they do venture out, typically it is in a bus with airconditioning and tinted windows which rushes through the countryside like an alien monster, with virtually no impact on the villages it leaves in its wake. Then its passengers see a dance, visit a temple, admire a view, go shopping, and are rushed back into quarantine again. Their cultural impact is minimal, limited to inserting some money into a society which needs it.

Is this to see more virtue in the system than really exists? Perhaps the tourist impact is greater and more damaging? But there is no doubt that the less restricted traveller who wanders down Balinese byways will find, even a few hundred yards from a highway, people who view him or her with surprise, the children shouting 'Turis' and their parents asking shyly if the visitor would like to come into their homes. Their older sons and daughters may be away working in hotels and shops and restaurants, they may explain, while village life continues.

There is also much change within the villages, of course, as there is change everywhere in the world. There would be no way of isolating them from the world, even if such an absurd idea should find favour. Tourism and development in general will continue to pose more questions than there are answers. Some of these questions will involve quixotic notions that Bali should be preserved as a kind of living museum, that there is something wrong in people wishing to reduce their considerable poverty, that higher aspirations are somehow wayward. There will also be an endless list of questions about the interplay of education and modernisation on one hand, culture and religion on the other. There are no clear answers.

The Indonesian government's perfectly respectable desire that Bali should be a centre of 'cultural tourism' is an example of these paradoxes. The idea is that visitors should want to know about Bali's culture and should be helped to satisfy their curiosity. But some people see this as posing more dangers to Bali than does the present and rising flood of cultural innocents. Urs Ramseyer had this in mind when he began compiling his Art and Culture of Bali. He feared, he wrote, that publishing such a book 'would shake the foundations of what it tries to describe'. Scientists make a similar point when they say it is impossible to study anything without changing it. In Bali's case, the 'cultural tourist', by his probing and his penetration into the heart of the Balinese way of life, must have a far more disturbing effect than has the casual visitor who is content to enjoy the surface of what he sees and leave the rest alone.

Then again, we must allow that Jakarta and Denpasar may know precisely what they are doing, and that 'cultural tourism', which is an elegant phrase, is just and only that — an elegant phrase.

Three Balinese Places—
1 Kuta

Just as rich people have been considered different from the rest of us, so Kuta is different from the rest of Bali, and for the same reason: It has more money. Having money, it attracts people who want some, and their efforts tend both to raise the activity level and to lower the social tone. Kuta, with Legian next door, is the honey-pot of Bali. It can therefore be a lot of fun. But it does not represent the rest of the island and with each year it moves still further away. It is so different as to be separate, a beach resort wherein the tourists provide entertainment for other tourists. It can be just as exotic as anything the Balinese may offer in other parts of the island.

Much of Kuta's verve comes from its newness. I have described how in Mads Lange's day it was a trading station. After his death, with shipping moved to Benoa and Singaraja, Kuta lapsed back into village life. Even in the 1930s, when tourist arrivals in Bali began to climb, there were few visitors. All that happened then was that some seeds were sown.

Sowing began one day in 1936 when an American couple, Bob Koke and Louise Garrett, his future wife, cycled through a coconut grove to find what they called 'the most beautiful beach in the world'. They leased part of it and within weeks had opened the Kuta Beach Hotel. 'We built it native style — little guest houses of bamboo and thatched roofs,' Bob Koke wrote later. 'The Dutch tourist agents snorted their disapproval and described our hotel as "dirty native huts". But that description seemed to do us more good than harm. . . . Soon we were turning

231

guests away.' Louise later wrote an enchanting book, Our Hotel in Bali, describing their adventure.

Visitors from all over the world came to enjoy that beautiful beach, to watch Balinese dancing in the gardens, to eat and drink — and to surf. Bob Koke had learned surfing in Hawaii and was its pioneer in Bali, using the long and heavy boards of the day which he made himself.

Also involved in the hotel was another American, Vannine Walker, who had seen a film about 'Bali the Last Paradise' and wanted to see for herself an island so aglow with 'peace, contentment, beauty and love'. After arriving she had been befriended by the royal family of Bangli, who named her K'tut Tantri, the name she has used ever since. She too was impressed by Kuta: 'The beach was magnificent', she wrote later in her book, Revolt in Paradise, 'and without a house or a hut. . . . What a site for a house!. . . .Or a hotel?'

Her relationship with Bob Koke and Louise Garrett did not last, however, and eventually she turned her house, just across the road from the Kuta Beach Hotel, into a smaller hostelry. Bob Koke and Louise Garrett left Bali just before the invading Japanese arrived in 1942. K'tut Tantri stayed on, underwent an appalling ordeal as a prisoner of the Japanese, and then joined the Indonesian side in the war against the Dutch.

After the Japanese surrender Bob Koke returned briefly to Bali to find that his hotel had been totally demolished. The site was bare and there were only jonquil borders gone wild to remind him of where it had been. A hotel of the same name was opened in 1955, but with different owners and on a different site. It is still in business, the oldest in Kuta.

Otherwise Kuta was left to slumber on through the 1950s and into the 60s. As recently as 1961 an English journalist, staying at the new Kuta Beach Hotel, expressed his delight: 'Crescent-shaped, fringed with coconut palms, and absolutely deserted. No beach huts, no souvenir stands, no drinks booths, nothing. Just a tiny bungalow hotel set back among the trees for the occasional guest. A paradise beach indeed.'

Now turn the calendar forward a couple of decades and what do we find? The fishing boats have vanished and all that is left to show where ricefields lay is an occasional bund between patches of weeds. Instead we find rambling, ramshackle, dirty, happy Kuta stretching along its inadequate road, a cheerful slum of cheap hotels, restaurants, bars, travel offices, curio, taped music and clothing shops, and lots of people. It is like this because Kuta, with Legian, is a do-it-yourself resort, created by individual entrepreneurs, not by companies. The person from whom you rent your room or buy your meal may actually be the owner. This helps lend Kuta a more engaging air.

Sanur, the sister resort on the opposite coast, is different in nature. It owes its rows of hotels, shops and restaurants less to its beach, which is not nearly as good as Kuta's, than to proximity to Denpasar and to the fact that the Bali Beach Hotel was built there in President Sukarno's time. The Bali Beach is the only tall building on the island, an ugly block which can be seen for miles. Local lore has it that it was ordered by Sukarno, and that when it was completed he ordered that no more like it be built, lest they spoil the view from his penthouse suite.

As a result of its example, Bali has been spared any more monstrosities. The rule is that no building will be higher than the coconut palms, and not even an ingenious Australian's scheme to plant palms four storeys up so he could build still higher has been allowed to break this rule. Even the luxurious new hotels in Nusa Dua, the coming tourist enclave, obey it.

But that has not stopped corporate businessmen, who tend to dislike making original decisions, from latching on to Sanur as a place to invest in. One big hotel demands many more, seems to be the reasoning, and the beach is now lined with them. They are run by professional managers and the workers are on wages, so the rapport one finds in Kuta is missing. The money you pay in Sanur goes into corporate coffers and probably leaves Bali. The money you pay in Kuta is more likely to go to some enterprising local family, or back to a village somewhere.

I came across an example of this process. In Jalan Padma, Legian, I found a losmen, or lodging house, The Three Sisters. The name rang a bell. 'Is this by any chance related to the famous Three Sisters food stall in Denpasar more than ten years ago?' I asked. 'The one known to travellers from all over the world for its mushroom omelettes?' It was indeed related. I was told how eight years earlier, when business was slowing down because travellers were forsaking Denpasar for beachier parts, the Three Sisters — Made, Nyoman and Ktut, of course — had decided to go with them. Not bad, really, for three women who had started their business selling meals to labourers on a building site. It was a time of hippiedom and travellers galore, and some of those who visited Denpasar called at the sisters' stall for food. The sisters expanded their menu, gave good service and became known from end to end of the travellers' pipeline extending all the way from Britain to Australia. You will not find Made, Nyoman and Ktut at the Three Sisters Losmen, however. They now live elsewhere while their mother and others in the family carry on the business.

Not all the enterprising families around Kuta are Balinese, however. Because Kuta is a honeypot, bees have flown in from all over Indonesia, especially from Java. There are also foreigners in business here, some of them playing a tense game with immigration officers as they fly frequently back and forth, pretend they have no business interests, pose as tourists, hide when necessary, and hope their Balinese partners and frontmen will not decide to do without them. All this just to get a share of the Kuta action, just to keep their fingers in the Bali till.

The action is dominated by Australians who have found that a holiday in Bali can be cheaper and more fun than staying at home. Signs invite them to 'drink more piss', which is Australian for 'real Aussie beer', but warn also that people unversed in a certain folk dance should not attend an evening's festivities: 'If you can't bloody rock and roll, don't bloody come.' Another sign offers a chance to hear a direct broadcast of the Melbourne Cup horse race 'while enjoying Aussie beer and hot Aussie meat pies'.

One popular bar, though it is housed in an excellent replica of a cockfighting building, presents a picture of men and women in shorts, singlets and rubber slippers, each one of them holding a tin or glass of beer, the crowd spilling out the front door, that could have been taken in Townsville or Darwin. Kuta has also learned to speak the language: 'Fucking right, mate,' says a small Balinese boy. It can be sad.

Down on the beach, which old-timers say is not as clean as it used to be, the Balinese women now wear t-shirts but the foreign ones are often topless. There is no complete nudity, by contrast apparently with the scene four or five years ago. The most substantial t-shirts, of good material and with long sleeves, are worn as a kind of uniform, along with pointed peasants' hats, by women who offer massages. They spread woven mats, kneel beside their customers and give them a good going-over right there on the beach, which many people enjoy. An expert massage in the warm sun, the breeze gentle, the oil soothing, the hands strong and clever, is one of Bali's more sybaritic joys.

And when it is over, you can perhaps spend time trading some oddments of clothing, t-shirts perhaps, for wood carvings or cheap jewellery. As a result of such business Kuta is the undoubted t-shirt capital of the world, with inhabitants wearing exotic specimens from scores of countries. There are many hawkers wandering along the beach despite signs which say hawking is forbidden. They can be a nuisance and some, the men, can be downright surly if their wares are rejected. But they can also be charming, like the girl who told me innocently that she had just sold a pair of cheap earrings worth 400 rupiahs for 10,000. That was still only US$10 so no harm was done; the girl was pleased, the buyer presumably content, and the rip-off no greater than countless others at higher levels of the tourist industry which are taken for granted.

Not all hawkers are local, or even Javanese. I met a Frenchman trying to sell a tawdry fake antique. He told me he was in distress but what could he do? Get a job? Impossible; the Indonesians would

Life on a Bali beach — a cartoonist's view.

not permit it, and even if they did he would still have to cut his beautiful long hair, his precious hair — he really did speak like that. Or go home? What about his spirit, he is so in love with Asia? Meeting this left-over hippy was like going back to the 1960s when such posing was common.

Goings-on like this are harmless and lend colour. More sinister ones are surprisingly rare. Three or four years before I arrived Kuta had a bad reputation for crime, drugs and prostitution but that has changed. Though there are few policemen or policewomen in sight, in fact the Balinese next to you on the beach or in the bemo could be one. The order from Jakarta is that tourists must be protected lest the tourist industry and the economy suffer, and they are. The security presence is invisible yet pervasive, and it links closely with the banjar and other community organisations.

In one week while I was in Bali not a single crime was reported in Kuta, which is astonishing for a place with so many tourists, such scattered accommodation and so many people around who would be delighted to make off with some valuables. A few Javanese prostitutes — rarely Balinese — haunt a couple of bars; if too many arrive, the police send them home again. Much of what crime there is comes from the tourists themselves in the form of drugs and gambling. Some thefts result, a senior policemen told me, because tourists insist on enjoying the fresh night air — and leave their room windows open. More thefts are reported of goods which in fact have been sold, to support insurance claims.

When I checked into a losmen in Kuta for my first night in Bali I found the room discouraging and could understand why some people might prefer not to close their windows. It was without a fan and without through ventilation. I imagined that with door and windows closed it would be an airless box. In the event I slept well and within a couple of days regarded my room as entirely acceptable. Lighting a mosquito coil each evening kept the pests away and I found that a mattress made from the cotton-like fibre which surrounds the seeds of the kapok tree is much cooler and sweeter than the foam rubber I encountered in more expensive places.

The following day I went visiting in an area beyond Kuta. I avoided the crowded and noisy main road and walked along quiet, sandy and shady footpaths to Legian, the next beach village. Seminyak, a little more Balinese, comes next and beyond that lies a region of mixed ricefields, villages and some exotic houses dotted along the beach. Many of these are 'houses of singing bamboo', holiday homes for foreigners built on land 'contracted' from villagers — foreigners cannot buy land in Indonesia — and some are whimsical creations indeed. But they age rapidly, thatching becomes untidy and they look like shaggy elephants, especially if absent owners leave them empty for months. One house, more substantial, featured an open-air bathroom in which a Balinese naiad had a shower rose in her headdress and hot and cold taps on her nipples.

Later I walked home along the beach, past lively surf with water so clean I could see right into the mounting waves. The setting sun coloured half the sky red, like my back. The beach was dotted with strollers and sitters enjoying the sight, or heading for the sea for a last swim before dark, or a last surfboard ride. It was a colourful, relaxed and interesting scene. Later I would learn more about Bali's marvellous offerings but that first day I needed nothing more from this island. Beaches are not all the same. Kuta's is special and those people who never get beyond it are not as daft as they are sometimes said to be.

A word about the water

Some of those people who never get beyond Kuta are surfers. Mostly they are Australians but as the sport becomes more international so does Bali's surfing community. Japanese exponents arrive in sufficient numbers to contend with Australians for the better stretches — there is only so much room on a wave — and the Balinese are also joining in.

Conversations in some Kuta bars are esoteric as surfers get down to technical detail about where to find the best left-hand and right-hand waves (breaking in different directions), the best boards, the best times, the tides, the damage that a coral reef can do to an unprotected human body. The people taking part in these sessions are young, ribald, drinking, determined to make the most of their time in Bali. Results can be extraordinary.

In 1983 an Australian surfing newspaper, Tracks, published in Sydney, printed a diary in which a surfer named Dick Bent had recorded his holiday. Here are some of the best bits. 'Filth' apparently is a word of praise:

May 6 — Wake early, the waves look big. Kuta Reef is 6 ft at low tide — will be big at high tide at two o'clock. Spending rupiah by the truckload. . . . Kuta is giant. A big offshore is howling too hard. Surf perfect lefts and rights at Legian Beachbreak. Absolute filth. . . . The scene on Kuta Beach today was amazing. There are a crew of Japanese surfers in town and the colours are so bright. Lot of people sell drinks at the beach. We all go senseless up at the bar.

May 7 — . . . There were about 50 guys surfing 4 ft waves. Offshore glass out at Kuta Reef. You could see the wind and swell were starting to really get straight. I am really sunburnt. I feel like I could glow in the dark. . . . So far the swell has just pumped every day we have been here. So much has happened in the last six days it has just been an incredible ball, like going to Disneyland. . . . We sink a few Bintangs [beers] at the Rum Jungle but it isn't raging enough so we go to the Pink Panther and meet two beautiful Javanese girls.

May 8 — Wake up and drive the girls home early. Swell is ultra clean glass, the offshore has slowed down. Should get magic waves today. . . . I am sunburnt to a great red glowing brown. My nose wants to leave. The gut rash I have from rubbing my board is turning into a great big crater of ulcer. . . . We hit it back to Halfway for the late arvo [afternoon] and sunset. Ketut Menda catches 50 waves before sunset. Back home to spruce up and suss out what to do tonight. This has been a heavy workout. I think I might be getting the Balinese paralysis. Starting to slow down and groove on everything we do all day. . . . Al reckons we deserve an iron man award for the pace we've been keeping up.

May 9 — Wake early. Go to Uluwatu. The tide is going down. Very large waves, the biggest day of swell yet. On the way in a few Balinese surfers said it was 10 ft. It is just O.D.ing itself but the wind is howling offshore. NO ONE OUT. So I thought, what the heck, I'd better go for it cause it wasn't really 10 ft, it looked about six on the peak, but the racetrack is closing out. Luckily a few guys said they would go out. Three of us. Two made it, one was washed down the line. We dogged huge sets. They were near impossible to take off on because of the offshore. My 6 ft 9 in pin felt like a toothpick. The other guy hit it in. During the next hour I saw some of the biggest waves of my life barrelling off the coral. You could have parked a semi-trailer in the tubes. So I finally get a little wave and go back into the cave. Just bullshit [i.e., filth]. . . . The Yankee guys one by one came in as it was dead low and the swell was not focussing very well. Waited till the tide came in a bit, it was late afternoon. The sets started getting bigger every set. 8 ft — 10 ft tubes. I caught the biggest left tube ride of my life. It was just bullshit. Copped the chop on a few of my rides on the last bowl section. It is just the heaviest place to be caught inside. Best tube — worst wipeout. The sunset on the walk back was classic. Huge lefts peeling down the reefs. I left my board with Wayan at Uluwatu because I think I'll get up early and go back to Ulu if the wind isn't so hard offshore and if the swell drops a bit. It could be all time. . . . All in all just the most ultimate day in my life. Also my board smashed me in the face. I think I might have broken my nose. . . .

May 10 — Wake and go check the swell and wind. My nose feels the size of old Schnozzle Jimmy Durante's. Rupiah runs like a raging river. We have a surf at Halfway. It's not too bad, four foot lefts and rights. Unfortunately in the heat of the moment I drop in on a Balinese surfer. He doesn't like it so he comes over crazy and punches me out. He told me it was his country and his waves. So much for the mellow Bali surfer. Luckily he didn't hit me on the nose as he held me under the water. After a while I left the beach. All his friends were patting him on the back and telling him what a great guy he was. [That night] chat up a Swedish girl. I hope I can make friends with the Balinese fighter.

May 14 — . . . Nights in Bali can last very late. Travellers have stories to tell, Sri Lanka, India, Istanbul, Iran, Amsterdam, London, Munich.

May 15 — Just got back from Ulu. It was great. Perfect heat, cloudy, heaps of sunshine. Lots of people, lots of bikini girls, perfect glassy 4 - 6 ft with lots of nice walls. Had a four-hour session.

May 23 — One week to go. We were off to surf down the beach. Good waves, perfect glass, offshore 3 ft - 4 ft. Everyone is going to Ulu for the day. . . . The big sea cow [dugong] was out the back today — I saw it about four times. Ate at the night market. We've just gone quarters in a large Jim Beam. Nights in Bali can last all night.

May 25 — Wake up in the dark and ride to Ulu for the early session. There was mist and smoke all the way there. Ulu is pumping, 6 ft. This is my personal best session there. Just filthy shape, glass feathering offshore. I caught a few of the larger sets, it was great. . . . A teenage Japanese chick nearly drowned at the beach today. One of the [Sydney] firemen saw some people trying to revive her so he bolted down and gave a hand too. The girl was just totally gone, no pulse, no breathing. Then after a few minutes she did a great chunder [vomit] and started breathing again, much to the surprise of the Aussie girl who was giving her mouth to mouth.

And so the time passes, wild days, wild nights, until time runs out.

May 29 — . . . The size the swell is pumping today there will be waves for the next week, no worry. Oh no! We have got to go home. I want to hide in the jungle. I'm broke, have enough money left for airport tax and the bemo to the airport. . . . I gave away all the things I don't want to take home. We're sitting with all our friends waiting for the bemo to go to the airport. . . . This has been the best surf trip of my life. I hope I can come back one day. One perfect day.

There are two reasons for quoting the unabashed Dick Bent at such length. First, any writing of such vigour deserves a fair run, to let its virtues shine through. Second, he stands stalwartly, sunburn and all, as a witness for the defence in an argument about what Australians like him may be doing to Bali. Early in 1984 Max Harris, a columnist in the newspaper The Australian, presented the case for the prosecution. Another part of this column was quoted earlier when writing about medical facilities:

'The Australian invasion [of Bali] began with the drop-out youth generation, the hippies, the yippies, and the druggies. As a contribution to a gentle and cleanly Balinese lifestyle, they brought with them their clap, their gonorrhea, syphilis, herpes, hepatitis, alcoholism, non-existent hygiene standards, violence, prostitution and a compulsive addiction to road slaughter, plus the whole evil drug culture unknown to the Balinese. [As a result] Kuta has all the civilised charm of a bikey rock festival. It is a place to meet a tribe of Australians behaving in a loud and larrikin way that can't be indulged at home.'

Before I read Dick Bent's account of his holiday in Bali I was inclined to agree with the Harris viewpoint. Bent made me think again, mainly because I saw in his writing an approach to life which fits well with the Balinese. The Balinese are not a delicate and genteel people. They are sturdy, vigorous, generous and given to fun. They have a robust sense of humour. Balinese men can be as addicted to drinking and gambling (in their own rice-wine and cockfighting forms) as Australian men can be. If Bent had managed to find that Balinese surfer who held him under water, there is a good chance they would have come to terms and become friends.

If there are Australians who do not fit into the Bali scene, it is not the hard-drinking, noisy, good-natured men and women of the Dick Bent class. It is the prissy, mean, unhappy men and women who want to find in Bali the kind of life they live in Australia, but cheaper. I overheard one of them in a money changer's office. 'Why do you want me to sign the back of my traveller's cheques?' he whined. 'I only have to sign the front. I don't have to sign the back. I work in a bank and I know. You people are wrong. There's no need for me to sign twice. Once is enough. I know because I work in a bank.'

Dick Bent would have thought that as funny as nearly breaking his nose on his own surfboard.

Three Balinese Places— 2 Denpasar

 n a world in which one spends too much time in cities and those cities all seem to be growing out of control, Denpasar is pleasant, suffering only from the superior attractions all around it. It is of convenient size, it has most of the facilities one looks for in cities, and it is easy to get out of. Despite the heat, noise and congestion of its main streets, it displays often a refreshingly indolent approach to life.

It is the only place where I have seen drivers park in the shade of roadside trees while waiting for traffic lights to change. Some banks have stools in front of their tellers' cages so customers can relax while their money is counted. It still has many pony carts ('dokka' they are called, from 'dogcart') with their ponies fancifully adorned with rosettes and metal floral sprays, and with sackcloth hung between their hind legs to help keep the streets clean.

In Denpasar you learn some essentials of the way of life. Taxis are hard to find and expensive, meant only for tourists, but tiny, three-wheeled bemos, unlike the big ones which ply the highways, are abundant. You learn to ignore whatever destinations are written on their sides and to check with the driver in his little cab. You do this by stating the name of your destination twice: Gajah Mada Gajah Mada, or Kerening Kerening. His reply is also a duplication, as if a place name spoken only once has no meaning. You learn to observe how much other passengers pay, and quickly the town is yours. Bemos can also be 'chartered' — using the English word —

Denpasar street scene, with bemo.

to serve as taxis and they give good, cheap service, so long as you settle the fare in advance. But beware that bemos vanish from the streets shortly after sunset; the Balinese value their family life.

You may also at times find motor-cyclists offering to taxi you around as a pillion passenger. In this way you can develop a feeling for the thousands of others on motor-cycles, and get a different angle on the girls riding sidesaddle on pillion seats. Some do this with great flair, leaning forward into the breeze, nicely profiled, black hair flying, left leg trailing, and a slipper dangling on a turned-up toe. This scene is most to be enjoyed in the streets around Udayana University, whose 13,000 students give the area a verve and energy lacking in other parts of town. I spent some time in the library there, by permission of the rector, and not all of it was with eyes downcast.

Having learned your way around, you see what there is to see, so long as this does not intrude much into enjoyment of Bali's other offerings. In essence, I suppose, you could reduce your calls to three.

The Bali Museum is a must. It was opened in 1932 (though proposed as early as 1910 by a Dutch official worried that the island was losing its treasures) and ever since has been vital to the preservation of Balinese culture. Prominent in its organisation and its first curator was Walter Spies, whose remarkable role has already been described. You pay 10 rupiahs to enter, and since no one ever bothers to carry such a meaningless coin and since the ticket seller never has change for a 100-rupiah note or coin, he at least does well. The museum is a series of galleries displaying artefacts from paintings and furniture to weapons and dance costumes. Barong masks are worth a special visit, and so is a display of carved and coloured woodwork — so much of it that you might overlook the carved pillars behind it.

The Bali Art Centre, Werdhi Budaya, is also a necessary visit. Designed as a showplace for Bali's performing and fine arts, it was opened in 1973. Among its offerings is one of the island's best art galleries. It can be a sleepy place around early afternoon — even the hawkers lose their enthusiasm — but if you go there to see a dance performance in one of the two open-air theatres your visit to Bali will be enlarged. A kecak performance with just one central stand of oil lamps throwing flickering light on surrounding trees and statues is a powerful occasion.

In June and July each year the centre is the focus of an arts festival which is becoming increasingly important. But you need not see a show. I was much impressed by a huge, carved tree-trunk standing in the grounds, its entire surface filled with monkeys scrambling to attack a formidable monster. Other carvings abound with cosmic conflicts between kingly warriors on one side and demons on the other. In one of them, two plump, buck-toothed, tiny figures huddle together in a shelter while the battle rages overhead, both with eyes closed, one with hands over ears to shut out the din as well. They are the eternal victims of their masters' warlike games. They are all of us.

A visit to the Bali Hotel is worthwhile, not necessarily to stay or eat or buy but to see the place where the Bali tourist business really got started. It was here that the visitors of the 1930s stayed, here that the first commercial dance performances were presented, here that the people who did so much to record the Bali of that time met often to compare notes. When it was built by a Dutch shipping company it was the latest in luxury. Since 1956 it has been under Indonesian control, as part of the countrywide Natour group, and despite extensive modernisation it retains some of its old character.

From the Bali Hotel it is only a short stroll, turning right at the Caturmuka (four-faces) monument at a nearby intersection, to Gajah Mada Street, Bali's main shopping area. A big market reminds one that Denpasar means 'beside the market' and that most Balinese prefer the old name, Badung. Certainly bemo drivers do, in its duplicated form. You hear hustling drivers calling 'Badung Badung' in every bus station on the island.

Government offices are being moved out of town to a new administrative complex at Renon. The complex is becoming splendid in its way with buildings in the Balinese style, all reddish brick and grey stone, but seems not to have allowed for the fact that many people may need to visit its offices. The immigration office and the main post office are both at Renon, which can be inconvenient.

Government offices mean government, and Renon is where it is. I met the Governor there and most of the other department heads I talked to. Renon is on the direct line to Jakarta, where real power resides. Some of it flows downward to the Governor, and through him to the officers of his administration. There is also a provincial assembly which meets from time to time in a modest building on the way to the Art Centre.

Denpasar is the headquarters of the media as well. Bali has three daily newspapers, with a combined circulation approaching 40,000, twelve radio stations (two on the Indonesian national circuit, two regional and the rest private), and a television station. About two and a half hours of regional material is televised each day, along with national material from Jakarta. The media overwhelmingly use the Indonesian language, though there are some magazine work and some radio programmes in Balinese.

What else? Another characteristic of Denpasar relates not to something present but to a vacuum. There is not much to do at night. A few cinemas show often deplorable films which are surely much more damaging culturally than anything tourists might do. There are some good Chinese restaurants. Not much else. Sleeping early and getting up early is good for you, and it is also the best way to make the most of Bali.

Three Balinese Places – 3 Ubud

ere surely is one of the world's most unlikely tourist 'destinations'. Ubud is tiny, a village of only about 7,000 people. It has no big hotels, no big restaurants, no nightclubs, no golf courses, only one swimming pool, none of the conventional trappings. Yet the tourists flock in by hundreds, or thousands — no one keeps figures. Some of them are puppets dancing to strings pulled by their travel agents but many get to Ubud as a personal decision.

They remain in the same way. The village is full of people saying to each other over their fresh papaya and banana juice drinks, or their black rice and fruit salad, that they were supposed to go to Java (or Japan or Singapore or Australia) last week (or last month or last year) but had decided to stay a little longer. Or, if they did fly, it was only to Singapore, to turn around in the airport terminal and to fly right back, picking up another two-month tourist visa on the way. There is a pavilion in the main street looking on to a lotus pond, part of an old temple, and lotus-eating pervades the air.

Why is Ubud so popular? The visitor newly arrived indeed may wonder, especially after walking up and down the main street for a couple of hours on a hot afternoon. But imagine that he shrugs his shoulders, finds lodgings, and decides to give the place a couple of days. He will be hooked. On the other hand, those more regimented travellers who are driven in and out in the course of a conducted tour will never begin to understand why Ubud is famous.

In the evening our visitor goes for a walk and finds himself in the ricefields which ring the village. The rays of the sinking sun reach upwards to illuminate the lower sides of hanging clouds, and this in turn spreads a radiance over the land. Far, far away down the long, gentle slope he may see a shining line of sea. Egrets and herons trace flight paths towards their sanctuary at Petulu. The air is fresher than it was in Sanur or Kuta. At dusk our visitor is in one of the dozen or so little restaurants where people chat between tables. A man in the street tells him there is a dance performance that night. He goes, just to pass the time, and with a bit of luck sees a show that would grace any city in the world.

The next morning he sits on his porch and enjoys the flowers which bloom everywhere and the birds which sing everywhere, while waiting for his breakfast of coffee, toast, eggs and fruit. He goes for a walk while the air is still balmy. There is more to see than he thought, and even that main street looks a little more friendly than it did in the previous day's heat. He falls into sampling Ubud's offerings one by one.

He walks to the 'monkey forest', to the heronry at Petulu, to Sayan for rustic scenery. He finds that there is more to Ubud's two art museums and its many art shops than he thought. And every night there is a dance performance somewhere not far away. He finds that Mas and Peliatan are just a short bemo ride away, that access to the entire tourist tract of south Bali is easy, and that Ubud can be a better centre for enjoying Bali than are Sanur and Kuta. Before our visitor realises it his couple of days have stretched into a week or more.

Two of Ubud's most efficient explainers (promoters would be the wrong word) are Nyoman Suradnya and Silvio Santosa. Suradnya, an artist who teaches in Australia for a few months each year and then spends more months in his beloved Ubud, is director of Bina Wisata, or 'Tourist Guidance', a foundation to protect nature and culture. Silvio is editor of the foundation's monthly newspaper, Napi Orti, or Ubud Post.

The foundation's task, in line with its motto, Ubud Indah Lestari, which means 'beautiful Ubud preserved', is to do everything possible to ensure that the rising numbers of tourists do not damage this quiet and beautiful little community. Its small office is worth visiting for free advice, for excellent cheap maps and for the newspaper. It says proudly that its role is not promoting or selling, but informing. The foundation is the only village organisation of its

Put the girl in traditional dress, and this would be a tourist shot. As it is, it represents real life in Ubud — real people in real courtyards.

kind in Indonesia. Lately it has moved on from protecting the village to trying to create jobs. Twelve people work in its tiny office, mostly at printing, it has people hand-colouring cards at home, and it has contrived that the street sale of tickets to dance performances is an occupation reserved for handicapped people.

Silvio Santosa, the editor, has been described as atoning for his past. He opened Bali's first disco in Sanur in 1970 and has also been involved in shops and restaurants depending on the tourist trade. When his disco ran out of money he escaped to Ubud, made his living as a writer and photographer, and delved deep into Bali's history and culture. Though he comes from east Java, he is from a community there which practises a religion similar to Balinism and is now totally at home in his adopted island.

The Ubud Post was meant to be an occasional newspaper but

a visiting minister from Jakarta praised its enterprise and virtually instructed it to appear monthly. Its contributors include cultural luminaries, tourists who want to express their affection for Ubud and students who feel they have discovered something new about the Balinese way of life. Suteja Neka, the art collector I have written about elsewhere in this book, is a frequent writer. When the contents are all in, the edition is typed on a borrowed typesetting machine in Denpasar. The paper has subscribers in many countries, all people who have fallen in love with Ubud and want it preserved as it is.

Not that subscribing is just an act of philanthropy. Buyers also get value mainly because of the newspaper's way with words. 'Tourism is not a simple thing to be handled as easily as frying an egg,' it says. On temple ceremonies, 'they are not tourist attractions. The parishioners are human beings, the priests are not your photo models, and the offerings are not for an art exhibition'. You may join in and be part of the ceremony, but with sensitivity: 'You are not visiting a zoo, are you?' Attend not as a tourist but as a villager, it says, properly dressed with shirt, sarong and sash and behaving respectfully. For people who might feel that local money changers are not giving them the best possible rate, the paper has succinct advice: Fly to Singapore.

This nice touch of asperity is not all that makes the Ubud Post different from most tourist town publications. It does not pander to anyone. It does not make deals to print puffs in exchange for advertising. It is a world removed from those glossy publications which pretend that every hotel, every shop, every restaurant in town is marvellous, so long as they buy space. The newspaper and the foundation which publishes it are beholden to no one except the people of Ubud, and the people respond in kind, as when farmers arrive unannounced with a load of thatch to repair the office roof. That Ubud, with clean lanes planted with flowering shrubs, regularly does well in island-wide 'beautiful village' competitions is another expression of the same sentiment. (In 1984 the Ubud Post had to suspend publication for some months but the foundation hoped it would reappear before the end of the year.)

Behind all this lies the reality that if Bali has a cultural heart, it is Ubud and the country for ten kilometres or so around. This has long been so. Even as the first Europeans arrived in Bali the village, then surely very small indeed, lay at the hub of a district abounding in musical, craft and performing talents. Walter Spies was so taken that he built his house nearby at Campuan, where it now forms part of the Tjampuhan Hotel. His being in Ubud brought in so many like-minded visitors that it became a kind of eastern Camelot, at times, one suspects, rather self-centred and resentful of other outsiders. One famous member of the Campuan circle, I was told, 'spoke little Indonesian, less Balinese, and had no local friends except boyfriends'.

They did make Ubud and its offerings famous, however, and therefore Bali as well, and today's arrivals tread the same path. This is especially so if they come, as many do, to learn music or dancing or some other aspect of Balinese life. In my time a young German worked patiently day after day in a mask carving shop, an English woman was learning gamelan and an American studied dancing. For a few weeks or months (visas are a major limitation) such people immerse themselves in just one aspect of the island's fascinations, and perhaps derive from that concentration much more than do those of us who leap from here to there and from this to that.

Ubud is changing. Denpasar is only 25 km away. During my time there we would go to Denpasar to make phone calls and be back in Ubud within a couple of hours. No doubt it will soon have a public phone of its own, just as it got electricity in the 1970s, and from that television. New losmens, shops and restaurants are reaching further down this road and along that one. But the tourist foundation and, it seems, a kind of village consensus are keeping Ubud simple. There is a total ban on big hotels and other major buildings. Ubud should survive. If not, poor Bali.

..and a Balinese Journey

was on Nusa Lembongan, one of the three Balinese islands — two small, one big — which lie between Bali and Lombok. I had gone there on the basis of information that turned out to be wrong. My intended destination was Nusa Penida, the big island ('nusa' means 'island'), but getting there was proving difficult. Never mind. The ride across in a bounding, bouncing outrigger sailboat with engine across the sparkling sea from Sanur had been fun. Being on the island, which has interesting walks, fine swimming and fine snorkelling if you can get out to the edge of the reef, was no great hardship.

There is also surfing good enough for a young Australian, Chris McHugh, to be building a hotel there specially for Japanese enthusiasts. 'The Japanese are not like Australians,' he says. 'Not even the surfers. They don't like to live cheap.' So Lembongan was fine, but it was not Penida. The big island was in plain view from a hilltop, where I shared the crest with a nervous cow, but getting there would involve a boat charter more expensive than I liked to think about, and then a chance of being stranded on a beach miles from anywhere. Penida could wait.

The trip back to Sanur early the following day was less bounding, more thumping, less sparkling, more pouring with rain, so we passengers were soon bedraggled. We sailed through a fleet of other sailing boats on fishing trips, and beautiful they were, until we got near Sanur and the designs on multi-coloured sails changed into advertisements for beer. Throughout the crossing a rooster in a small basket kept crowing protests, though in principle roosters cannot crow without stretching their necks. Perhaps Balinese fighting cocks are different. Another mystery.

From Sanur I set out on a day's travelling by bemo to Denpasar, to Gianyar, to Klungkung, to Candidasa (passing Kusamba on the way, where I should have gone to get a boat to Penida). When I reached Candidasa I was still salty from my dawn drenching while sailing from Lembongan. But the salt did not matter. I was now able to relax on one of Bali's finest beaches, with soft sand, 'water like silk' as a Canadian traveller described it, a spectacular view of Penida, a sea dotted with colourful fishing craft skittering across the sea like insects, and fresh water newly hand-pumped from a well for washing in.

The sunset view from Candidasa was spectacular as the sun appeared between clouds and serried hills and produced a flamboyant panorama which changed as I watched. In the process, that evening, Penida away on my left became darker and grimmer. In Balinese lore Penida (even the name has a grim and penitential sound) is an island of demons, monsters and exiles. It is barren, surmounted even with what travellers have called a desert, and, well, unBalinese. Some old European charts call it 'the Island of Bandits'.

An Australian told me that on Penida he had seen a man with all-black eyeballs. 'I was fascinated but found I couldn't look at him for more than a moment or two at a time,' he said. 'It was like looking right inside his head.' That is the kind of story that the Balinese expect to hear about Penida, stories which fit well into its frightening barrenness. The island is an upthrust seabed, much as Bukit at Bali's southern tip is, soilless, losing its rainwater rapidly to the sea. A considerable government effort, with American aid, has gone into building reservoirs and the aim now is to bring about a greening of this desert island. Eventually Penida will come into its own, partly as an agricultural producer, partly as an extension of the tourism machine because, I was told, it has splendid beaches, superb surfing and snorkelling, many caverns and spectacular walks.

The following morning I asked at the food stall where I was having breakfast why the village is named Candidasa, which seems to mean 'ten temples' or 'ten shrines'. A guidebook says the people there are eager to show visitors the shrines that can still be found. But the woman cooking my breakfast showed me something different: A temple nearby, in the shadow of a cliff, with a ten-tiered gateway. It was the only time in Bali, where odd numbers normally prevail in temple architecture, that such an even-numbered structure was brought to my attention. There may be many others; one does not go around counting.

Later I walked to the nearby crossroads where motorcyclists wait to carry visitors pillion-style to Tenganan, which I have already written about in excessive detail. I have also written about the destruction of the coral reef and the erosion of the shore, so that leaves little else to say except that eventually I caught another bemo and went through scenic country to Amlapura, the capital of Karangasem regency. (The two names, one Balinese and one Indonesian, mean the same thing, a kind of sour fruit, and can be interchanged.)

Amlapura is the main town of eastern Bali, but not such a main town that you can change money there; for that you must retreat to Klungkung. It was badly damaged in the 1963 Gunung Agung eruption and today is spartan and raw, not a place to delay one long unless you enjoy old palaces. Amlapura's has much character, crumbling away with time and weather, though the American husband of a royal princess has begun some restoration work.

In the main porch there is a photograph, dated 1939, showing a handsome, moustachioed king wearing a heavily decorated and bemedalled jacket and a plain sarong, and with bare feet. Another shows him posing with a son as they study a palm-leaf book.

This king is said to have had 35 wives, some of whom can be seen in more photographs on the same porch. Across the road, in an even older palace, I found a porch on the verge of collapse decorated with old paintings similar to those in the Klungkung courthouse; this too I have written about elsewhere. This royal family had two retreats, one a few kilometres away by the sea, the other a few kilometres away in the foothills of Gunung Agung. The first, at Ujung (which means 'the end', as of a road), was undistinguished even when it was built in a mock European style. Today it is even more undistinguished because it was badly damaged in an earthquake in 1979. There were two main shocks. The first caused the six people in the palace to flee; the second did the damage and there were no casualties. There have been no repairs and there is no prospect of any. The lagoon around the palace is full of fish and lotus flowers.

The second retreat, Tirtagangga, 'Water of the Ganges', is a much more recent creation. Work began a year after World War II ended

A motorcycle can be ideal for seeing Bali off the beaten track — if you are not careful, right off.

as a sign that good times had really returned, though perhaps not so good for the villagers conscripted for corvee labour as the king's right. It was an astonishing time to start such a project, with the island still suffering from the Japanese occupation, with independence in the air and with signs increasing that a war with the Dutch lay ahead. But then, it was an astonishing creation. Right at the far end of Bali was an unlikely place for a water palace with elaborate dining room, bar, chalets and even a boat fitted out for entertainment. Perhaps because it was so outlandish it succeeded, surviving right through political and economic confusion until 1963. It was famous enough even for President Sukarno to visit it, by helicopter, for a few minutes. Then came the Gunung Agung eruption, and destruction.

In recent years, though its buildings are virtually all gone, Tirtagangga has been brought back into operation as a public bathing place. On holidays hundreds of people flock in to swim and splash in the deliciously cool water. In 1974 an enterprising Amlapura printer opened a tiny losmen alongside the water garden, and today Wayan Dhangin's enterprise provides a place to stay, eat, drink and sit in a pretty garden. The air is full of birdsong and the sound of tumbling water and the nearby countryside (which includes Budakling, the Buddhist community I have written about elsewhere) is splendid for wandering in. One never knows when villagers are going to invite you into their homes, perhaps to stay as long as you wish.

Later, at the other end of the island, I met an American I had talked to at Tirtagganga. He had been with a friend then. I asked about the friend, and a pretty story emerged. The two had been invited to stay with a village family near Tirtagangga, and some fine parties they had. Then one, the man I was talking to, had to leave. The two men arranged to meet later.

The man who stayed behind later found his traveller's cheques were missing. The whole village made the issue theirs, searching everywhere and displaying great concern. Eventually the man who had lost his cheques had to leave, however, to meet his friend — to find that the friend had the cheques with him. So he turned right around and made the long journey back, to tell the villagers all was well and that they need not feel that someone among them was a thief.

'That's thoughtful of him,' I said.

'No choice,' was the reply. 'They're such nice people. We couldn't let them go on thinking they had done something wrong. A telegram or a letter might never arrive. Besides, now they'll have some more parties.'

One moves on, which is a simple matter of waiting on the roadside for a bemo. With a little luck one catches a ride within minutes; with a little more luck one gets a seat; with really good luck the bemo will be of the minibus variety which also provides windows to look out of. A guidebook advises sitting on the left when travelling northeast from Amlapura, the better to see the beetling heights of Gunung Agung. They are worth seeing, and worth seeing also is the achievement that has greened so much of the countryside. The coast road passes through many villages, not as luxuriantly foliaged as in the south of the island but not noticeably poorer either. The road is sealed for all its length, there is considerable commerce and it seems that the area is not as backward as it was earlier kept by isolation.

I stopped briefly in Tejakula because a guidebook referred to the 'horse baths' there. I imagined some degenerate ruler building marbled pools for his pampered steeds, leaving his subjects to sit in the dust outside. But it was not quite like that. Whoever he was, ruler or Dutchman, he built an excellent bathhouse with water gushing from many spouts into separate compartments for men and women. Then, since there was water and space to spare, he added an extra enclosure where people might scrub down their horses and cows. They no longer do so but the compartments for men and women are still in use.

The turn-off to Sembiran, or turn-up, since it is a steep road which follows, is a little further on. Sembiran is one of the three Bali Aga villages described in the first chapter of this book. Then comes Bondalem, not apparently different from a dozen other places along the way but a name to conjure with because this is where Indonesian and Dutch engineers are building an electricity station which will tap heat from the sea, as mentioned earlier. Next stop is Yeh Sanih, where a prolific freshwater spring feeds a wide, well-made swimming pool adjacent to the beach. Then Kubutambahan, for that temple carving of a man with a bicycle, and Sangsit for the most ornately carved temple in Bali, and perhaps a side trip to Jagaraga and Sawan.

And so to Singaraja. I like dusty and dirty and rundown towns, so I enjoyed Singaraja. Since it faces the Java Sea, that unifying stretch of water in the centre of the Indonesian archipelago, it was much more often visited much earlier than any point on the south coast of Bali. The Muslim community in Singaraja is of venerable age, and so is the Chinese, and the Dutch came here before they concerned themselves with the rest of the island, fighting their most ferocious battles around Jagaraga, just a few kilometres away.

Here too was the port where the tourists of the 1930s landed, to be driven over the mountains to the Bali Hotel in Denpasar. Singaraja has some good Chinese restaurants to provide a change from nasi campur, a banjar called Bali, a marvellous old library called Gedong Kirtya with old lontar books, many more in Dutch and some in English I had not been able to find elsewhere. But most travellers go straight through Singaraja west to Lovina, which its landlords hope will one day be as famous a beach resort as Sanur and Kuta are today.

A peculiarity of this region is its black beaches. The sand is greyish when dry but when wet is so dark that it does not reflect sunlight. As a result the bottom of the sea at times is invisible. You plunge in, enjoy the warmth, swim through immeasurable space, imagine you are well out of your depth, and then find the water is only waist-deep. On my first evening there, after a long day's travel, I was enjoying this soft, clean water, and the sunset over mountains to the west, and the passing fishing craft, when I met two Balinese girls swimming topless. They took care to keep their bodies underwater but their fair skins were luminous against the dark background and the effect was agreeable.

The next day I asked around about the origin of the word 'Lovina', patently unBalinese, and received no good answers until I met an elderly gentleman sitting behind the desk in a restaurant opposite my losmen. He said the name was created by his father, just before World War II. His father was the Raja of Buleleng and the family had a kind of resort in this beach area — but not for swimming: 'Too dangerous. Too many crocodiles.' My informant was Anak Agung Ngurah Agung, the first two words of his name indicating his Ksatria caste and his noble birth. But Bali had had too many kings, with too many wives and too many children, and the royal coinage had become devalued. Not that Ngurah Agung resents this. He runs his restaurant, looks after his remaining rice land, dandles his half-Australian grandson on his knee. The child, on holiday with his parents from Queensland, knew English well but in Lovina refused to use it lest he be taken for a tourist.

That night I went to the pictures with the two young swimmers I had met the previous evening. All day a little lorry with placards on its sides and a blaring loudspeaker on its roof had toured the neighbourhood, advertising that night's film. Soon after dusk people began streaming through Lovina. I wondered that there should be a cinema to accommodate so many. Eventually I met the girls, and their entire family, and we joined the drifting throng. I asked when the show would begin but no one seemed to know, or care.

Half a kilometre down the road we turned off, walked through a vast number of parked motorbikes, on payment of a tiny fee (150 rupiahs each) passed through a gate in a temporary palm-leaf fence, and found ourselves on the beach. A screen had been strung between two coconut palms and all around the area hawkers had set up little stalls selling coffee, soft drinks, sweets, fruit, small meals, cigarettes. Children ran everywhere, made little campfires, stretched out on mats and went to sleep. Their elders sat, strolled, met friends, flirted, enjoyed the activity. The event was not all that different from those described in accounts of shadow play performances in earlier days, and the social function of giving people a reason to gather was identical. But instead of seeing a Ramayana story we eventually, about 11 pm, when there was not a child left awake, sat to watch a cheaply-made kung-fu movie.

That event had nothing to do with the tourists of Lovina and screenings like it can be seen in most parts of Bali. It is not a happy development but I doubt that the films do any more harm than those which the villagers of the western world turned out to see in similar circumstances in the 1930s. We survived a great deal of trash and so will the Balinese.

But talking of trash — Lovina, as its losmens and restaurants spread further along the beach, is generating a great deal of it. After a stormy night the beach was littered not only with sea wrack but also with much plastic, as if the ocean had vomited back litter we had thrust into it. I saw the same thing happen in Kuta. Everywhere in Bali, as plastic wrappings take over from banana leaf and other degradable ones, there lies enduring evidence of physical pollution.

Some local habits do not help much. Restaurants routinely drop their garbage into roadside drains. I repeatedly saw household waste, from prosperous homes where people should know better, being

All Bali is Balinese; you find Bhoma everywhere.

dropped into irrigation channels. Right in the centre of Ubud, one of the cleanest places in Bali, there is a rubbish dump spilling down into a stream much used downstream for bathing.

I stayed in Lovina for several days because there is much of interest in north Bali, from the wildlife reserve away to the west to waterfalls in the hills behind to the string of sights east from Singaraja. Lovina is a good base for them all. But eventually the time came to complete my journey around Bali and I bemoed on, through ricefields, miles of new vineyards and forest, to Gilimanuk, beside the narrow straits so important in Balinese history, and then to Negara.

Neither Gilimanuk nor Negara, I was told, has tourist 'obyeks' but Negara, capital of Jembrana regency, is known for its bull-racing. An illuminated statue of two buffaloes harnessed to a simple cart and a driver urging them on stands in the town centre. Some tourist information material says the races are held every second Sunday but this is wrong, for the good reason that they can be staged only when the fields used for racing are not growing rice. Races are held in September and October. Some bulls, specially bred and fancifully decorated, are said to reach speeds up to 50 kph. The races are an old institution, recently revived and similar to those held on Madura Island off northeast Java. Covarrubias described bull races in north Bali in the 1930s in which the referee chose as the winning team not the fastest one but the one with the most stately bearing. 'It is typical of the Balinese to place style before mere physical speed,' he commented. But the object today is to come first.

From Negara the road runs about 90 km back to Denpasar, all the way through attractive, rolling ricelands, with the sea on the right, mountains on the left, and on a clear day Gunung Agung in the distance. Eventually the traffic thickens and you are back in the capital, able to say smugly that unlike most visitors you really have been all around Bali.

Masculine and feminine mountains

Around, but not through. Two more tourist-type excursions must be added to the circumnavigation, just to complete the picture of an island which deserves to be seen in all its aspects. Both trips involve volcanoes, Catur and Batur. The first, Gunung Catur, huddles over its crater lake, Bratan, like a hen over her chickens. The mountain is high and protective, the lake placid. The setting is serene, cool, beautiful, garden-like, feminine. It is the place to sit by the water's edge, admiring the mist drifting across the mountainside, the platinum sheen of the lake, the temple with its eleven merus, and eat a durian. Right beside the temple stands an austere Buddhist stupa and while I was there a mosque loudspeaker called the Muslim community to prayer.

The lake is important in Bali's irrigation system, the headwaters of many subaks, and the cool, moist air around it helps produce a torrent of vegetables for the towns and tourists down on the plains. Tourists come here to admire this gentle valley, to walk amid the pines, to enjoy the fresh fruit — or to play golf. The Bali Handara Country Club course is described as the only one in the world set in the crater of an extinct volcano — but then, many people thought Gunung Agung was extinct, too.

The club is spectacularly located, with a view from its clubhouse down towards another lake, Bujan, though the course does not in fact reach that far, and is said to be superb to play on. The Asian Golf Digest has described it as 'truly splendoured, peaceful, immensely challenging and highly memorable,' one of the top 50 in the world. A golfer who tried all 50 said the Bali course was the most beautiful of all of them. Altitude is over 1,000 metres, mean daytime temperature is around 18 degrees, and the 18-hole course is 6,400 metres long.

Golfers pay for the privilege of playing here, of course, because Bali can be as expensive as it can be cheap and because the club — which calls itself 'the ultimate getaway' — is a big-money operation. It is owned by Dr Ibnu Sutowo, an army doctor who built Pertamina, Indonesia's state oil corporation, into a giant and was then sacked because of its huge overseas debts. Its name derives from the first syllables of the names of two of his children.

Just how Sutowo came to control 135 hectares of the most spectacular land in an island which tries to keep its land to itself is yet another mystery. Golfers are Japanese, American, Australian, sometimes Javanese and Sumatran, rarely Balinese. The Balinese caddy, cut the grass, fetch the drinks, serve the meals, and remember that 1,500 of them helped build the course, digging and carrying earth in wicker baskets.

Catur is extinct, they say, and Bratan is gentle and Bedugul is a calm retreat. About 20 kilometres away across country, much further by road, is Gunung Batur, with a lake of the same name, and the villages of Penelokan and Kintamani. This is not soft and

Gunung Batur, with its three craters.

gentle country. If the first is feminine, the second is masculine. There is no question of one being better than the other, but it is fair to say the first is more beautiful, the second more spectacular.

It is an element of local lore that travellers should arrive at Penelokan or Kintamani after dark, to awaken the next day to a stunning and — if passages like this have remained unread — unsuspected view of a volcanic peak looming in the eastern sky. The peak rises from within a crater nearly ten kilometres across which contains a lake, a field of lava, some villages and farms — and that peak looming against the sunrise.

The landscape has not always been thus, not even in recent times. In 1917 the volcano, then much smaller than it is today, burst into violent eruption, killing 1,300 people and destroying 65,000 homes and 2,500 temples. The lava engulfed most of a village at the foot of the volcano but stopped at the gateway to a temple. Villagers took this as a sign of divine favour and continued to live there, only to be driven out in another eruption in 1926, when the temple was also buried. Most villagers moved out of the crater, to the rim communities of Kintamani and Penelokan (which means 'lookout'). The volcano was active again in 1963, in association with Gunung Agung, and many villagers moved away for up to six months.

I joined a small party to climb Batur. Our guide was Wayan

Ngedap, of the village of Kedisan which stands beside the crater lake almost directly beneath Penelokan, about 200 metres lower down. He takes tourists up the mountain two or three times a week, and the rest of the time tends his small maize, peanuts and oranges farm. A pleasant, rather bucolic man, homely in sarong, t-shirt and rubber slippers. On our walk up the mountain he appeared never to hurry, never to strain, but in fact set a cracking pace which had us sweating to keep up. Nor did he stumble or dislodge as much as a pebble from the steep pumice and scoria-strewn slopes which marked the last stages of the climb. We strangers on the mountain by contrast slid and stumbled and floundered and started small avalanches of volcanic debris, and found frequent reason to pause to admire the view.

And a view to admire it can be, whether on a clear day, with Gunung Agung hard against the sky beyond the crater, or on a misty one, with the lake shimmering silver and with occasional snatches of sun-speckled views across the greening lava fields.

Eventually we reached the summit of this Young Smokey, or summit enough. There are three craters stepped down the mountain side, and most visitors are taken to the top of the middle one. The topmost involves another hour's climbing and offers less spectacle. Most people are content to say they have been up Batur without specifying exactly how far. On our climb we at last reached a ridge which sloped away gently on one side, precipitately on the other. Wayan poised nonchalantly on the very edge while we crept up cautiously, to peer over into a caldera, a cauldron, the mouth of a volcano.

There was no bubbling lava, no fiery heat; just a rocky basin with gouts of steam here and there and the smell of sulphur. The ground was cold, but one had only to move a boulder and feel again to detect heat from the bowels of the earth. Dig a little, and one could cook a meal. The warm steam mingled with the cool mist, producing a confusing and slightly alarming atmosphere of moving lights and shadows. It was a place for unusual sensations, worth the climb.

From this point we descended to lunch in a warung beside a hot spring at the lake edge, and to prepare for the second venture of the day, a visit to the Bali Aga village of Trunyan, across the lake, which is where this book began.

Books about Bali

A complete list would take pages. The books named here are among those more readily available in English. Some of them contain considerable bibliographies.

Baum, Vicki: A Tale of Bali, London, 1937, recently reprinted.
Belo, Jane: Trance in Bali, New York, 1960.
Covarrubias, Miguel: Island of Bali, London, 1936, recently reprinted.
Dalton, Bill: Indonesia Handbook, Chico, California, USA, 1983.
de Zoete, Beryl, and Spies, Walter: Dance and Drama in Bali, London, 1938, recently reprinted.
Geertz, Clifford: Negara — The Theatre State in Nineteenth- Century Bali, Princeton, 1980.
Geertz, Hildred and Geertz, Clifford: Kinship in Bali, Chicago, 1975.
Gorer, Geoffrey: Bali & Angkor, London, 1936.
Hanna, Willard A.: Bali Profile — People, Events, Circumstances 1001 - 1976, New York, 1976.
Hooykaas, C.: A Balinese Temple Festival, The Hague, 1977.
McPhee, Colin: A House in Bali, London, 1947, recently reprinted.
Mathews, Anna: The Night of Purnama, London, 1965, recently reprinted.
Powell, Hickman: The Last Paradise, New York, 1930, recently reprinted.
Ramseyer, Urs: The Art and Culture of Bali, Oxford, 1977.

Index

Abang, Gunung (Mt Abang) 16
Abu Bakar, Sultan of Johor 179
Administrative districts — see Regencies
Agama Tirta, the Religion of Holy Water 104 115
Agotini, Nyoman 154
Agricultural society — see Subak
Agung, Gunung (Mt Agung) 16 22 24 60 86 107-8 110-1 148 184-90 192-3 220 224 252-4 258-61
Airlangga, Emperor 171
Airport 18 79 224 228
Amlapura 18 29 153 187-190 193 252
Anak Agung, Ksatria title 46
Ancestor worship 98
Animality 62-3
Anom Styari, Anak Agung 133-4
'Antik' painting 154-5
Area 16
Areca nut 74-5
Art Centre 130 157 166 243
Artists' community 160-1
Arts festival, annual 243
Ashram, Gandhian 119
Astawa, Dr I.B. 197-200
ASTI 139
Australia, Australians 207 224 234 237-40
Australian, the, newspaper 208 240
Babel, Tower of 109
Badung 18 172 180 243-4
Badung Tourist Promotion Board 62
Bali Aga 25-34 87 128 255 261
Bali Barat National Park, proposed 216
Bali Barat Wildlife Reserve 213-6
Bali Beach Hotel 224 233
Bali-Ha'i 106
Bali Handara Country Club 259
Bali Hotel 138 224 243 255
Bali Museum 140 157 158 166 181 242-3
Balinism 86 92 98-105 116
Bali starling 214 217 222
Bambang Swartha, Made 59
Bangbang Gde Rawi, Ktut 58-9
Bangli 18 172 210-2

Banjar 38-44 46 48 54 127 142-3 197-8 212 236 255
Baris 140
Barong, barong dance 140-3 145 167 171 243
Bat Cave 219
Batubulan 141-3
Batukau, Gunung (Mt Batukau) 16
Batu Renggong 87 172-3
Batur, Gunung (Mt Batur), crater and lake 18 25 33 108 258-61
Baum, Vicki 93 157 182
Bedugul 259
Bedulu 121
Beef eaten 70
Belo, Jane 102 132 141 144-6
Bemo 18 100 241 254
Benoa 18
Bent, Dick 237-40
Besakih 107 111-2 114 185-6
Betel 73-5
Bhoma 80 114 218 257
Bicycle carving 163-5
Bina Wisata 246-8
Bird-watching 214 219
Birth customs 62
Birthrate 198
Black magic 20
Blacksmiths 14
Blanco, Antonio Mario 160 162
Blimbingsari 118-9
Bondalem 205 255
Bone 143-6
Bonnet, Rudolph 157-9 161 162
Books about Bali 262
Borneo 7 42 171 180 196
Borobodur 109
Brackman, Arnold 191-2
Brahma 75 108 109
Brahmanas 45-8 104
Brahma Vihara Arama 117-8
Bratan, lake 258-9
Brayut, Men 114
British Embassy, Jakarta 189
Brooke, James 178-9
Bualu 131
Budakling 116-7 254

263

Buddhism 98 111 113-4 116-8 254 259
Buffaloes, buffalo racing 42 205 258
Bujan, lake 259
Bukit 113 173 205 228
Buleleng 18 172 173 176-7 255
Bumblebee dance — See Oleg Tambulilingan
Burning of widows — see Widows
Cakra, Nyoman 150-2
Calendar 33 56-63
Campuan 249
Candidasa 220 251
Candrametu 139
Carangsari 78-84 87
Carving 48 153 157 163-8 243
Caste — see Gentry
Catholics — see Christians
Cattle, wild 214
Catur, Gunung (Mt Catur) 16 258-9
Caturmuka 199 243
Celebes — see Sulawesi
Celuk 58
Celukanbawang 204-5
Ceramic research station 168
Chaplin, Charles 129
Chinese, the 59 117 119 173 175 179 180 255
Chinese lion dance 140
Cholera 209
Christians 59 118-9 181
Christian Science Monitor 191
Cili 60-1
Cinemas 244 256-7
CITES, Convention on International Trade in Endangered Species 221
Civets 214
Cloth, 'double ikat' hand-woven 31-2
Cockfighting 48 64-6 211
Coffee 72-3 203-4
Cokorda, Ksatria title 46
Commoners as opposed to gentry 45-8
Communist Party, communists 190-2
Congregation, temple — see Pemaksan
Co-operation 38
Coral, coral reefs 170 220
Cosmos depicted 90 110
Cousin marriage 47-8
Covarrubias, Miguel 21-2 34 62-3 84 86-8 95-7 129 131 138 153 155 157 159 258
Cows 42 67 70
Cremation 33 47 63 77-97 159
Crime 40 236

Crosby, Bing 134
Cultural tourism 200 230
Dalai Lama 118
Dalang 146-7 154
Dalton, Bill 26 76 210-2
Dancers, dancing 52 124 126 129-46 243 246
Darling, John 156 158
Darwin, Charles 218
Dead bodies, exposure of 26 34
De Houtman, Cornelis 173-5
Denmark, connection with Bali 177-9
Denpasar 18-9 33 40 48 57 68 72 75 88 92 117 121 130 180-1 188 193 197 204-5 207 209-10 224 228-9 241-4
Development Planning Organisation 200
Dewa Agung 172-3 175
De Zoete, Beryl 5 84
Dhangin, Wayan 254
Diarrhoea, ricewater as cure for 76
Dilantik Dharma, Gde Wayan 116-7
Djuwito Chayadi 73
Dogs, dog-eating 55 67 70 170 209 219
Drake, Francis 173
Drugs 212 235
Ducks 70
Durian 71-2
Dutch, the 45 47-8 116 118 122 133 137 157 173-83 196 223-4 231-2 255
Dutch East India Company 175
Dutchmen in carvings 164-5
East India Directory 177
Economic development 200-6
Economist, The 191
Eka Dasa Rudra 111 185-6 219
Eiseman, Fred 75
Electricity 55 205-6 255
'Elephant Cave' 113-4
Elizabeth, Queen 226
English, the 176
Erlangga — see Airlangga
Europe, Europeans 124 172-183 248
Exile, exiles 30 46 118-9
Exodus from Java to Bali 172
Expectation of life 209
Extended family system 37 39
Fabius, Dr 182
Family planning 35 197-9
Feudalism 48
Fire dance 143-4
Food 52 67-73
Forest Service 193 213-8
French, the 176

Friend, Donald 160 162
Fruit 71-2
Fuller, Buckminster 37-8 108
Gajah Mada 171-2
Galungan 60-1
Gambuh 138
Gamelan 78-84 120-8 153 156-7
Gamelan museum, proposed 121
Gandera, Wayan 121
Gandhian ashram 119
Ganesh 113 'Gang Tuan Langa' 178
Garment industry 204
Garuda 13
Garuda Indonesian Airways 13 207
Gateway, split 108-9
Gateway with ten tiers 251-2
Gde, Gede, personal name 35
Gedong Kirtya library 255
Geertz, Clifford, and Geertz, Hildred 22 36 47 64-6 84-5 95 97 102 170 172
Gelgel 172-4 181
'Genealogical amnesia' 36 39
Gentry 45-50 104 105
Gestapu, the September 30 incident 191
Gianyar 18 93 113 166 171 172
Gilimanuk 258
Giri Rakkito Thera, Bhikku 117
Goa Gajah 113-4
Goa Lawa, the Bat Cave 219
Golf 259
Gong, kettle 7
Gorer, Geoffrey 54
Government Tourism Office 226
Governor of Bali — see Mantra, Prof Dr Ida Bagus

Grinsing cloth — see Cloth
Gua Gajah 113-4
Gua Lawar, the Bat Cave 219
Guides, tourist 226-7
Gusti, Ksatria and Weisya title 46
Hanna, Willard A. 22 86 102 173 180 185 196 223
Hariti 114
Harris, Max 208 240
Health 207-12
Helms, L.V. 93-5
Heronry 219 246
Hinduism 13 86 113 117
History of Bali 169-193
Holy water — see Agama Tirta
Hood, Mantle 120 122
Hooykaas, C. 102
Hope, Bob 134
Horses, horse baths 67 255
Hotels 229
Hughes, John 191-2
Ibnu Sutowo, Lt-Gen Dr 259
Ibraham, Sultan of Johor 179
Ida Bagus, Brahmana title 36 46
Iksan, Dr A.Y. 208-11
India, Indian dancing 116 125 137 170-1
Indonesia 13 16 45 105 196
Indra 116
Infant mortality 209
Inflation 201
Irrigation 17 18 41
Islam, Muslims 59 119 172 192 221 255 259
Jagaraga 164 177 255
Jakarta 13 175 183 186 191-2 204
Janger 138-9

265

Japan, Japanese 59 139 157 182-3 185 196 232 237 250
Java, Javanese 16 40 42 64 108 122 129 170-2 176 196 181-6 192 198 202 204 234 236
'Java Minor' 173
Jembrana — 18 258
Jilantik, Gusti Ktut 176-7
Jones, Howard Palfrey 186
Kahyangan tiga 43 107
Kamasan 154-5
Kapal 168
Karangasem 18 172 173
Kawi, old Javanese 147
Kawi, Gunung 114-5
Kebyar 126 138
Kecak 130-1 140 143 157 243
Kedisan 25 27-8 261
Kennard, Allington 20
Kerambitan 68
Kerta Gosha 153-4
Ketu, Drs Ngurah 226-8
'Kidnap marriage' 54-5
Kintamani 18 25 259-60
Klungkung 18 29 145 153 172-3 180-1 187 252
KOKAR 121-2 139
Krakatau, Krakatoa 183-4
Krause, Gregor 21-2
Kreisky, Bruno 167
'Kris dance' 140-1 143 145
Ksatrias 45-8 62 135
Ktut, K'tut, Ketut, personal name 35
K'tut Tantri 22 232
Kubutambahan 163-5 255
Kuningan 61 70
Kusamba 251
Kuta 18 28 68 140 178 204-5 228-9 231-40
Kuta Beach Hotel 232
Kutri 171
Lamour, Dorothy 134
Lange, Cecilia 179
Lange, Emil 179
Lange, Mads 177-9
Language 16 49-50
Lebih temple festival 100-1
Legian 89 231-7
Legong 7 131-4 138 140 144
Lembongan, Nusa 250
Le Meyeur de Merpres 160
Lempad, Gusti Nyoman 158-9 161 162
Leopard cats 214
Leucopsar rothschildi — see Bali starling

Library, Gedong Kirtya 255
'Life-cycle' ceremonies 62-3
Lim Chong Keat 150
Lombok 172 173 177 179 189 216-8
Lontar books 32 65 110
Lovina 255-8
Macagues 214
Made, personal name 35
Magellan, Ferdinand 173
Mahabharata 111 137 146
Mahendradatta 171
Mahmood, Sultan of Johor 179
Majapahit 13 98 171-2 180
Malaria 209
Malaysia 179 189
Mandera, Anak Agung Gde 123-6 129 133-4
Mantra, Prof Dr Ida Bagus, Governor of Bali 17 52 88-9 201 206 218 244
Map of Bali 10-11
Margarana 183
Mario 127 138
Markets 48 52 56
Marriage 46-8 54-5
Mas 18 166 246
Mas, Cokorda 121-3
Masks 140 166-8 243
Massacre 190-2
Massage 234
Mass ritual suicide — see Puputan
Mathews, Anna 22 187-9
McPhee, Colin 22 71 90-3 118 121-8 145 157
McVey, Ruth 120
Mead, Margaret 225
Mediums 104
Meier, Theo 159-60 162
Melanesia 106
Menjangan, Nusa 216
Menstruation 110
Mental health, mental hospital 210-2
Meru 90 109
Michener, James 106
Missionaries — see Christians
'Monkey Forest' 246
Mudraswara Foundation — 121 136
Museum of Gamelan, proposed 121
Museum Subak 42-3
Music, musical instruments 19 33 52-3 120-8 181-2 211
Muslims — see Islam
Names, personal 35 52: effect on family planning 199
Napoleon Bonaparte 176
National Geographic Magazine 225-6

Nature worship 98
Negara 18 118 172 258
Neka Museum 161
Neka Wayan Suteja 162 248
Newspapers 244
New Year 57 61
New Zealand 205
Ngedap, Wayan 25 33 260-1
Ngurah Agung, Anak Agung 256
Ngurah Rai, Col Gusti 79 183
Nieuwenkamp, W.O.J. 7 164 165
Nusa Dua 18 80 131 228-9 233
Nusa Dua Hotel 228
Nyepi 61-2 64 142
Nyoman, personal name 35
Offerings, how system developed 99-101
Oka, Nyoman 123-4 225-6
Oleg Tambulilingan 134
Olivier, Tarquin 194-5
'Once in a Lifetime Ceremony' 111
Opium 175
Padangbai 117
Padmasana 109-10
Painting 148-62
Palaces 68 108 153 181-2 196 252
Palasari 118-9
Palm-leaf books — see Lontar books
Paramount Ruler of Malaysia 179
Parisada Hindu Dharma 59 111
Pearson, Muriel 231 'Peasant painters' 149-52
Pegok, turtle slaughterhouse 221-2
Pejeng, Pejeng gong 7 114 168
Peliatan 18 123-5 129 132 134-6 246
Pemaksan 43-4 107
Penelokan 25 28 259-61
Penestanan 150-2
Pengosekan 7 160
Penida, Nusa 205 250-1
Petulu 219 246
Philip, Prince 225
Pig, roasted 68-70
Pita Maha 157 158 162
Police 40 235-6
Pollution 257-8
Polok 160
Polynesia 107
Population 16 196-9
Population decline in Tenganan 30
Portuguese 173-4
Pottery 168
Pournama, Beny 7
Powell, Hickman 22
Prembon 139
Priests 57 61 102-4 187

Prijono Winduwinoto, Prof 137
Prostitution 40 235-6
Protestants — see Christians
Provincial Assembly 244
Puppets — see Shadow play
Puputan 180-3
Pura, puri, distinction 108
Puri Lukisan 159 161
Purnama 57
Putu, personal name 35
Pyramids 109
Qantas 207-8
Rabies 93 209
Raffles, Stamford and Sophia 176
Rainfall 17
Ramayana 111 119 130 137 146 154
Ramseyer, Urs 22 29 34 99 101 110 123 230
Rangda 140 171 231
Ratih Iryani, Cokorda Istri 132-6
Rayon 244
Red Cross, Indonesian 188
Reforestation 193 218
Regencies 18
Reincarnation 86-7
Religion 43-4 53-4 98-105
Religious Affairs Department 105
Republic of East Indonesia 183
Restaurants 229
Rice, Ricefields 23 41-3 170 201-2
Rice goddess — see Cili
Ricewater as cure for diarrhoea 76
Rice wine 73
'Runaway marriage' 54-5
Sangeh 218
Sanghyang dance 144
Sang Hyang Niratha 113
Sangsit 165 255
Sanur 18 80 180 204-5 228-9 233, 250-1
Saraswati 62
Sarawak 178
Sate 70
Sawan 128 255
Sculpture — see Carving
Seafood 71
Sembiran 34 255
Sexual equality 52-3
Sex, attitudes to 54
Shadow play 140 146-7 154
Shipwrecks as a political issue 180
Silvio Santosa 114 246-7
Singapore 40 176 178-9 187 245
Singaraja 18 93 173 204 255
Siti, Made 160
Siva, Siwa 75 98 108 109 116-7

267

Slavery 39 175
Smit, Ari 149-52 156 162
Snel, Han 160 162
Spices 75-6
Spies, Walter 130 156-9 162 242
Starling, Bali — see Bali starling
Straits Times 11 187
Subak 41-4 46 48 259
Subak Museum 42-3
Sudras — see Commoners
Suharto, President 191-3 201
Sukarno, President 116 125 184-6 191 197 201 233 253
Sukawati family 156 158-9
Sulawesi 43 119 127 196
'Surabaya Sue' — see K'tut Tantri
Suradnya, Nyoman 246
Surfing 237-40
Surya, the Sun God 109
Suteja Neka, Wayan — see Neka
Swiss, Switzerland — 30 128
Tabanan 18 42 48 166 172 183
Tagore, Rabindranath 137
Tampaksiring 115-6 185
Tanah Lot 107 113
Tantera, Dr Ir Gusti Made 193 213 216 218
Tantri, K'tut 22 232
Tantrism 98
Tawfiq Effendi, Lt Col 40
Teeth-filing 62-3 67
Tejakula 34 255
Teknonymy 36-7 46
Telephones 206
Television 55 244
Teluk Terima 214
Temperatures 17
Temple as a stage 110
Temples, temple festivals 43-4 53-4 62 100-1 106-116 165
Tenganan 28-34 128 252
Ten-tiered gateway 251-2
Thong, Dr Denny 210-2
Three Sisters Losmen 233-4
Tigers 170 213-5 231
Tilem 57
Time zone 17
Tirta Empul 115-6
Tirtagangga 70 116 252-4
Tjampuhan Hotel 157 249
Tolkien 14
Tourism, tourist industry 13 16 122 139 185-6 200-1 203 205 207-10 212 223-230 243
Tourist Development Corporation 228

Tourist Guidance Foundation, Ubud 246-8
Tracks, surfing newspaper 237-40
Trance, trance dance 104 130 140 143-6 211
Transmigration 196 213
Triwangsa — see Gentry
Trunyan 25-9 34 261
Turtles 70 220-2
Ubud 7 18 28 37 46 72 92 121 130 136 140 149 156 159-62 195 203 206 218-9 245-9
Ubud Post 246-8
Udayana, King 171
Udayana University 135 242
Ujung 252
Uluwatu 107 113
Van Helvoort, Bastian 214
Van Kol, Heer H. 223
'Village republic' — see Banjar
Vineyards — 203 258
Vishnu, Wisnu 13 75 108 109 114
Volcanoes 16-7 183-90 192-3 261
Wallace, Alfred Russel; Wallace Line 71-2 216-8
Wars between Dutch and Balinese 176-80
Wayan, personal name 35
Wayan, town 127
Wayang kulit 140 146-7 154
Wedagama, Drs D.M. 200-4 206
Weeks of different length 56-7
Weisyas 45-8
Werdhi Budaya 243
Wicarna, Pan, gamelan maker 127-8
Widows, burning of 47 93-97
Wig-making 203
Wildlife 213-222
Wilhelmina, Queen 124
Wiranata 139
Wisnu — see Vishnu
Women, girls 39 40 51-5 122 204
Women slaves killed during queen's cremation 96-7
Workers Federation, Indonesian 204
World Health Organisation 228
World Wildlife Organisation 214
Yang Dipertuan Agung — see Paramount Ruler of Malaysia
Year, Balinese 56-7 112
Yeh Pulu 113
Yeh Sanih 255
'Young artists' 149-52
Young, Capt Thomas 97
Ziggurat 109

From the same publisher

Three more fine books about Bali..

Our Hotel in Bali, by Louise G Koke

In 1936 Bob Koke, a young Californian, and Louise Garrett, his future wife, landed in Bali, fell in love with the fabled isle, and decided to stay. Within four months they had opened a tourist hotel on 'the most beautiful beach in the world.'

Louise Koke's account of their adventure, written during World War II, came to light nearly half a century later with masses of drawings and photographs. All are here combined in a book which reviewers have described as 'wonderful' and 'absolutely delightful'.

Paperback, 288 pages, nearly 150 drawings and photographs. 15cm x 21cm. ISBN 0-9597806-1-0.

In Praise of Kuta, by Hugh Mabbett

Kuta, home to tens of thousands of visitors to Bali each year, is trying hard to live down its rambunctious past. It is no longer the hippy haven of the 1960s, when it was noted for drugs and nudity. The new Kuta is cleaning up its act, improving its offerings, and making the most of its superb beach.

But this book is not just about tourists having fun or about Kuta's eventful history. It also describes how the original villagers of Kuta have stood up to a tidal wave of change, coping with huge numbers of visitors yet at the same time preserving their Balinese-ness.

Paperback. 160 pages, more than 50 colour photographs. 30 other illustrations, 15cm x 21cm. ISBN 0-9597806-0-2.

Bali 1912, photographs and reports by Gregor Krause

More than 70 years ago a young German doctor working for the Dutch East Indies government fell in love with Bali. To mark his devotion the doctor, Gregor Krause, took more than 4,000 photographs — making him the forerunner of the vast numbers of visitors who have been photographing Bali ever since.

This new selection of Gregor Krause's best work, made from his original glass slides, offers a unique view of traditional Bali and proves once again that good black-and-white photography can easily hold its own against today's glossiest work in colour.

Hardcover. 112 pages, 26cm x 19cm. ISBN 0-9597806-2-9.

.. One about the most famous building in the world ..

In Praise of the Taj Mahal, by Hugh Mabbett with photographs by Fiona Nichols.

Sparkling text about the Taj Mahal and more than 80 brilliant colour photographs make this a book to cherish. It is all here — everything from the romance of Shah Jahan and Mumtaz Mahal to the present day conservation and management of the monument. In Praise of the Taj Mahal is praise not in the sense of extravagant tributes, but in the form of an honest description of everything that makes the building so entrancing.

The Taj Mahal, a monument to love and the outstanding symbol of India, draws more than a million visitors a year. This book explains its astonishing appeal. It will fascinate those who have seen it and those who hope to; as a companion to take to Agra with you, it has no equal.

Paperback, 176 pages, more than 80 colour photographs and 20 other illustrations and maps. Index. 15cm x 21cm. ISBN 0-9597806-5-3.

.. And another about Borneo

A Stroll through Borneo, by James Barclay

With no precise route mapped out, with no timetable to keep to, James Barclay wandered for months through central Borneo. He travelled up mountains and down rivers and lived with fascinating people — Ibans, Kenyahs, Kayans, Kelabits and the nomadic Penans. And then he went back for more.

This is his account, always engaging, often hilarious, at times exciting, of his adventures in one of the world's most surprising wildernesses.

Paperback, 208 pages, more than 40 drawings and photographs, 15cm x 21cm. ISBN 0-9597806-3-7.

All published by January Books Ltd,
c/o Design Business, 809 French Road #06-160,
Singapore 0820. Tel: 2942811, Fax: 2911285